HiB

TRANSPORT AND THE DEVELOPMENT OF THE EUROPEAN ECONOMY, 1750–1918

Also by Simon P. Ville

ENGLISH SHIPOWNING DURING THE INDUSTRIAL REVOLUTION:
Michael Henley and Son, London Shipowners, 1770–1830

Transport and the Development of the European Economy, 1750–1918

Simon P. Ville
Lecturer in Economics
University of Auckland

MACMILLAN

First published 1990

Published by
THE MACMILLAN PRESS LTD
Houndmills, Basingstoke, Hampshire RG21 2XS
and London
Companies and representatives
throughout the world

Printed in Hong Kong

British Library Cataloguing in Publication Data
Ville, Simon P.
  Transport and the development of the European economy,
  1750–1918.
  1. Europe. Transport, history. Economic aspects
  I. Title
  380.5'094

ISBN 0–333–43602–4

In memory of Steve Jones

Contents

List of Tables

List of Figures

List of Plates and Acknowledgements

Preface

The title of this book and much of its form arose out of a course which I taught at UMIST between 1983 and 1989. In teaching this course I soon became aware of the need for a comparative study of European transport in the modern period. There are precious few studies of developments in individual countries or of particular modes of transport. The collection of essays on European railways edited by O'Brien provides one of the few worthwhile studies of individual sectors although it concentrates too much upon some of the specific quantitative debates of the new economic historians to produce an overall account of the rise and impact of the railway. The other forms of transport have received no noteworthy treatment for Europe as a whole. Several national transport studies exist, such as those by Bagwell and Toutain, but they are now mostly out of date in terms of coverage and interpretation. The recent volumes edited by Aldcroft and Freeman, though, are a welcome addition to the British picture.

The explanation of the absence of surveys of European transport lies in the division of most transport studies between the antiquarian and econometric schools. The antiquarian school has concentrated upon the production of specific case studies without indicating their wider significance or employing rigorous social science techniques. The econometricians, mainly confined to railway history, have emphasised equally specific issues, of a quantitative and theoretical nature, without showing an awareness of broader and often non-quantifiable developments. The huge gulf that exists between popular and the new economic history can be illustrated by the juxtaposition of two articles in the *Journal of Transport History* bibliography of 1977: C. M. White, 'The concept of social saving in theory and practice' and Reg Wilkinson, 'A railwayman recalls his days at Wantage railway station'. While these are both legitimate studies in their own right they serve to indicate the confused picture presented to the student of transport history searching for work which is both rigorous in its methods and sympathetic in its coverage.

This division also helps to explain why so few studies have examined the role of transport in European industrialisation. This topic has received some attention in railway history but largely in terms of assessing the social saving method. Maritime history, alas, is overflowing with antiquarians who refuse to recognise that shipping played an important role in economic development though in a less dramatic manner than the railways. Inland waterways and road transport, both before and after the coming of the motor car, await further assessment of their economic importance although the work of Price and Laux is moving in this direction.

It is one thing to identify the shortcomings of generations of historians, it is quite another to put them to right. Neither this book nor this historian claim to be embarking on a single-handed attempt to do just this. Rather the intention of the present writer is two-fold. The book offers a general and comparative survey of European transport from the middle of the eighteenth century to 1918, something which, as I have indicated, is sadly missing. The book is divided into chapters on particular modes of transport as the most logical manner of approaching the subject. Themes such as urban transport, the impact of war and competition between different modes are dealt with in appropriate sections. The aircraft industry is not covered separately because it remained very much in its infancy in 1918 although the role of car manufacturers in early aviation production is discussed.

Like all general surveys it must eschew some of the more specific detail of the subject in order to indicate the main trends and developments. An extensive bibliography of many of the major works, which also serves as a system of references, is included for those wishing to delve more deeply into particular issues. More extensive coverage is given to those areas and countries where transport developments were greatest. Thus, there is more attention to north-western than south-eastern Europe. This, of course, is not to deny that transport developments were sometimes damaging for a country or that lack of improvement helped to shape the pattern of European economies in the nineteenth century. Consideration is also given to countries where transport featured large in the economy but there was little change in its nature. Such was the experience of the Norwegian shipping industry for much of the nineteenth century. In places coverage must inevitably extend beyond Europe. It would make little sense to examine the rise of the European motor vehicle industry without accounting for the importance of American influence. The building of the Suez Canal and the growth of long haul routes beyond Europe were essential features of the European shipping industry in the nineteenth century.

The emphasis is upon the dynamics of change rather than structures and institutions. This approach is significant for the second aim of the book: to look more closely at the relationship between transport and European economic development during the course of the eighteenth and nineteenth centuries. The book assesses the limited amount of existing work in this field and offers a pointer towards fertile new grounds for study by discussing where further links between transport and development may exist. Each chapter contains a section which specifically assesses the economic impact of that mode of transport but the relationship between transport and development is discussed in various forms throughout the book. It also attempts to encourage historians to employ more rigorously the methods of transport and development economists by indicating how their work has impinged upon the discipline.

I should like to thank Professor Malcolm Falkus for encouraging me to write this book in the first instance and Tim Farmiloe of Macmillan for supporting the project and bearing with me when the events surrounding the closure of the European Studies department at UMIST delayed the book's completion. I have frequently benefited from the ideas and issues raised and discussed by the many students who attended my transport seminar over the course of six years. I am also grateful to Susan Spence for typing several drafts of the book and Sue Ville for press and publicity information.

The book is dedicated to my good friend and former colleague Steve Jones who died tragically in a road accident on Hallowe'en 1987. Steve was an outstanding academic both as a patient and thorough teacher and as a prodigious writer of three books and more than 20 articles on labour history. Above all else, however, he was a kind and thoughtful person who will be missed greatly by his many friends.

SIMON VILLE

1 Transport and Industrialisation

TRANSPORT AND DEVELOPMENT THEORY

Transport is normally viewed as a form of social overhead capital (SOC) because it provides an activity essential for primary, secondary or tertiary production. Other forms of SOC include law and order, education, public health, and power and water supply. The alternative to SOC is investment in industrial production known as direct productive activities (DPA). Development economists have looked at these alternative forms of investment to try and understand whether one or the other, or a combination of the two, has been more important in explaining economic development.

A group of economists have supported the idea of balanced growth, that progress in the two sectors went hand in hand (Rosenstein-Rodan; Nurske; Scitovsky; Nath; Lewis). They held that the two sectors had to remain in equilibrium: more rapid growth in DPA would be impossible without the infrastructure offered by SOC while expansion in SOC could not be justified without accompanying progress in DPA. Nurske argued that investment in a particular industry would be discouraged by the smallness of the existing market. The balanced growth theory received support from Milward and Saul in their economic history of nineteenth-century Europe in which they argued that, 'everywhere successful development required balanced development' (1973, 529).

In 1958 A. O. Hirschman in his important study, *The Strategy of Economic Development*, cast doubt upon the theory of balanced growth. In a rather literal interpretation of the theory he argued that balanced growth was unlikely because it involved repeatedly laying an entirely new economic structure on top of an old one which required unavailable amounts of skill, capital and technology. This could be achieved through foreign assistance but might lead to colonisation. Government intervention was an alternative but Hirschman believed this would foster a less innovative structure. Moreover, the indivisibility of social overhead capital schemes and the lack of necessary expertise made balanced growth an unlikely eventuality. In support of Hirschman, Hughes, in his study of indus-

1

trialisation, argued that whether or not balanced growth was theoretically possible historically it had never happened. Nurske, looking at the theory from a demand perspective, helped to confound its historical importance by arguing that balanced growth could only occur where there was no external trade stimulus to particular industries, which was clearly not the case in the nineteenth century.

In opposition to balanced growth, Hirschman argued for the idea of unbalanced growth. For him growth was not a process of 'creation' but rather a gradual 'transformation' from the old to the new. He believed that disequilibrium between the sectors was essential to maintain the momentum of progress, 'if the economy is to be kept moving ahead, the task of development policy is to maintain tensions, disproportions and disequilibria' (Hirschman, 66). Thus, in the manner of a seesaw, progress in one sector will trigger off induced investment in the other as bottlenecks occur. Hirschman's theory of unbalanced growth won wide support. Rostow, for example, emphasised the importance of sector-led development when cost-reducing innovations in a particular industry induced expansion elsewhere in the economy through spreading effects or 'linkages' (1960). A recent attempt to test the validity of balanced and unbalanced growth theories for nineteenth-century Italy, Sweden and Germany by correlation analysis, however, found no consistent relationship between either theory and overall growth rates (Geary). Further research and conclusions along these lines will, however, be necessary before the weight of opinion is turned against unbalanced growth.

For Hirschman, the problem then arose of which sector, SOC or DPA, was the dynamic variable in the relationship. Expansion in industrial output would stretch existing resources of SOC and therefore encourage further investment in such areas as transport, communications, education, health and energy supply. This is known as development by shortage (DBS) of social overhead capital. On the other hand, investment in social overhead capital, by improving the infrastructure, could induce investment in DPA. This is known as development by excess (DBE) social overhead capital. Figure 1.1 illustrates the possible paths of development. The curves A, B and C indicate the cost of producing particular outputs of DPA from a given DPA investment as a function of the availability of SOC. XY indicates balanced growth where SOC and DPA are maintained in perfect equilibrium. Zig-zag growth through $Xabcde$ constitutes development by shortage and $Xafcge$ development by excess. Hirschman decided that the most likely and effective route was DBS. SOC

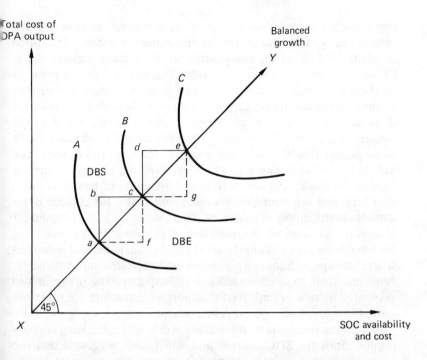

Figure 1.1 Paths of Economic Development

investment, he argued, was essentially permissive, reinforcing motivations which already existed and therefore it made more sense to invest in DPA which would lead to increased SOC once bottlenecks began to appear. Moreover, the indivisible nature of SOC investment and the problems measuring its capital-output ratio made for costly and irreversible mistakes if the DBE route was pursued.

For transport, as the major form of SOC in the eighteenth and nineteenth centuries, this implied a supporting rather than a leading role in the process of economic development. However, the relative merits of DBS and DBE vary according to time and place; the present study will examine their validity in the context of transport's role in European industrialisation.

The debate between DBS and DBE lies in deciding which is more effective in inducing development in the other. The elasticities of supply and demand in both sectors are thus of some importance. The price elasticity of demand for transport is generally high, particularly where competition exists between different modes, and therefore cost-reducing innovations are likely to encourage increased DPA investment to take advantage of these improvements. The price elasticity of demand for commodities is much more variable but is likely to be low for essential goods. The increase in the price of foodstuffs and fuel, which constituted a large proportion of transport volumes in the nineteenth century, is therefore less likely to choke off demand sufficiently to force transport improvements which would assuage rising costs. The elasticity of supply for transport is also likely to be greater than for industrial goods, in the short run at least. The uniqueness of each journey, which prevents the storage of surplus capacity as stock, together with the indivisibility of transport infrastructure and the irregularity of demand make for chronic over-capacity in the supply of transport. Thus, increases in the demand for transport can often be absorbed within existing capacity, nullifying the effectiveness of DBS in the short run. Within individual industries where storage is frequently possible and capital is more divisible, firms are likely to operate closer to full capacity. The opportunities presented by new or improved transport infrastructure are therefore more likely to induce new DPA investment.

One of the problems with DBE is the difficulty calculating capital–output ratios for SOC. Hirsch and Klein have suggested that the longevity, lumpiness and externalities common to transport investment makes it unsuitable for cost-benefit analysis and therefore unreliable as a means of inducing DPA investment. On the other hand, the expertise involved in making a decision on SOC investment has often been considerably greater than that available to the individual firm. Transport investments in the eighteenth and nineteenth centuries frequently encompassed the views of many entrepreneurs, local officials, the government and Parliament. Although there were failures and frequent opponents, many transport investments of the previous two centuries were successful in terms of the Hicks-Kaldor criterion of yielding a potential Pareto improvement.[1] Most industrial firms, however, failed.

There is no reason to suppose that the emphasis should not change between DBS and DBE in the course of a country's expansion. While many of the earliest canals and railways were a response to the expanding needs of local manufacturers, later projects frequently occurred ahead of demand. The experience of the early canals and railways stimulated a 'demonstration effect' as industrialists elsewhere hoped that transport investment would yield similar benefits. Freeman has indicated a similar behaviour pattern in road construction (1983, 18). Sometimes the demonstration effect took on a more negative aspect as an attempt to prevent trade diversion to areas with improved communications. The geographical widening of investment sources in the later projects implies DBS was of less significance although this may reflect greater speculative activity and interest in the profitability of transport projects rather than a move to DBE.

Evidence of the 'demonstration effect' can also be seen at an international level. Four out of five major development processes for backward countries involve some form of imitation of more advanced nations.[2] In the nineteenth century backward countries frequently copied the heavy investment in transport pursued by the more developed nations especially in relation to the railways which contemporaries correlated with economic modernisation. The views of R. D. Baxter in 1866 were typical of many: 'Railways have been a most powerful agent in the progress of commerce, in improving the conditions of the working class, and in developing the agricultural and mineral resources of the country' (Button, 245). Ironically, however, they were often substituting a DBE policy for what had been DBS in the developed country.

Hirschman was particularly critical of the potential for DBE policies in backward regions and countries which, he argued, were hardened in their reluctance to develop and so were unlikely to respond to the opportunities presented by additional SOC. Conversely, one could argue that given the absence of entrepreneurial spirit and capital, DPA investment was even less likely by itself. The traditional interpretation of Spanish railways, introduced as a DBE policy, was that they did little to foster Spanish economic development. However, Gomez-Mendoza (1982) has argued that development in the Spanish economy would have been even less likely without the railways which overcame a tremendous transport bottleneck. By the final decades of the nineteenth century railways had begun to stimulate the expansion of Spain's heavy industries. Germany also built railways as a DBE policy but here the stimulus was much quicker. The more immediate success of the policy in Germany can be explained by the more conducive environment: industry was at a maturer stage of development, there was greater capital available and the government supported the policy with import controls to ensure the benefits went to domestic rather than foreign industries as had been the case in Spain. A further influence upon the efficacy of DBE policies was the quality of other forms of social overhead capital which could heighten a nation's propensity to grow. According to Heymann, 'where these qualities are deficient, no amount of transport investment will be likely to create an economy-wide dynamism' (31).

THE ECONOMIC IMPACT OF TRANSPORT

There has been a long historiography supporting the central role of transport in economic development. In the eighteenth century Adam Smith saw transport as the mainspring of economic development through its market-widening effects. Neoclassical economists such as Young followed Smith in emphasising the importance of transport in establishing competitive markets. More recent studies have confirmed its central importance. Flinn's study of Britain's industrial revolution saw transport expansion as an essential precondition while Youngson suggested that the central role of transport in economic development 'is one of the few general truths it is possible to derive from a study of economic history' (73). The work on railways by the new economic historians, however, has adopted a more circumspect interpretation.

There are two critical elements to this problem: was there a profound change in the efficiency and extent of transport in the eighteenth and nineteenth centuries and, if so, how did these changes bear upon European industrialisation? Support for a transport revolution is widely held. Bagwell's study of Britain, entitled *The Transport Revolution from 1770*, is one of many works which sees a major discontinuity in transport development from the second half of the eighteenth century. More recently Freeman has dated the major change in Britain as coming with the application of steam to transport in the middle decades of the nineteenth century noting that the earlier road and river improvements were of limited significance. Similar timing, within a decade or so, occurred in France, Belgium and Germany and somewhat later in Spain, Italy and Russia. The application of oil and its by-products gave a further stimulus to motor vehicles and shipping at the beginning of the twentieth century. While there was undoubtedly a quickening in the pace of transport development in the eighteenth and nineteenth centuries it may be wrong to look for specific short term discontinuities within this period as reflected in major technological developments. The traditional Schumpeterian interpretation which emphasised the role of great innovations in economic development has now been replaced by the idea that the impact of technological change was more gradual. Cootner has shown how this interpretation can be applied to American transport history and a similar view for Europe is reflected in the current work.

The diffusion of transport innovations was a lengthy process which was delayed by conservatism and the unreliability of new technologies. The process was extended by the varying rates of relative competitiveness between modes of transport in different markets. The steamship replaced the sailing ship earliest in the European trades where coal was cheapest. Rail replaced road transport more quickly over the long hauls where its higher terminal costs were less significant than on short hauls. Thus, second-best technology continued in operation often complementing the new innovation. In Figure 1.2 road transport, with its low terminal costs but higher journey costs, is cheapest over the short haul *ab*. Rail is cheapest on the medium haul, *bc*, and shipping with the highest terminal but lowest journey cost is most effective over long distances from *c* onwards. Not all the

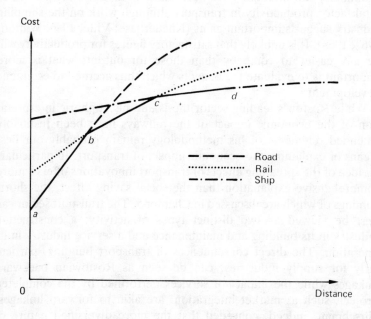

Figure 1.2 Transport Cost Functions

changes taking place in transport were associated with new technology. A series of organisational improvements can be identified such
as the growth of occupational specialisation in the shipping industry
and the standardisation of capital stock and timetables.

Identifying these changes is much easier than trying to measure
them. The dynamic nature of transport can be illustrated by the fact
that its share of GDP more than doubled for most European countries
during the course of the nineteenth century. In France, Britain and
Belgium freight output grew at more than double the rate of commodity output between 1830 and 1913 (O'Brien, 1982, 339). Less is
known about more backward countries such as Spain, Italy and
Russia but since their transport provision was much more primitive in
1800 the growth differential may have been greater. The fast growth
in transport output can be explained by the elasticity of demand at a
time of rising incomes and falling freight rates. A shift in the demand
curve resulted from changing tastes which demanded a greater range
of consumption from other regions and countries which in turn
produced longer average leads.

Similarly few attempts have been made to measure the growth of
total factor productivity in transport although work on the shipping
industry suggests important gains (Knauerhase; Ville, 1986; Walton,
1967, 1968). It is unlikely that satisfactory figures for productivity will
be any easier to come by than those for output; what is more
important is to evaluate the benefits which thus accrued to economic
development.

While Rostow's leading sector thesis and his euphoric interpretation of the economic impact of the railways have been justifiably
amended, elements of his methodology remain probably our best
means of explaining the economic impact of transport. In particular,
his idea of the spreading effects of transport innovations offers a more
comprehensive explanation than the social saving effect, the shortcomings of which are discussed in Chapter 5. The transport sector can
best be viewed as two distinct types of activity: a construction
industry in its building and maintenance and a service industry in its
operation. The direct consequences of transport building, particularly for supply industries, can be seen as Rostowian backward
linkages while the impact of services performed by the completed
project, such as market integration, are akin to forward linkages.
Hirschman, indeed, conceded that the more diversified nature of
SOC than DPA investment meant it was likely to generate more
widespread effects.

Backward linkages were most important to industries supplying materials and know-how for transport construction and therefore particularly included coal, iron and steel, engineering and timber. In addition, the managerial experience of handling unprecedentedly large organisations was important. The capital intensity of many transport projects influenced the development of the financial markets and encouraged the evolution of new forms of finance. The largeness and capital intensity of projects made for long investment gestation periods. This suggests many projects which had been floated in periods of prosperity and optimism were often completed in economic downturns several years later, thereby imparting a counter-cyclical influence upon the economy. Transport building was likely to provide work for the unemployed and fill the empty order books of supply firms. Thus the social cost to society, or 'shadow price', would be less than the wages paid because there would be no opportunity cost of production foregone elsewhere in the economy. The extent of backward linkages varied with the nature of the transport construction not all of which were long-term capital-intensive projects. Many road and river improvements of the eighteenth century involved little capital and therefore had a minimal effect upon the output of supply industries or the demand for finance.

Forward linkages arose from the improved efficiency of transport services. The productivity growth resulting from an improved transport system manifested itself in three main ways: the reduced cost of transport, greater regularity and higher speeds. The work of Toutain and Fremdling indicates that transport costs in France, Germany and Britain declined in real terms suggesting that transport played a leading rather than an accomodating role (Toutain, 1967(2), 283; Fremdling, 1975, 57–60). The share of transport charges in total industrial costs therefore fell. This decline was particularly important for bulky goods such as coal and iron where transport costs were likely to figure large but which were essential items in the early stages of industrialisation. Freeman, on the other hand, warns against concentrating on the significance of cost reductions and lays more emphasis upon the importance of increased speed and reliability. Tighter schedules, the introduction of timetables, overnight travel, and improved infrastructure and means of conveyance all helped to produce a more regular, reliable and rapid transport service.

These improvements to the efficiency of transport services imparted a substantial influence upon the location of industry, the development of markets and the pattern of urban settlement and growth. By reducing factor costs and increasing their mobility transport improvements offered greater flexibility and therefore more cost-efficient industrial location. With the increased speed and regularity of transport, industries could reduce their stocks of raw materials and unfinished goods and convert this circulating into fixed capital. Lower transport costs enabled goods to find a wider and larger market. This gave firms the opportunity to expand output and gain scale economies or specialise in a particular line of production in which greater efficiency and expertise could be developed. Speed and regularity particularly improved the market for perishables and enabled firms to receive more accurate, up-to-date information concerning market trends and orders. Cheaper, faster and more regular transport also encouraged population movement away from the city, on the one hand, and from the subsistent village community on the other. Transport systems largely shaped the pattern of suburban expansion during the eighteenth and nineteenth centuries.

Isotims show the influence of transport costs upon industrial location. They represent the shape produced by transporting materials or manufactures from the central point to any position on the circumference at equal cost. Isotims can be drawn for each material and product and joined into a locational map in a series of concentric shapes to represent rising costs. The points where the shapes cross and total transport costs are the same are joined to form isodapanes. The lowest cost isodapane is the most cost-efficient area of location (Stubbs, Tyson and Dalvi, 134). Changes in transport costs will affect both the size and shape of isotims and therefore affect the position of the isodapane. Though frequently drawn as circles, isotims are more likely to be star shaped. This was particularly the case in the first half of the nineteenth century because proximity to a railhead would make some long hauls cheaper than short hauls to less well served areas. Thus, in Figure 1.3 it is as cheap to travel from M to A as from M to B because MA represents a major rail link. The filling in of the detail of the transport network in the second half of the nineteenth century with more secondary railways and roads helped change the shape of the isotim closer to its circular ideal.

In practice two provisos must be inserted into this picture of easy automaticity between transport improvement and economic modernisation: were there any major obstacles to the transmission of these benefits and did the transport sector bring problems or cause any lagging in economic progress? The major obstacle to the economic transmission of transport improvements was the actions of

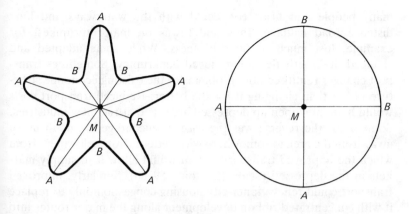

Figure 1.3   Circular and Star-Shaped Isotims

monopolists. Technically, most forms of transport operate in a monopoly because each journey is unique but in practice varying degrees
of competition exist. Competition between modes of transport is
frequently limited as the less efficient form is eliminated or forced
into a different market. Competition thus more often existed between different firms operating the same type of transport. In
nineteenth-century Britain, railway companies bought up many competing canal companies and benefited from lack of inter-firm competition after the rationalisation of the 1850s and 1860s to maintain
prices above marginal costs. In the shipping industry liner rings
attempted to fend off tramp competition by collusive action which
maintained higher freight rates but produced a more systematic and
reliable form of service. O'Brien has suggested that government
intervention, concerned more with public revenue than consumer
welfare, was a further obstacle to the transmission of economic
benefits (1982, 343). However, there were many occasions, particularly in the French experience, where government action aided
productivity growth through increased standardisation and by head-
ing off monopoly action. What is probably more significant is the lack
of planning which prevented transport projects maximising their
economic potential.

The external costs of transport development were among its major
disadvantages. These included pollution, congestion, noise and the
destruction of some communities. Each new innovation brought
losers. The coming of the railways, for example, adversely affected

many people and firms connected with the waterways and long distance road haulage. Inns and towns on major turnpikes, for example, lost much of their business. While some adapted and changed their activities others faced bankruptcy. Sometimes transport changes reinforced the problems of the existing economic structure rather than changing it for the better. Reduced transport costs would hopefully open up depressed areas and attract new industries. Sometimes, the reverse was the case: it encouraged firms to move away from the area to somewhere with better factor endowment from which the improved transport system would allow it to supply markets in the depressed region (Button, 259–60). Similarly, improved transport could relieve inner-city housing congestion only to replace it with concentrated ribbon development along the major routes into the city, with scant regard for urban development upon fertile agricultural land. The star-shaped isotim thus remained a problem. The capital intensity of transport projects brought a heavy opportunity cost of investment foregone in other industries. Thus any assessment of the economic impact of transport developments must incorporate a form of cost-benefit analysis in order to establish whether it has yielded a potential Pareto improvement where society as a whole has benefited from the change.

Notes

1. A potential Pareto improvement occurs where the gains of the beneficiaries are greater than the losses of the losers to the extent that the former can compensate the latter but still yield a net gain.
2. Teheranian, Hakimzadeh and Vidale (26–7) cite the demonstration, fusion, compression, preventive and stylisation effects.

2 Road Systems

This chapter looks at roads and their services from the eighteenth century until the coming of the bicycle and then motorised transport in the last four decades of the nineteenth century. Eighteenth- and nineteenth-century developments in road transport were less revolutionary than changes taking place in shipping and the railways. While the motor industry clearly transformed road haulage, progress in road construction and transport in the eighteenth and nineteenth centuries was important for several west European countries as a significant break from previous practice and a much neglected contribution to the early industrialisation of those particular countries.

ROAD SYSTEMS IN 1750

We possess few useful or reliable figures for the size of the road networks of European countries in the eighteenth century. This is hardly surprising since most roads were little more than unmaintained mud tracks or bridlepaths. It was the condition rather than the size of the road system that mattered most. Poorly maintained roads were unable to support coaches or carts and would be blocked to most traffic by snow and rainfall in winter. The quality varied on stretches of the same road; in France the road from St Étienne to Lyons was good as far as Rive de Gier but of poor quality thereafter. In the mid-eighteenth century Russia was said to have no roads of any worth. Wide dusty tracks existed in summer which turned to impassable bogs for most of the rest of the year. Much the same could be said of the rest of eastern Europe particularly the Balkans. Improved routes between Moscow and St Petersburg were completed in the second quarter of the century. Several roads were built in Austria-Hungary by Charles VI but, similar to the Russian experience, they were intended primarily for military purposes. Karlstadt was linked to Fiume and Vienna to Trieste, both providing communications between central Europe and the Adriatic.

In several west European countries there is evidence of improvements and extensions to the road system before 1750. An Act of 1555 formed the basis of road policy in Britain. Responsibility for the upkeep of local roads lay with the parish but this duty was often neglected. An Act of 1663 took the important precedent of authorising the collection of a toll from road users to finance the cost of maintenance. A turnpike was erected on the road for the collection of these dues. This measure applied solely to a particularly heavily used section of the Great Irish Road between London and Holyhead and was regarded as exceptional and temporary. Scepticism of the scheme prevented its extension beyond a few roads before the early eighteenth century. In 1706 responsibility for the turnpikes was transferred from the over-worked justices of the peace to a body of local trustees. By 1750 143 trusts had been established covering 3000 miles (Albert, 1983, 60). In France the future road network was mapped out and building begun in the 1730s and 1740s under the supervision of the Controller General of Finance, Orry (Arbellot). This task had been made easier and more professional by the existence since 1716 of the Corps des Ponts et Chaussées, the first government body of civil engineers in Europe. In 1747 a training school, the École des Ponts et Chaussées, was opened.

ROAD IMPROVEMENTS, 1750–1860

The main period of improvement and extension of the European road network came after 1750; earlier developments in Britain and France had established little more than a spring-board for expansion. French and British attitudes towards road development began to change in the later eighteenth century. Economic growth, population expansion and the neglect of responsibilities by local authorities was causing a deterioration in the condition of the roads. Much of the opposition to turnpikes dissolved as they came to be understood and the benefits of the early improvements digested. The offer of concessionary rates quelled local opposition. Legislation governing roads was more readily enforced with government surveyors ensuring that local authorities and trusts undertook sufficient maintenance. In France a law of 1798 enacted that responsibility for local roads (*chemins vicinaux*) rested with the commune. This law, together with legislation in 1824, was rarely enforced. A further law in 1836 more clearly defined the responsibility of the commune. A tax of up to five per cent could be levied towards the cost of road maintenance and each family had to provide three days labour (*prestation*) from each male aged between 18 and 60 and for each cart they owned.

Of much importance was the movement away from the minimalist policy which had addressed the problem of deteriorating roads by discouraging their use rather than improving their quality. British Acts of 1662, 1670 and 1691 restricted wagon weights and the number of animals in draught while the 1773 General Turnpike Act contained 28 clauses governing weights, carriage construction and wheel sizes. As late as 1806 a French order limited the weight of carts and required a minimum width of wheel rim. However, insufficient surveillance and weighbridges made enforcement of these policies difficult. The high cost of enforcing minimalist legislation could be better used in improving the road system.

Road building technology changed little before the late eighteenth century when John Metcalfe, Thomas Telford, John Macadam and others began to apply more scientific methods. Macadam constructed roads with the correct degree of convexity for effective drainage. Steep gradients or long contour routes were avoided by more tunnelling and bridge building. Increased strength and durability were achieved by packing broken stones into the road's surface. In the nineteenth century new materials were introduced to preserve and strengthen roads. Concrete was used on the road between Highgate and Archway in London in 1829 and on Austrian roads by the 1850s. Asphalt, a mixture of bitumen, pitch and sand, became popular on French roads. It was first used in a mastic form in 1835 on the Pont Royal and Pont du Caroussel in Paris. The alternative, more popular in Britain, was the tarmacadam surface which added tar to the basic Macadam stone surface. This was first used on part of the Nottingham to London road in 1845. The main impetus for the extensive use of tar surfaces, however, came with the introduction of motorised vehicles at the end of the nineteenth century.

The 'demonstration effect' helps to explain the quickening of activity in the century after 1750. The perceived benefits of road improvement and extension in one area encouraged action elsewhere. Sometimes the motive was to prevent the diversion of trade to another area or the estimated profits to be derived from toll charges. This helps to explain the cyclical nature of road investment in Britain and the emulation of one state by another in Germany. It also explains the attitude of the Swiss bund which in 1848 ordered the construction of new roads to capture the trade between France and Italy through the Mont Cenis pass.

Road extension and improvement was concentrated initially upon main routes. A French decree of 1776 defined the *routes nationales* and at the end of the century Napoleon began to build a series of *routes impériales* designed to serve military purposes. Between the end of the French Wars and 1850, 7000 km of new main roads were built together with 23 000 km of departmental roads (Price, 1983, 37). After 1850 several *routes nationales* were built in remote areas such as the Hautes- and Basses-Alpes but attention was concentrated upon the *chemins vicinaux*. Road construction in Britain was concentrated into several spurts or 'manias', notably 1750–72, the early 1790s, 1809–12 and the mid-1820s. Roads built and improved in the first period were frequently on major routes. The later booms more specifically served the needs of the industrialising northern cities though some late eighteenth century roads were designed for military purposes including 15 in the vicinity of the Kent ports (Albert, 1983, 41).

In spite of good river and canal systems, Belgium and the Netherlands built reasonably extensive road networks. Helped by turnpike tolls the Belgian network expanded rapidly between the end of the French Wars and 1830 by which time a network of over 3000 km of maintained roads had been established which was particularly extensive in Flanders, Brabant and Hainaut (Placq). The network had doubled by 1850 but then grew more slowly to 1880 with more emphasis upon minor routes and poorly covered regions such as Campine and Ardennes. Dutch roads were built up in the eighteenth century to a network of around 3000 km to complement the extensive waterway system (Milward and Saul, 1973, 112). Several major routes were built including a link between Rotterdam and Antwerp in 1751 but more emphasis was laid upon connecting services with the long distance passenger waterway service (*trekvaart*).

Most of the German states lacked a decent road network before the nineteenth century. Frederick the Great of Prussia had opposed road building arguing that it might aid potential invaders. His death in 1786 facilitated an expansion of road building which gained greater momentum after 1815 when Bavaria and Westphalia began developing their road systems. Berlin was linked with the chief towns of Prussia and roads were built connecting states including a major north–south link from the North Sea to Switzerland which brought Prussia into closer economic and political contact with the south German states. In addition it attempted to attract trade to the Zollverein by running via Magdeburg and Nuremburg rather than through Bremen, Hanover and Frankfurt-am-Main. The formation of the Zollverein encouraged inter-state co-operation in road building and maintenance (Thimme, 4). Two major highways were also built from the Ruhr, one travelling south-west to Nuremberg and the

other north-west to Soest. Secondary roads were built for the movement of agricultural produce to local markets, for example in the
county of Mark. After 1815 Westphalia, under the presidency of
Ludwig von Vincke, actively expanded her road system. A successful
period of road expansion occurred over the next quarter of a century
including the completion of a major arterial road across the state
from Wesel to Minden.

In Spain a system of royal highways (*calzada*) was begun which was
financed by indirect taxation and turnpike tolls and was supervised by
qualified civil engineers. By the 1830s 5000 km had been built but the
planned network remained unfinished. In the following two decades
construction accelerated causing a doubling in the size of the network
(Gomez-Mendoza, 1981, 5–6). Roads of good quality were built with
low gradients and convex surfaces but in a country with irregular,
mountainous terrain this spelled high costs and delays to build many
bridges, tunnels and causeways. The highways were designed for
military purposes and linked Madrid directly with coastal towns such
as Barcelona, Cartagena and Cadiz. They bypassed major towns like
Toledo and Valladolid and did nothing to open up backward areas of
the inland economy. A network of local roads (*caminos*) evolved
although most remained primitive and unsuitable for wheeled traffic
before the twentieth century. This was partly the fault of carriers who
often varied their route along minor tracks in search of good grazing
ground for their draught animals.

Little progress was made in road building in most other parts of
Europe. Italy gave scant attention to road building before unification. Even after the 1860s road policy was subordinated to the further
expansion of the railways and was allocated a small budget. Only in
the northern plains was a reasonable plan of road communications
established. In central and southern Italy and Sardinia and Sicily few
roads of commercial benefit were built.[1] In many areas there remained a heavy reliance upon Roman roads unsuitable though they
often were for the economic structure of nineteenth-century Italy
(Friz). Several passes across the Alps were built such as the Arlberg
pass in 1782–5 and the Simplon pass in 1805. Further roads were built
over the St Bernard and Splugen passes in the 1820s. Few roads were
built in Scandinavia where greater reliance was placed upon coasting
and the waterways as means of transport. Several good roads were
built in Russia including the Siberian highway in 1781 which connected Moscow with Perm, Tobolsk and Irkutsk. Macadam surfaces
were introduced by the end of the eighteenth century. In most areas

of the country, however, roads remained few and primitive throughout the nineteenth century. Communications were even worse in the
Balkans where, it was reported to the British Foreign Office in 1897,
'peasants [were] quite ignorant of 10 or 15 miles distant' (Pounds,
430).

Initiative for road expansion and improvement was a mixture of
public and private action. Several examples have been cited of
military-induced road building by eighteenth-century governments.
By the early nineteenth century governments began supporting road
schemes for economic rather than political reasons. Vincke's policy
of road expansion in Westphalia was born of the belief that this was
the best way to develop the considerable economic potential of the
Ruhr. Bypassing the problems private enterprise faced in raising
money during the depressed postwar years, he raised a loan in 1822
and kept down costs by putting work out to competitive tender and
by hiring the unemployed as a form of winter relief work. In France
the state planned the network, defined the *routes nationales* and
supervised their development. It was also responsible for developing
the local roads and improving communications in remote areas. The
identification of better roads with economic development may be
seen by the fact that the Minister of Public Works estimated in 1860
that a reduction of 0.01fr. per tonne/km in the freight rate would
yield an annual saving of 16 million francs on the movement of goods
on the *routes nationales* alone (Price, 1983, 260). The engineers of the
Corps des Ponts et Chaussées supervised and inspected road building. Central government was the major source of finance for the
routes nationales and local roads were supported by local government. Successive pieces of legislation, culminating in the 1836 law
had failed to ensure sufficient financial provision for local roads with
the result that the state periodically intervened with increased support. A law of 1868 granted 100 million francs of state aid over ten
years which was followed by a further 80 million in 1880 (Price, 1983,
263–4). In Spain the state was responsible for the construction of the
expensive system of royal highways. Maintenance of local roads was
undertaken by local authorities with a greater or lesser degree of
diligence. The few respectable roads built in Austria-Hungary in the
nineteenth century were privately sponsored in contrast to the state
support for military roads in the previous century (Blum).

Road construction, like most areas of economic activity, lay principally in the private domain in Britain. The turnpike trusts were the
main agency of road improvement and these resulted largely from the

initiative of individual merchants, farmers, landowners and local government authorities who stood to benefit from the scheme although they required parliamentary consent before they could come into being. They were responsible for the financing, management and operation of the roads. There were periodic road grants from the government including £20 000 towards the improvement of the Great Irish Road in 1815 and by 1830 over £700 000 had been spent on the building of roads, bridges, harbours and similar civil engineering works (M. Hughes, 200). However, there was no support policy for turnpikes when toll receipts began to decline after the 1830s. Annual Turnpike Continuance Acts omitted or repealed particular turnpikes. Exceptionally in South Wales, where the Rebecca riots of 1843 had been focused on the turnpikes, an Act of the following year consolidated tolls, established a road authority for each county, compensated old turnpikes and appointed road surveyors and a General Superintendent of County Roads.

ROAD TRANSPORT, 1780–1860

While road extensions and improvements were important much depended upon how road users, particularly specialist hauliers, responded to the new conditions. Better roads presented opportunities for improved vehicles and a greater range of services which encouraged new entrants into the industry and heightened competition. At the same time, road hauliers faced increased competition from canals in the second half of the eighteenth century and then from the railways after 1830.

In the eighteenth century there were two main types of carrier, the professional common carrier and the local or peasant carrier. The former worked full time in the haulage industry owning a series of animals and carts which he operated from specialist premises. He carried consignments under specific conditions over mostly long but sometimes short distances and frequently ran on a regular route though not to a fixed timetable. In some countries his activities were governed by a series of regulations relating to such issues as freight rates and the nature of the service in return for which he received certain privileges. Pickfords were an important example of a professional carrier in England. In the mid-eighteenth century they owned six wagons and 50 carts which they deployed in a regular service between Manchester and London (Turnbull, 1979, 17–21). In

Spain the government encouraged professional carriers with a series of privileges which included grazing rights and tax and military exemptions. This policy was self-defeating because the government then dominated the services provided by professional carriers for the sake of military and administrative duties to the exclusion of private merchants and farmers. These included the movement of munitions, ships' timber, and the salt and tobacco monopolies together with mercury from the Almaden mines and gold and silver to the mint at Seville. Peasant carriers were sometimes requisitioned in a random fashion to supply Madrid with food and fuel.

Spanish professional carriers sometimes consolidated their carts into cart trains (*cuadrilla*) of around 25 to 50 vehicles. These were entrusted to a professional train captain who hired a crew, arranged the cargoes and overnight stops, kept the accounts and distributed the profits among the owners. Trains of 40 to 50 carts carried copper to the mint at Segovia (Ringrose, 1970, 36). Professional carters operated for most of the year from March to about November or December. Low demand and poor weather conditions discouraged winter deployment. This gave them an opportunity to fatten up their draught animals in winter in the rich pastures of the valleys in the southern and western regions of the country and therefore helped to resolve the problem of insufficient grass for satisfactory roadside grazing during hot Spanish summers. In the more temperate climate of northern Europe seasonal pasturage was less of a problem and with substantial road improvements all year round operation became the norm in the nineteenth century.

Peasant carriers operated over shorter distances and frequently conducted business on a part-time and seasonal basis according to the vagaries of farming which was often their main source of income. However, they were responsible for the bulk of road transport provision, in Spain as much as 90 per cent (Ringrose, 1968, 68). They were prominent in local market towns operating to and from outlying villages within a radius of about 25 to 35 miles (Chartres and Turnbull, 92). They might make one or two journeys to market each week leaving the rest of the week to farming, merchanting or a cottage industry. Farming was the most likely combined occupation since it shared the cost of animals. Most carriers owned only a few animals and sometimes operated for as little as one to four months a year. This made for significant seasonal variations in the supply of transport. Their main duties included taking agricultural produce to market, carrying passengers on local routes and acting as shopping agents for villagers. The number of local carriers in Britain doubled to about 25 000 from the eighteenth to the end of the nineteenth century though they were more likely to work full time in the haulage industry than their Spanish counterparts (Everitt, 186).

Improvements in road surfaces enabled more and larger coaches and carts to be used. Pack animals were gradually replaced by towed carts carrying heavier loads as wheeled vehicles could be used on the new surfaces. In Britain the maximum permissible load rose from 30 to 120 cwts between the early eighteenth century and 1765 and in France average loads carried by road increased from 650 kg at the end of the French wars to 1350 by 1865 (Price, 1983, 270). In Spain medium-sized wagons (*galera*) were increasingly used by professional hauliers though the larger *carreta*, which was built more like a wagon and pulled by four to eight mules, was less common. Smaller carts were introduced by local carriers though in Spain the poor state of local roads made pack animals the more suitable form of transport. Even the substitution of the horse for the mule, common in other western European countries, was discouraged in Spain by a government keen to retain horses for military use. Well into the nineteenth century the mule continued to be used for heavy loads and the donkey for light ones. The design of coaches and carts also improved. Steel springs became common in late eighteenth-century coaches which permitted higher speed and the carriage of outside passengers. Further refinements included the introduction of brakes and a variable front axis. In general, better roads permitted lighter designs and therefore less dead-weight.

While a range of freight services were available before 1700, it was the eighteenth and nineteenth centuries which witnessed a growth in the volume, range and nature of passenger road services. The number of passenger miles completed in England grew rapidly from 183 000 in 1773 to 2 043 000 by 1816 (Chartres and Turnbull, 69). In particular there was a rising number of regular inter-city services linking the capital with the major regional cities. In Britain these included connections to London from Manchester in 1754, from Liverpool in 1757, from Leeds and Sheffield in 1760 and from Holyhead in 1776. By the end of the eighteenth century many lesser towns with populations of 1000 to 1500 had direct road services to London. Short haul and suburban passenger services expanded around major cities like London, Bath, Birmingham, Bristol, Liverpool, Norwich and Nottingham. Direct communications between provincial centres remained less common and often necessitated a series of short hauls or travelling via London. The falling real price of passenger transport explains the rapid increase in output given the high price-elasticity of its demand. Demand was also highly income-elastic which accounts for the concentration of growth in the north of England and the Midlands, the areas most affected by the 'industrial revolution'. The types of services offered expanded under the pressure of heightened competition. Services of a faster or slower and more or less comfortable nature were offered with the tariff fluctuating accordingly. Post chaises offered faster and more luxurious travel while the slow coaches took longer and offered more primitive facilities. In France a distinction was drawn between *roulage ordinaire* and *roulage accéléré*. Many of these changes also affected freight transport services particularly the increased frequency and diversity of service.

Road carriers had to face competition from inland waterways and the railways. Waterway competition was the less serious because of its limitations of speed and terrain. Rivers and canals proved most effective in lowland areas surrounding coalfields and industrial towns where competitive rates could be offered for the carriage of coal and other high-bulk low-value items with a low dispersion rate. Elsewhere road services were frequently more efficient because of their ability to deal with multiple consignments and cope more easily with the vagaries of climate and terrain. Flooding, ice or drought could cause a shift of freight from the waterways to the roads. High value goods such as textiles and light metalwares were carried by road, though it was often the needs of the consignment rather than the nature of the product which determined the mode of transport. Complementarity as well as competition governed the relationship between road and river. Road transport often dispersed consignments from the quayside to areas beyond the reaches of the waterways. The greatest road traffic density frequently occured in areas with the best waterways, for example Normandy, Paris, the Loire, the Rhône and the Puy de Dôme in France.

The railway had a much greater effect on road transport output. It did not face problems of terrain and climate, travelled much faster and, unlike most road carriers, continued to operate after the hours of darkness. The substantial time-saving of the railway can be seen by the fact that in France *roulage ordinaire* achieved about 30–35 and *roulage accéléré* about 60–80 kilometres per day. The railways could cover this distance in a matter of a few hours. The proportion of merchandise carried by road transport in France declined from 53 per cent in 1830 to only 9 per cent by 1905–13 (Toutain, 1967 (2), 248). The most notable feature was the rapid displacement of road services by the railways over long distances where the latter's comparative advantage was greatest. On short hauls the relative cost advantage of the railway was much reduced. Time savings were less and the railways faced high station handling and trans-shipment costs. Nor could railways provide the high rate of dispersion which was required of many short distance services. Indeed, the very existence of the railways increased the demand for 'feeder' style services to and from railheads for which road carriage was most suitable. The more enterprising road hauliers changed the basis of their services from long to short hauls. Pickfords changed from a Manchester to London service to operating as short-haul carriers for several railway companies. A report from Hérault in 1866 showed a 48 per cent rise in traffic on its *chemins vicinaux* between 1856 and 1864 and that transport on the roads leading to railway stations had more than doubled. The rapidity of nineteenth-century urban growth and the suitability of road transport called forth a fleet of around 30 000 carts and wagons in Paris in 1845 belonging to 4500 transport firms (Price, 1981, 9). Moreover, even at the height of the railway boom, there remained many rural villages unconnected to the rail system which continued to rely upon the services of the local carrier.

THE ECONOMIC EFFECTS OF THE ROADS

Road extension and improvement exerted few backward linkages to supply industries. The methods of Macadam and others were achieved at low cost and required little in the way of capital and materials. Road improvement involved little more than remodelling the existing surface. Even labour requirements could be fulfilled with statute labour and the employment of paupers thereby providing little income stimulus to the economy. Nor did road construction introduce any new methods of industrial finance though it did set a precedent for government financing of social overhead capital. In Britain the turnpike trusts were supported by the local mercantile and agrarian classes who stood to benefit from road developments. By the end of the eighteenth century they were joined by a growing group of passive middle-class investors who were more interested in the turnpikes as a remunerative form of investment. In this sense the turnpike trusts may have served as an important link between middle-class savings and economic improvement. Identifying such 'conduits' had been viewed by Postan as a significant problem in the history of economic development.[2] Albert, in his study of English roads, believes the trusts were an important example of Postan's missing conduits (Albert, 1983, 54).

If roads were important in shaping the process of industrialisation in Europe, it lay more in the forward-linkage consequences of the extension of road networks, particularly the integration of markets. Faster and more extensive passenger and mail services encouraged the evolution of more standardised tastes and fashions on a national scale. Citizens of provincial cities read in newspapers and witnessed through travellers the changing social trends in fashionable capitals like Paris and London. It was in the receipt of information, and particularly commercial intelligence, that early road services had their greatest impact on European economy and society. In the carriage of the bulky goods of industrialisation, road transport remained relatively inefficient. While road building in the German states aided the early development of the Ruhr as an industrial area by improving the movement of coal, iron and engineering products to and from the Rhine and Weser, it was the improved postal system and coach services for Ruhr entrepreneurs travelling to the Rhinelands and Berlin which was most important for their businesses.

Pawson has illustrated the benefits of a better road system to the Crowley and Dowlais iron companies. Crowley's business was spread around England particularly in the north-east, the Midlands and London. Improved postal communications were particularly important in coordinating the different regional operations. The Dowlais Iron Company also found improved postal services an important issue. It sent representatives around the country to drum up business from blacksmiths and retailers who then reported back progress and orders by letter. Some roads helped the early growth of the coal trade. The Liverpool to Prescot turnpike, for example, carried a large amount of coal in the first half of the eighteenth century. Such progress, however, was soon overshadowed by the impact of the canals. Agricultural production also benefited from road improvements. Kentish market gardening expanded under the influence of improved communications to London. Corn, fruit and hops were carried to market along the London to Dover road. The Vale of Evesham flourished as a market gardening centre in the eighteenth century as a result of improved communications with urban centres. Price (1983) has shown how road improvements in France transformed agricultural marketing while also improving access to the countryside for industrial products. On the other hand, Lepetit argues that France's extensive road network failed to overcome market fragmentation, privileged trade axes and significant regional differences, problems which were to be solved more effectively by the railway.

French roads were often built or improved in areas of greatest economic activity, thereby accentuating regional economic disparities and hindering the development of a national market. There was a concentration on the north, north-east and Paris Basin while the underdeveloped south witnessed less than its share of construction. In the more remote areas of the Pyrenees, Alps and the central highlands, road building was discouraged by the high cost of bringing materials to the area.

A similar theme is that economic expansion in one area, as a result of improved roads, could divert trade away from other areas rather than increase its overall volume. Eighteenth-century mercantilist ideology was based on the assumption of a fixed volume of economic activity and this can be illustrated by the trade-diversionary road policies adopted by several German states, Switzerland, Belgium and the Netherlands. The diversionary effect could sometimes occur inadvertently. The expansion of the Santander wool trade was partly at the expense of Bilbao. The Forest of Dean declined as a centre for coal and iron production because of the failure of the Crown, which controlled much of the surrounding land, to keep up with road improvements occurring elsewhere. Agricultural areas already close to an urban market or with existing good communications could suffer a loss of trade with the construction of new roads. Road improvement frequently strengthened regional markets at the expense of local ones. Producers could travel further afield to larger regional markets specialising in particular products rather than rely upon smaller and more general local markets. The development of regional markets was also connected with transport developments through the expanding stage coach services for whom regional markets provided conveniently distanced stopping points. In mid-seventeenth century England there were around 800 market towns. By the 1770s this figure had fallen by a third as markets became concentrated upon those towns with good roads and existing facilities (Pawson, 323).

Road building had only a limited economic impact in Spain. It has already been seen that the network of main highways were of political rather than economic benefit and that most of the local roads remained in a primitive condition. One significant exception, however, was the road from Santander to Reinosa and Alar del Rey which encouraged some economic growth of this area of the Castilian plateau. Opened in 1752 it soon carried a substantial volume of traffic principally wool for export through Santander. It also provided outlets for Castilian grain via the northern ports and to Madrid southwards. In 1778 the Spanish crown opened its American empire for direct trade with most Spanish ports which, helped by good road communications, enabled flour-milling and leather-processing to develop in the area. As a result flour exports through Santander grew from virtually nothing in the 1770s to 60 000 barrels by 1793 (Ringrose, 1970, 29–30). In general, however, the Spanish road system contributed little to the economic development of Spain in the eighteenth and nineteenth centuries. Indeed, overland transport before the railway acted as a bottleneck retarding economic progress in Spain. With population rising rapidly, particularly in the grain-deficient cities, road policy was insufficient to cope with the growth in the demand for transport. The government monopoly of professional carriers and the attachment of peasant muleteers to the farm made the supply of transport services highly inelastic and helped to create 'a degree of stagnation and backwardness unmatched in western Europe' (Ringrose, 1968, 79). The problem was highlighted by the Madrid supply crisis of 1804–5 when the government struggled to transport sufficient grain to Madrid during a poor harvest.

In the eighteenth century a series of cities began to spread out along their major arterial roads in a form of ribbon development which encouraged the growth of suburbs and dormitory centres. Summerson's study of Georgian London identified four types of road-related development: villages, country villas, roadside and estate development. The villages of Tottenham and Edmonton were connected with London by the Stamford Turnpike Trust. Country villas were to be found at Richmond and Wimbledon and roadside development at Islington. Access to spa towns, such as Bath and Tunbridge Wells, and seaside resorts was facilitated by turnpikes. It was seen earlier that the coming of the railway altered the pattern of road sevices from long to short hauls, particularly in the distribution of goods from rail termini to surrounding urban areas. As a result, while the road lost much of its importance in long-distance commercial communications, after the middle of the nineteenth century it became important in the provision of retailing services in and around many towns and cities, thereby reinforcing the eighteenth century urban expansion.

Road improvements increased the cost efficiency of transport in a number of ways. Better road services facilitated faster travel and therefore greater utilisation of carts, coaches and animals. The use of more and larger carts with fewer draught animals, as a result of better roads, also reduced the unit cost of transport. Improved surfaces minimised the damage to carts and horses. Tighter schedules, as well as better roads, help explain the faster journey times as coaches and carts were kept on the road for longer periods each day. Regular changes of horses at set intervals also increased speeds. In France the average speed rose from about 3.4 km per hour in 1800 to 9.5 by 1848 (Price, 1981, 10). One historian has estimated that journey times in Britain fell by between a third and a fifth in the period 1750–1830 (Jackman, 339). The greatest time reductions occurred in the period 1750–80, when turnpike construction was at its peak, and the 1820s, when the influence of Telford and Macadam was being strongly felt. The journey from Edinburgh to London, for example, fell from ten to four days between 1754 and 1776 while that from London to Holyhead fell from 41 hours in 1815 to 28 hours in 1831 (Pawson, 289; M. Hughes, 206–7). Besides reducing the cost of transport, quicker journeys enabled more rapid commercial communication and allowed firms to hold less capital in the form of raw materials and inventories thereby releasing more resources for use as fixed capital. Thus the average time taken for a letter to go from London to Durham was reduced from three to one and a half days during the course of the eighteenth century (Pawson, 306).

There was less need for seasonal laying-up as many roads became passable all the year round except in times of severe bad weather. Thus many coach services which had not run in winter-time at the beginning of the eighteenth century began to change their policy from around mid-century and by the last few decades many routes could be travelled all year. This enabled coach and cart owners to use their vehicles continuously and so reduce capital costs. Seasonality was less easily overcome in Spain where peasants returned to the farms in the sowing and harvesting seasons and professional carriers sought winter pasturage for their animals. The elimination of seasonality is an important consideration in the development of a modern capitalist economy because it enables capital equipment to be used all the year round and for stocks of inventories and raw materials to be reduced and converted into fixed capital.

Several costs of transport increased through the course of this period. The existence of tolls on many previously free roads was the main increase although the requirements of highway legislation, such as broader wheels, and periodic rises in the price of winter fodder also exerted an upward pressure. Taken together, however, the cost reductions more than offset these increases. The extent to which these cost reductions were converted into lower freight rates depends on the nature of competition in the transport industry and the manner in which these savings were used. A high degree of perfect competition existed in road transport services and so there is little reason to believe that cost savings were converted into higher carrier profits. Rate regulation by the government was introduced in Britain in 1691 and lasted until 1831. It was long believed that these rates soon became a 'dead letter' (Willan, 1961–2) though more recent historiography has argued that they continued to be effective and were kept closely attuned to market forces (Albert, 1968; Turnbull, 1985).

Cost savings were used to improve the quality, range and speed of services as well as reducing their price. It has already been seen that speeds rose and a wider range of services became available. Evidence on rates is sporadic and suffers from the problem of trying to compare services of different quality. Moreover, climatic changes and the availability of a return freight affected the rate charged. In 1816, for example, freight rates between Marseilles and Lyons rose 250 per cent after flooding on the Rhône at a time of heavy grain imports caused a reversion of traffic to the roads (Price, 1983, 44). Higher rates were often charged on long hauls because of the reduced likelihood of finding a return cargo. Pawson (297) calculates that average freight rates were falling in real terms in Britain in the second half of the eighteenth century, a conclusion similar to that reached by Toutain (1967 (2), 56) for France in the first half of the nineteenth century. In Spain Ringrose found no real fall in peasant carrier rates, 1773–87, and a significant rise in those of professional carriers, reflecting the severe transport bottleneck which was afflicting the Spanish economy (1970, 84).

While the impact of improvements in roads and their services was less important than the railways and affected fewer countries they at least set in motion many of the economic changes which were to achieve their maximum impact with the railways. Pawson's conclusion for Britain could equally be applied to France and Germany: 'many of the changes which have been traditionally ascribed to the railways – coalfield industrial concentration, regional agricultural specialisation, the destruction of small markets, suburban growth and the development of the resorts – were already in motion in the eighteenth century encouraged by the modernisation of road transport services and public highways' (339).

NOTES

1. R. S. Eckhaus, 'The north–south differential in Italian economic development', *Jnl. Econ. Hist.*, 21, 1961, 285–317.
2. M. M. Postan, 'Recent trends in the accumulation of capital', *Econ. Hist. Rev.*, 6, 1935, 2.

3 Inland Waterways

The improvement of rivers and the construction of canals was an important feature of transport development during the eighteenth and nineteenth centuries. While waterway improvements occurred in previous centuries, particularly in the Dutch economy, there was a concentration of activity into these two centuries. It was seen in the previous chapter that the coming of the railways caused a shift in the pattern of road services rather than their catastrophic decline. Similarly, the railway did not spell the collapse of waterway services in most countries and in some areas it was followed by an increase in waterborne traffic.

WATERWAY IMPROVEMENTS

River improvements and canals were not new in the eighteenth century. Artificial waterways were built in Russia as early as the twelfth and fourteenth centuries. Sweden had canals by the sixteenth century while the Exeter Canal of 1566 was possibly Britain's first deadwater canal with pound locks. In France the Canal de Briare was completed in 1642 and the Canal du Midi in 1682. The Dutch had built an entire river and canal network in the seventeenth century. The rapid growth of the Dutch economy had provided both the demand and the finance for an improved transport system ideally suited to the country's geology. Dutch waterways expanded rapidly in the 1630s and 1640s and then again between 1656 and 1665. In the earlier period four regional networks were established respectively upon Leiden, Delft, the Hague and Bruges. Links between these systems were drawn during the second phase (De Vries, 26–34). It was during the eighteenth and nineteenth centuries, however, that the waterways of France, Germany, Britain and Belgium witnessed their main expansion.

Demographic and economic growth in Europe in the eighteenth century exposed the limitations of the existing system of inland waterways. The Dutch had faced these problems a century earlier. In 1772 traffic on the Moselle was at a virtual standstill because of customs dues, tolls, navigational obstacles and the ravages of war (Cermakian, 27–34). The unnavigability of stretches of many rivers

Table 3.1 European Canal Systems, 1800–1914 (km)

Country	Britain	Germany	France	Russia	Netherlands	Belgium	Spain
Length	7,200	6,600	4,170	500	650	450	300
Year	1,850	1,914	1,847	1,914	1,800	1,830	1,856

Note: Figures include canals, canalised rivers and navigations.

Sources: Duckham, 1983, 109; Milward and Saul, 1973, 377, 441; Price, 1981, 16; Hanson, 4; De Vries, 42–3; Gomez-Mendoza, 1981, 11.

was a major drawback. The Rhône was notorious for its shallows as it meandered between different channels (Rivet, 1956). The circuitous nature of the Weaver in Cheshire made for extended journeys and awkward navigation. River improvements, or 'navigations', aimed at deepening and concentrating the channel, building up the riverbanks and cutting off long curves in the river. Some navigational obstacles were man-made, particularly the tolls and prescriptive rights demanded by riverside settlements. In the eighteenth century there were more than thirty separate tolls and prescriptive rights on the Rhine. Cities such as Cologne and Mainz could oblige passing vessels to unload their goods and offer them for sale (*Stapelrecht*). At other points cargoes had to be loaded onto another vessel considered more suitable for the next part of the journey (*Umschlagsrecht*). Reducing or eliminating these rights required an attack on local vested interests. Where the river ran though several countries, as did the Rhine, freedom of navigation required international agreement. Nor did the existing waterways serve adequately the needs of growing industrial economies for links between major towns or between industries and their materials and markets.

In Britain about forty rivers were improved between 1660 and 1750 (Duckham, 1983, 101). The Mersey and Irwell Navigation (1734) linked Manchester to Liverpool and the sea via the Irwell and Mersey rivers. In the second half of the eighteenth century, however, increased economic activity and the success of the early schemes turned interest towards deadwater navigations beginning with the Sankey Brook Navigation (partly opened in 1757), which connected the coal mines of St Helens with the Mersey, and the Bridgewater Canal (1761) which linked the Duke of Bridgewater's coal mines at Worsley with Manchester. In the following decade and a half at least fifty Acts were passed authorising individual canals and navigations (Duckham, 1983, 101). These included a series of long distance trunk canals which took many years to complete. The Trent and Mersey Canal Act was passed in 1766 but the project only reached completion eleven years later. Its promoter, Josiah Wedgwood, used the canal to ship his pottery to the ports of Liverpool and Hull and to receive coal and clay. The Forth and Clyde Canal, designed to give Edinburgh merchants access to the Clyde, was begun in 1768 and not completed until 1790 while the building of the Leeds and Liverpool Canal took from 1770 to 1816. Many of these early canals were designed to carry industrial raw materials such as coal and iron ore and were concentrated in the industrialising towns of the Midlands and the north of England. Between 1759 and 1774 thirty-three out of fifty-two projects were thus located (Duckham, 1983, 105). While many schemes were intended to ease transport bottlenecks, such as the Trent and Mersey and the Bridgewater Canals, others attempted to induce industrial expansion. In the later nineteenth century, the Manchester Ship Canal was conceived as a solution to the slow down in the city's cotton industry (Farnie, 1980, 72).

The mid 1770s and early 1780s witnessed a decline in the number of new waterway projects due to the economic downturn of those years. This was followed by another canal boom as economic conditions improved in the early 1790s. Similar to road building, the good profits of some early canals attracted more passive investors interested in dividends rather than better transport. In this period developments were spread more widely around the country including southern agricultural regions. Few canals were built in Britain after the French Wars and none at all after 1830 except for the New Junction, which was really a rationalisation of the Aire and Calder network, and the Manchester Ship Canal which linked Manchester to the Mersey for ocean going vessels and turned Salford into a busy inland port.

In France waterway development was likewise concentrated in the industrialising regions which meant the north, north-east and Paris basin. Construction was concentrated around the period 1815–50 when two-thirds of the canals were built. The Canal de la Sensée (1820), the Canal d'Aire à la Bassée (1825) and the Canal de St Quentin (1828) were all designed to improve the market links of the northern coalfields. Existing rivers were improved and links made between the major rivers (Loire, Seine, Rhône- Saône and Rhine). The Rhône-Rhine Canal was completed in 1832 and the Marne-Rhine Canal in 1853. The Canal de Bourgogne (1832) linked the Seine and Saône and provided a more direct route between Paris and

Lyons. Earlier, in 1793, the Canal du Centre had connected the Loire at Digoin with the Saône at Chalon.

The problems of navigation on the Moselle were tackled in the eighteenth century by the Lecreulx Plan which recommended improvements (dredging, removing obstacles and repairing the banks) and canalising sections. Progress, however, was halted by the French Wars. After 1815 the river benefited from the declaration of the freedom of navigation. This was of particular advantage to the movement of bulk materials such as coal and iron produced in the area because many of the taxes had been based upon the volume rather than the value of the cargo. In 1837–42 further improvements were made to the river and in 1867 government authorisation was given to a plan to canalise the Moselle between Frouard and Thionville (Cermakian, 47–8). In contrast to Britain, French waterways continued to be developed and improved throughout the nineteenth century, for example, in 1882 the Canal de l'Est linked the Nancy region with Belgium to the north and the Rhône-Saône corridor to the south.

German waterway development came even later and postdated the arrival of the railway. In 1845 the Ludwig Canal was built to connect the Rhine and the Danube and so provide a link between the Black Sea and the North Sea. In spite of this and several other projects there were only 750 km of canals in the German states by 1850 and about double that amount of rivers. Between 1873 and 1914, however, the length of canals and canalised rivers doubled from 3400 km to 6600 km (Milward and Saul, 1977, 43). The rapidity of German industrialisation together with the high potential of her rivers led to a surge in the demand for waterborne inland transport. In 1886 the Main was canalised between Mainz and Frankfurt so that the larger Rhine barges could travel upstream. In a similar vein the Elbe was improved in order to increase the volume and size of traffic which could reach Magdeburg. In 1895 the Kiel Canal was completed as a wider, deeper and stronger version of the Eider Canal built in 1784 to link the North Sea and Baltic while by-passing the Kattegat. The Dortmund-Ems canal (1899) provided a link between the coalfields of the Emscher Valley and the port of Emden, via the river Ems, for the import of iron ore and the distribution of coal. The Dortmund-Ems Canal was also part of a policy to link the Rhine, Elbe and Oder. The Herne Canal completed the link between the Rhine and the Elbe in 1914 while connections between the Elbe and the Oder were improved by canalising the Havel and the Spree.

Improvements to navigation on the Rhine, however, were most vital to German inland transport. In 1809 the engineer Johann Gottfried Tulla drew up plans to improve the navigability of the Rhine. His proposal to cut a channel through the upper river and secure it with dykes leaving the current to scour the channel was enacted between 1824 and 1832 (Valdenaire). Although this improved navigation in the upper reaches it made two-way trading more difficult until the introduction of steamboats powerful enough to combat the increased current. Strasbourg experienced little trade for much of the third quarter of the nineteenth century as a result. The greatest obstacle to Rhine traffic was the exaction of tolls and prescriptive rights which made long-haul movements on the river slow and expensive. In 1792 the French Revolutionary government had declared freedom of navigation on all rivers. This principle was reaffirmed in the Treaty of Vienna in 1815. The terms of the treaty, however, were open to various interpretations. Navigation was to be free from the point of navigability to the river mouth. The Dutch interpreted the river mouth as being where the influence of the tide was felt which meant about 90 km up river from the North Sea and that the Lek was the only true continuation of the Rhine. By this interpretation tolls could be levied along most of the Dutch Rhine. This 'quarrel of the river mouths' remained unresolved until the Mainz Convention of 1831 established rules for the navigation of the Rhine and the collection of some dues for river maintenance and the 1868 Mannheim Convention declared free navigation on the Rhine from Basel to the open sea. All tolls were also to be abolished on Dutch waterways and those between Belgium and Holland for craft of the Rhine's riparian states. The convention, moreover, established the Central Rhine Commission as an advisory body (Cermakian, 44–6).

Russia possessed a series of navigable rivers although their north –south flow made them inappropriate for overland intra-European trade. In the early eighteenth century Peter the Great began a canal-building programme to link St Petersburg with the main river systems. The Vychnyvolotschok Canal was built to provide a link between the Baltic and Caspian Seas. The project was a success and by the second half of the eighteenth century more than 3000 craft were using the canal (Pilkington, 554). In 1805 a more direct link between the Black Sea and the Gulf of Riga was achieved by a canal between the Beresina and Dvina rivers. Between 1808 and 1811 the Tikhvine and Mariinsk canals linked the Neva and Volga. By the

1820s a continuous navigable link had been established between the Black Sea and the Baltic. The Volga was the longest and most important river in European Russia. Its major settlements served as distribution points particularly Astrakhan, Nizhnii Novgorod, Kazan, Rybinsk and Tver.

Little progress was made in waterway improvements elsewhere in eastern Europe. The Danube received only occasional attention as a result of its comparatively low usage. The Fritz Canal connected the Danube with the Tisza in 1802. The Treaty of Vienna in 1815 established an international commission to supervise navigation of the Danube but the Austro-Hungarians, Russians and Ottomans showed little interest in improving the river. After the Crimean War a commission was established with more extensive powers which supervised several measures, especially the improvement of navigation on the Sulina Channel between the Danube and the Black Sea. In 1898 canalisation of the Danube at the Iron Gates was completed thus overcoming the major hurdle to navigation along the river (Hajnal, 189–91).

Belgium added many improvements to its waterway system in the nineteenth century. Connections between existing rivers and port access were both improved. In 1823 the Pommeroeul-Antoing canal connected the Haine and Scheldt basins. Access to the port of Ghent was improved by the construction of a canal to Terneuzen on the western Scheldt in 1827. Several canals were built to connect the Meuse and Scheldt rivers: in 1827–32 they were linked by way of Brussels and Charleroi and in 1844–59 by way of Liège and Antwerp. These waterways facilitated coal distribution in the central industrial region as well as improving communications with the port of Antwerp.

The Dutch waterway system was in decline by the nineteenth century but new waterways were required for land drainage or improved access to the ports. By the nineteenth century access to Amsterdam was becoming more difficult with the growth in ship sizes beyond the capacity of the shallow river Ij. Between 1819 and 1824 the North Holland Canal was built northwards from Amsterdam along the length of the peninsula to Den Helder. This soon proved a long and difficult journey as ship sizes continued to grow and was superseded in 1876 by the North Sea Canal which took the much shorter westward route to the sea. Aware of the importance of the growing trade of the Rhine, Amsterdam improved its links in this direction culminating in the building of the Merwede Canal

(1883–92). Rotterdam had to face up to the siltation of the Brielsche Maas and the growth of ship sizes. The Voorne Canal was built in 1823 across the island of Voorne to Hellevoetsluis. Increasing ship sizes meant it too became rapidly obsolescent and was superseded in 1872 by the New Waterway which went westwards to the sea. Connections with the Rhine were improved by the building of a cut between the Lek and the Waal.

The rivers of southern Europe contained little potential as trade arteries, most being short and frequently unnavigable in summer. The exceptions were the Douro, Tagus, Guadalquivir and the Ebro in the Iberian peninsula. Part of the Ebro was canalised and the Castile canal was built to connect Valladolid and Alar del Rey, and the Aragon Canal to link Zaragoza and Tudela. In general the geology of Spain was unsuited to waterway development and financial support was intermittent so that by 1850 only 300 km of canals existed (Gomez-Mendoza, 1981, 6). Indicative of Spain's financial and physical problems is the fact that it took over one hundred years to build the Castile Canal (1751–1852). Italy possessed few waterways outside the Po Valley and even here navigation could often be difficult and toll charges high. Several canals, such as the Cavour Canal, were built for irrigation rather than trade.

In much of continental Europe the planning and finance of waterways lay predominantly in the public domain. The development of Dutch waterways in the seventeenth century and their improvement in the nineteenth was largely under the auspices of local and national governments who financed much of the construction and supervised their operation. The North Sea Canal was a joint public and private venture but the burden of finance fell on the state after the costs rose far above the original estimates. In France, Belgium and Germany the waterways were built and maintained mainly by the state with some help from the municipalities and private enterprise. French governments played a central role in the development of the waterway network between 1814 and 1848, initiating 80 per cent of new projects and using the Corps des Ponts et Chaussées to organise construction (Geiger, 330). Becquey, the General Director of the Corps, decided in 1817 to begin a major expansion of the waterways in order to ease the transport bottleneck of the economy. In a report of 1820 he argued that the state should plan the network and encourage the support of private capital. This policy was pursued in the following years with the state granting concessions and special privileges to joint stock companies formed for the purpose of waterway development. The government guaranteed cost overruns and gave the companies a veto over changes in tolls (Geiger, 330–6). It also financed major projects which were unable to attract private capital. The lion's share of financing came from the public purse; between 1821 and 1853 the state spent 536m fr. on the waterways compared with 101m fr. by the concessionary companies (Price, 1983, 32). In contrast to Britain much of the private initiative and capital came from the wealthy bankers and entrepreneurs of Paris rather than local sources.

The planning and finance of waterway construction lay in the private sector in England. The motives of major canal promoters and builders like Josiah Wedgwood and the Duke of Bridgewater have already been indicated. On other occasions the planning and finance would be organised by groups of local trustees or commissioners whose businesses and farms would benefit from the scheme. Tolls were used to finance development which was mostly non-profit making although the Aire and Calder proprietors recorded large profits. The third form of promotion and financing was through joint stock companies although this was also largely of a local nature. With share denominations in excess of £100 this form of finance was aimed at the landed and mercantile classes rather than a mass investing public. Ward has estimated that 24 per cent of the finance for British waterways came from the landed classes and 40 per cent from the mercantile sector (18, 74). In the mania of the 1790s, denominations were reduced in order to attract a wider field of investors in an increasingly competitive capital market for canal shares. The state lent some money for waterway schemes under the 1817 Exchequer Bill loan facilities but this was after the main era of expansion. The Manchester Ship Canal's promoters were bailed out by the city government when its cost expanded beyond their expectations and resources. In return the local administration claimed a majority representation on the Company's board. In Scotland the Caledonian Canal was one of several projects built and improved from Parliamentary grants. In Ireland the state and county authorities supplied much of the finance for waterways.

While planning and development mistakes were made by both the private and the public sectors, waterway users in continental Europe benefited from low or non-existent tolls. In Britain tolls were charged by private enterprise and in some cases they were high, reflecting a monopoly position. The barge owner in Britain therefore had to absorb higher charges in freight rates and faced the problem of calculating a through rate on a long haul over several waterways. The real differences between the public and private systems, however, emerged with the coming of the railways. In Britain waterway transport was allowed to fade into insignificance while on the Continent governments intervened to revive the waterways. Between 1830 and 1900 French governments spent £56m on the waterways, the Belgian £16m and the German (Prussia only) £27m (Waterways Association, 15). In 1853 the French government moved into canal ownership in order to increase competition with the railways and to reduce the cost of the waterways through rationalisation plans. By the end of the Second Empire only 569 of 4700 km of canals remained in private ownership (Price, 1983, 280). The French government pursued an interventionist rates policy to ensure fair competition by fixing a higher rate for railways than waterways to offset their advantage of greater speed. This was supported by the Freyçinet Plan of 1879 which aimed at standardising the waterway network in terms of dimensions and tolls. By 1914 nearly a half of French waterways accorded to the standard criteria laid down by Freyçinet. Standardisation was an important source of productivity growth and contributed to the 73 per cent growth in traffic between 1885 and 1905 (Waterways Association, 15). The monopolistic rates charged by British canals left them uncompetitive and vulnerable to takeover by railway companies who in turn used their monopoly to increase charges.

The interventionist model was not always a successful one. While the decline of Dutch waterway traffic in the eighteenth century was primarily due to the stagnation of the economy, the situation was aggravated by a poor response from the municipal managers. Decisions on rationalisation and fare reductions had to be agreed by the municipal authorities which could be a lengthy process particularly if several authorities were involved. To achieve agreement on changes for long-haul through traffic required more wide-ranging bureaucratic consent. Extensive fare reductions to improve competitiveness were only agreed in the 1840s, many decades too late. More scientific and spontaneous management was required to cope with a capital-intensive transport system operating in a mass market. Some British canals, promoted and operated by private enterprise, proved very successful. An estimate of 1825 calculated the average return on British canal companies as 5.75 per cent (Duckham, 1983, 122–3). The Swansea Canal returned ten per cent and the Loughborough Navigation managed double that (Duckham, 1983, 107; Pollins,

1953–4, 145). It was generally the canals in industrial and coalfield regions, where a high demand for bulky products existed, that fared best. Failures were common among canals in rural areas.

WATERWAY TRANSPORT

Most waterway traffic consisted of bulky low-value cargoes, frequently industrial raw materials and agricultural produce. On French waterways the staple cargoes were coal, stone, cement, bricks and grain though the Moselle carried a wider range of consumer products such as brandy, wine, olive oil and furniture (Bourquin; Cermakian). On the Elbe salt, grain, coal, timber and flax were most frequently transported while Russian rivers carried grain, iron, hemp and lumber (Root; Haywood). British waterways supported a large trade in coal, lime, manure, corn, sand, gravel, stones, bricks and timber (Duckham, 1983).

At the end of the eighteenth century these cargoes were carried in a range of craft, mostly small. River barges were most common with a crew of three, skipper, helper and a jockey for the towing horse. Most boats were built long and narrow with a shallow draught in order to pass through locks and cope with meandering rivers of variable depth. Developments in engineering, improved river navigation and growing industrial demand led to improvements in boat design and a regular growth in their size. The introduction of the steam hammer, for example, encouraged the establishment of specialist boatyards on the Saône and Rhône in the 1840s. By the end of the nineteenth century many purpose-built Rhine barges were in excess of 1000 tonnes. In France the Freyçinet Plan encouraged barge standardisation into just two sizes of which the smaller *peniche flamande* of 300 tonnes was to be suitable for most waterways (Price, 1983, 275). In Britain many of the improvements in river-boat design were ignored because of the narrowness of most canals, the lack of standardisation and the decline of the waterways in the second half of the nineteenth century.

More primitive than horsepower was towage by manpower. Towage by boatmen (*burlaki*) was most common on the Volga in the early nineteenth century but it was very slow and high wage costs made it expensive. The Russian *burlaki* managed little more than seven miles per day which meant that a voyage upstream from Astrakhan to Nizhnii Novgorod could take two to three months (Haywood, 139).

In 1810 an emigré French engineer, Jean-Baptiste Poidebard, introduced the horse-powered kedging machine to Russia. It was adopted
slowly at first until the numbers on the Volga and its tributaries
jumped from 35 in 1836 to 200 in 1846 with the expansion of Russian
trade (Haywood, 140–1). This reduced the cost of barge transport by
lowering wage bills and increasing speeds, allowing freight rates to
fall by 20–25 per cent (Haywood, 141-2). By the 1850s French horse
barges were completing 30–40 km per day (Price, 1983, 280). Man
and horse power were popular on Belgian waterways in the early
nineteenth century. However, their labour was needed in the
country's coal mines. Consequently, traffic on the Charleroi to Brussels canal was sometimes halted through lack of available draught
power. In the harsh winter of 1837–8 Brussels suffered a fuel shortage
because barge traffic on the canal was delayed by lack of available
haulage power (Pilkington, 557–8). Sailing boats were frequently
used on the Rhine but the river's growing traffic in the nineteenth
century cramped their tacking room. Rowing boats were sometimes
used, for example on the Moselle, but these were neither quick nor
cheap.

Steamboats began to appear on the rivers of Europe from the end
of the French Wars including the Elbe in 1816 and the Havel and
Volga in 1817 but they were only used regularly on the Rhine before
the 1830s. Some of the earliest Rhine steamships were used for
travelling against the current whose force had been increased by
improvement and canalisation projects. Previously it had not been
uncommon for simple wooden barges to be broken up at their
destination and used for timber because returning against the tide
was too difficult. In 1826 the Preussische Rheinische Dampschiffahrt-
gesellschaft began regular up-river services from Cologne initially
for the carriage of passengers but increasingly to carry cargoes.
Steamboat services began on the Rhône and Saône in the later 1820s
encouraged by American entrepreneurial initiative and financial
support from the banks of Lyons and Geneva. The success of these
early operations led to a burgeoning of companies offering steamboat
services on the two rivers including the Compagnie Générale de
Navigation. The Moselle, which had relied previously upon rowing
boats and horse-drawn barges, turned to steam in 1839. By 1845
steam services on the river were carrying 47 000 passengers and 3835
tons of freight. Steamboats gained popularity on the Volga from the
1840s (Cermakian, 50). The earlier designs had been too clumsy and
unsuitable for the Volga's shallows. A law of 1843 removed existing

monopoly rights and encouraged private entrepreneurship into steamboats. In the same year the Volga Steamboat Company was formed which proved to be the most successful company on the river for many years and whose formation was largely the responsibility of foreign enterprise and capital with the British entrepreneur Edward Cayley playing an important part. Six years later the Mercury Company was formed which also proved successful but many smaller firms failed (Haywood, 148–65). A further improvement in the second half of the nineteenth century was the replacement of the steamboat by the steam tug which was able to tow a long train of barges.

A varied pattern of boat ownership existed from the skipper who owned a single barge to the large specialist firm. In the eighteenth century haulage services were offered by some canal companies such as the Thames and Severn Canal which began operating in 1788 and by 1800 had a fleet of over 50 boats. Like many other canal companies, however, the Thames and Severn found itself unable to compete with the more specialist firms and ceased operating in 1805 after bearing a series of losses (Duckham, 1983, 125). Fragmentation of the ownership structure in France can be illustrated by the fact that in 1891 nearly one half of the 13 604 owners each had just one barge. At the other extreme there were several very large firms including one with 410 craft (Price, 1983, 278). In Britain Pickfords moved into barge owning on a large scale in the first half of the nineteenth century, increasing their fleet of craft from 10 in 1795 to 116 in 1838 (Duckham, 1983, 125). On the Rhine Matthias Stinnes operated a fleet of 66 barges in 1820 (Pounds, 438).

The output of waterway services continued to grow in most European countries through the course of the nineteenth century in spite of road and railway competition. At the beginning of the nineteenth century Telford was claiming that roads were preferable to canals and John Grieve calculated that canals cost £5000 per mile to build in comparison with only £1600 for roads (Duckham, 1983, 109). In fact road competition was rarely a problem. Waterway transport was cheaper though more susceptible to climatic interruptions. Most important is the fact that the two modes generally operated in different markets with waterways picking up much of the high bulk but low dispersion traffic in industrial areas. The improved efficiency of the waterways also led to a significant expansion in their long-haul services in contrast to the short-haul operations of most road carriers in the nineteenth century. The waterways more often complemented than competed with shipping by improving access to and from ports.

In the Netherlands regular shipping services (*beurtveer*) were arranged to connect with timetabled waterway passenger services (De Vries, 51–2). In France combined coasting and waterway services could sometimes reduce the journey: Bordeaux to Le Havre was reduced from 20–40 days to about eight by going inland along the Loire from Nantes (Price, 1983, 35).

Railway competition was more serious because it operated in similar markets and conveyed the goods much more quickly. The journey from Amsterdam to Utrecht took seven hours by barge but only one hour and ten minutes by train. Sometimes the effect of railway competition could be immediate and devastating. In 1841 the Haarlem to Leiden *trekvaart* had carried 32 400 passengers but in 1843, the first full year of railway competition, the number collapsed to only 1800 (De Vries, 206). Waterway traffic on the Elbe and Havel in the 1840s had declined to only a third of its volume of the previous decade as a result of the railway (Milward & Saul, 1973, 378). Traffic on the Rhône declined from 634 000 tonnes in 1855 to 273 000 in 1859 after the completion of the Paris–Lyons–Marseilles railway (Price, 1983, 284). The decline came earliest and was most defined in Britain where private enterprise set its heart against waterways in the early years of the nineteenth century. In Russia railways and river transport frequently complemented each other because many railways were built as a link between the rivers and major towns rather than running parallel to the waterways. The Moscow to Nizhnii Novgorod line, built in 1862, is a case in point.

It was seen above that the attitude in many continental European countries was rather different from that in Britain. Governments displayed a more interventionist role by encouraging further improvements to the waterways and a fair tariff policy. By the end of the nineteenth century freight rates on French waterways had, as a result, declined by around 50 per cent since the middle of the century. In Belgium waterways were estimated to be 40 per cent cheaper than railways by the end of the century and German waterways were a 36 per cent saving on coal carriage by rail, 49 per cent on corn and 37 per cent on sugar (Waterways Association, 17–18). This enabled waterway traffic to expand and operate on a large scale on many rivers and canals. The Saar Coal Mines Canal carried 473 000 tons of traffic in 1867, mostly coke and iron ore, at a freight rate of 3.9 fr. per ton/km which was half the price charged by the railway. In 1873 the Marne–Rhine Canal carried over 600 000 tons of coal, coke and iron ore (Cermakian, 63). By the 1860s railways connected most of the ports along the Rhine and in the following years there was a decline in river traffic. However, water traffic began to grow once more from the 1890s as more industries sprang up beside the Rhine, particularly on the upper river, aware of the cheapness of river transport. Between the mid-1880s and 1905 the volume of tonnage on French waterways grew by 73 per cent; on Belgian by 114 per cent; and on German by 274 per cent. In contrast a growth of only eight per cent was recorded in Britain despite the opening of the Manchester Ship Canal in 1894 (Waterways Association, 15). This rapid growth halted the relative decline of the waterways in continental Europe. In France the share of inland traffic going by canal had declined from 37 to 15 per cent between 1851 and 1882 but by 1903 had grown once more to 21 per cent (Caron, 1979, 32).

Table 3.2   Traffic on Inland Waterways, 1885–1905 (m ton/km)

Country	Austria[1]	Belgium	England[2]	France	Germany	Netherlands[2]
1885	1 649	760	36 462[3]	2 453	3 801	5 200
1905	3 422	1 143	39 499	5 085	11 692	21 000
% Increase	108	50	8	107	208	304

Notes: 1. Goods carried by the Danube Steamship Company.
　　　　2. Thousand tons.
　　　　3. 1886.

Sources: Mitchell, 1975, 635; Waterways Association, 15.

THE ECONOMIC EFFECTS OF THE WATERWAYS

The waterways, like the roads, yielded few backward linkages in their construction and operation. The demand for labour and materials was comparatively small and they exerted little influence upon the industries of the industrial revolution such as coal and iron. Nor did canal building contribute appreciably to engineering technology although it did familiarise builders with the methods and problems of large civil engineering works such as tunnels, cuttings, embankments, bridges and aqueducts which were to be faced by railway builders in subsequent decades. The canal engineers in Britain were important in the early organisation of the civil engineering profession. In 1771 a group of canal and harbour engineers, led by Smeaton, formed the

Society of Civil Engineers, which in 1818–20 gave birth to the modern Institution of Civil Engineers with Telford as its first president. Since financing was organised by the state in most countries canal building had little impact on capital markets. Exceptionally, there was a heavy reliance upon private finance in Britain where canal building encouraged the wider use of preference shares and debentures thereby helping to lay the ground for their more extensive use by railway companies.

The main benefits of canals lay in their forward linkages. By improving the navigability of waterways, connecting different rivers, reducing journey lengths and abolishing many charges, the improved waterway system made it viable to carry many goods over longer distances. This was particularly the case with bulk raw materials such as coal, iron ore and building materials. Indeed, many canals were built for the precise purpose of facilitating the movement of coal. The Bridgewater Canal halved the price of coal in Manchester. The Oxford Canal permitted the carriage of Staffordshire coal to Reading and North Wales coal to Shrewsbury. The canals were important in opening a national market for the growing output of the coalfields of northern France. The Rhône-Rhine and Marne-Rhine canals solved the problem of high costs facing the Alsatian textile industry if it converted to steam power. Moreover, the government undertook to preserve the Paris market for French coal producers by offering them subsidised canal rates. Most remarkable was the growth of the Rhine coal trade. Coal loaded at Duisberg-Ruhrort was carried upstream to Mannheim and downstream to the Dutch ports. The volume of this trade expanded from about 300 000 tonnes in 1831 to 7m by 1900 (Zorn; Pounds, 438). The canalisation of the Moselle benefited the iron and steel industries of the Ruhr by improving access at lower rates to sources of phosphoric iron ore. In the Netherlands the Maastricht-Liège Canal completed a web of waterways which enabled the transportation of stone, coal and steel from the Meuse and Sambre industrial areas to most parts of the country. Agricultural materials and produce were also conveyed by water. The Aberdeenshire Canal gave farmers better access to their markets while also improving their supply of lime and manure.

Many more individual examples exist but on a national basis the integrating effects of the waterways were severely limited. Waterways could only operate efficiently in regions with a sympathetic geology and even there remained susceptible to frequent interruptions. While French waterways helped the mining and metallurgy industries of the Nord and Loire basin as well as stimulating commercial agriculture in the north and viticulture in Bordelais and the Loire valley, they could not prevent the dispersal of many other industries and the survival of semi-subsistent polyculture in many areas. On the Volga severe winters meant the river was often blocked with ice between October and April. With the spring thaw floods caused shoals and sandbanks. In the summer navigation was made difficult by lack of water especially upriver between Nizhnii Novgorod and Rybinsk. On the Rhine traffic was disrupted during 199 days as late as 1899 (Pounds, 435). Even when navigation was uninterrupted progress was slow in the face of many locks. The Trent and Mersey Canal, for example, had 75 locks in the course of 93 miles and the Canal de Bourgogne 189 locks in 242 km. Such regular stoppages limited the benefits to be gained from steam navigation. Many of the canals built in the eighteenth century suffered from their narrow and circuitous nature. They were built with locks only seven feet wide which excluded larger vessels and they traced the contours in hilly areas thereby extending the route considerably. These factors help to explain why Britain's canals, built ahead of most of the networks of continental Europe, had already fallen into decline by the second half of the nineteenth century.

It is of little surprise, therefore, that it was the major rivers which witnessed the most substantial growth in traffic in the late nineteenth century, particularly the Rhine and Moselle which supported large ports growing under the impact of locally-concentrated industrial development. Cologne and Mainz began modernising their shipping facilities in the last two decades of the century while Düsseldorf built four modern dock-basins in the 1890s. A dock complex was built at Mannheim-Rheinau between 1896 and 1907.

Port expansion also took place where its communications with the sea or the surrounding hinterland were improved by the waterways. The Aire and Calder Navigation was important in the development of Leeds and Wakefield in the late eighteenth and early nineteenth centuries and Goole from the 1820s (Duckham, 1967). It was most important, however, for the growth of Selby between 1774 and 1826 by linking its coastal trade with the rich hinterland of the West Riding (Duckham, 1965–6). Other British ports whose growth is explained by the waterways included Stourport on the Severn, Runcorn and Ellesmere Port on the Mersey and Grangeforth on the Forth and Clyde. Nearly all the consignments moving through the port of Hull in the late eighteenth century used the waterways for some part of their journey. The rise of Liverpool in the eighteenth and nineteenth centuries was due not only to its growing foreign trade but also to its inland waterway links with Lancashire, Cheshire and Yorkshire. In the Netherlands improved access to the sea enabled a rapid revival of the fortunes of Amsterdam and Rotterdam at the end of the nineteenth century. Shipping arrivals at Amsterdam rose from 0.7 million tonnes in 1879 to 2.6 million tonnes in 1911 and those of Rotterdam from 1.6 to 11.3 million tonnes (Milward and Saul, 1977, 196).

By locating at the point of major trans-shipment rather than close to the market or the raw material source, port and riverside industries benefited from lower trans-shipment costs. This was particularly important for bulk industries such as iron and steel, engineering and chemicals which crowded the banks of the Rhine at the end of the nineteenth century. In Figure 3.1, A is the source of the raw materials, B is the point of trans-shipment and C the market. If the industry was located at A it would have distribution costs of $AhgcdC$ and if it was located at C it would have procurement costs of $AabfeC$. At the trans-shipment point B, however, it would have combined distribution and procurement costs of only $AabcdC$. The opening of the Manchester Ship Canal effectively converted the location of many of the city's industries to the point of major trans-shipment. The stimulus imparted to Manchester by its ship canal can be illustrated by the growth of imports from £2.8 million in 1894 to £30.4 million by 1907 which was dominated by timber, grain, raw cotton and oil (Farnie, 1980, 26, 53).

The limited improvements to the waterways of southern Europe meant that these countries derived few economic benefits. In Spain, several canals were built but the Castile Canal soon lost most of its traffic to the Norte railway company. The Aragon Canal only connected with the outskirts of Zaragoza and Tudela and therefore necessary trans-shipment made it uneconomic.

Several attempts have been made to assess the impact of the waterways using the social savings model. Jones's study of malt movements from Hertfordshire to east London by the brewers Trumans, expressed social savings as a percentage of the company's total expenditure. By this method he found the waterways to be a 1–3 per cent saving on the roads and the railway to be a saving of only 0.19–0.29 per cent on the waterways (E. Jones, 1986, 12). De Vries undertook a national social saving calculation for Dutch waterways in 1670 by which he found barges to render a 0.8 per cent saving on road services while coasting vessels were a 0.08 per cent saving on the

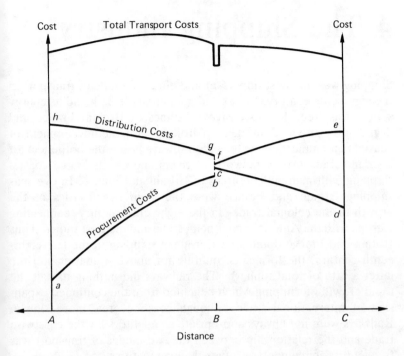

Figure 3.1   Industrial Location at the Point of Major Trans-Shipment

waterways (194). De Vries, dissatisfied with the social saving method because of its failure to make full allowance for speed, seasonality, flexibility and comfort, substituted Walton and Hayden Boyd's consumer surplus approach. This time he found the canals to be a 0.2–0.23 per cent saving on vessels and a 0.44–0.58 per cent saving on stage coaches. By 1750 even this small differential had fallen by half (198).

4 The Shipping Industry

Shipping was the most important and effective mode of transport in the eighteenth century. It required no man-made path and its energy source was free. The extensive coastlines of Britain, France and Scandinavia provided an ideal environment for the development of coastal communications before the railways broke the bottleneck of overland transport. A network of rivers and canals linked coastal shipping with many inland areas of Britain and France. In overseas shipping Britain and France were the main beneficiaries of the growth of the colonial trades in the eighteenth century, connecting Europe with the American continent, India and the East Indies. Thus Britain and France dominated European shipping in the late eighteenth century, the former accounting for above a quarter and the latter a fifth of total tonnage. The railways did nothing to halt the rapid growth of shipping which benefited from the continued expansion of international trade although coasting grew more slowly. Railways were not always appropriate competitors for the coastwise trade and the relationship between the two modes of transport was frequently complementary rather than competitive.

In the nineteenth century Britain dominated world shipping almost as fully as America subsequently did the car industry. By the First World War, Britain owned half of the European fleet, carried more than half of world seaborne commerce and built two-thirds of new European vessels. Her fleet was the most modern and her shipbuilders were responsible for most of the technological advances associated with the change from sail to steam and wood to metal. A British Departmental Committee of 1918 attributed maritime dominance to industrial leadership, empire, and coal exports. Industrialisation brought Britain into a complementary trading position with many less-developed countries who exchanged their primary goods for her manufactures. The strength of Britain's engineering and metallurgical industries enabled her to build iron steamships. Her colonies and former possessions provided a series of worldwide shipping routes including to India, Australia and New Zealand. British coal exports, sought after by industrialising countries and bunkering stations, provided a valuable outward bulk cargo which enabled British shipowners to offer competitive homebound freight rates.

In contrast, the French mercantile marine grew only slowly in the

48

nineteenth century and her share of European shipping dropped to
only six per cent by 1910. French industry developed more gradually
than Britain, her coal output was small and her empire and political
influence was already waning by the second half of the eighteenth
century. A new breed of fast American sailing clippers briefly challenged Britain in the North Atlantic in the first half of the nineteenth
century before civil war and the change from wood to metal ended
this competition. Germany's share of European shipping rose from
eight to twelve per cent between 1890 and 1910 as her liners began to
pose a threat on various shipping routes but made little impact
overall on British domination of the industry before the Great War.
Norwegian and Greek shipowners, employing cheap second-hand
British tonnage, offered some challenge to British tramps. The First
World War marked the turning point for British shipping accompanied
as it was by a loss of overseas markets, the accelerated decline of coal
as a source of power and Britain's faltering industrial status.

SHIPBUILDING AND TECHNOLOGICAL CHANGE

The shipbuilding industry was transformed in the nineteenth century
by the change from wood to metal and sail to steam in vessel
construction. Geographical location, job skills and workplace organisation all altered as shipbuilding moved away from its craft skill
tradition to become a heavy engineering industry. The comparative
advantage Scandinavia, Canada and the United States possessed in
access to timber and other shipbuilding materials counted for little as
the industry began to build with iron and later steel. Shipbuilding
became concentrated into particular regions and ports where coal
and iron were available. The rapid expansion of the heavy engineering industries of the Ruhr in the later nineteenth century provided
the raw materials for shipbuilding in north German ports including
Danzig, Stettin, Lubeck, Hamburg and Bremerhaven. Rotterdam
and Amsterdam were also provided with shipbuilding materials by
way of the Rhine. Sometimes vertical integration brought together
shipyards and iron and steel firms. Both Krupps and Schneider-Le
Creusot owned shipyards at Le Havre. Locational changes occurred
regionally within individual economies. In Britain, traditional centres
of wooden shipbuilding in the south-west and south-east were replaced by Clydeside, the north-east and north-west of England which
were close to sources of coal and iron.

The introduction of iron and steam technology involved four principal changes: the development of the marine engine and its complementary boilers, the alliance of these to effective propulsive devices and consequent alterations in the design of the hull. Co-ordinating similar rates of technological advance in these interdependent mechanisms was essential. Early steam-shipping was regarded as two separate technologies: the shipyard construction of the hull and fittings and the engineering provision of engines, boilers and paddles. Early progress also laboured against the absence of a scientific basis for steam-shipping, the lack of standardisation of boilers, engines, paddles or other parts and the inter-firm and inter-port rivalry which discouraged the sharing of ideas.

Steamboat experiments were conducted on the Clyde at the beginning of the nineteenth century but interest soon spread to the Humber, Mersey and Thames as steam found its earliest use in river craft and tugs. By the 1820s and 1830s larger engines and more efficient paddles brought steam into the coastal trade. Early steamship companies, such as the General Steam Navigation Company, operating in the British coastal and near trades, battled to keep their vessels fully employed in order to cover the higher capital costs of steamships. It was not until later in the century, with improved steam technology and a modified infrastructure, that steamship owners could be more certain of making profits. In the 1840s paddles were replaced by the screw propeller which acted upon a consistently large volume of water and was more efficient in rolling seas. The partially submerged paddle was more or less effective according to the depth of the vessel in the water. This was particularly significant on long journeys when a large coal reserve was carried.

Engine efficiency was increased substantially when Elder and Randolph patented their compound engine in 1853 but its effective use had to await the introduction of higher pressure boilers and surface condensers in the following decade. The compound engine accounted for three-quarters of the horsepower of the British shipping industry by the mid-1870s (Slaven, 1980, 111). Twin screws were introduced in the following decade along with the improved triple expansion engine. The introduction of Siemen's improved quality mild steel permitted the necessary increase in boiler pressure. Boiler pressures rose progressively from 5–10 lbs per square inch in the 1830s and 1840s to 20 lbs in the 1850s, 50 lbs in the 1860s, 100 lbs in the 1870s and 200 lbs by the end of the 1880s (Graham, 82–8). In 1884 Parsons built the first steam turbine and an improved version was used to power

Turbinia a decade later. The early turbines only achieved sufficient advantage to offset their greater capital costs at high speeds and so found their earliest use in passenger and naval vessels. Its greater mechanical complexity required the retraining of engine room staff and the supply of new spare parts. In 1909 reduction gearing made the turbine more suitable for slower-moving cargo vessels. Finally, in the years leading up to the First World War the internal combustion engine was introduced into shipping. The engine was smaller than coal-powered engines, required no boiler and its fuel was lighter, less bulky, easier to load and could be stored in the ship's double bottom where it did not occupy potential cargo space. In 1909 Royal Dutch Shell ordered *Vulcanus*, the first ocean-going motor vessel.

Auxiliary vessels, combining sail and steam, were introduced in the 1850s and 1860s but met with little success because they combined the worst of both systems: high manning and fuel consumption. The introduction of steam-shipping represented the substitution of coal for labour and, in some cases, for fixed capital. Steamships required lower manning ratios and in the cases of the more efficient vessels towards the end of the nineteenth century their increased capital cost over sail was more than offset by greater productivity. Thus, reductions in fuel consumption from improved engines and stronger boilers was important. Coal usage declined from 10 lbs per horsepower per hour in the early engines to 3.5 lbs with the introduction of the compound engine, 1.8 at the time of the triple expansion engine, 1.3 following the introduction of the steam turbine and 0.45 with the diesel engine (Henning and Trace, 365–8; Fletcher, 1958, 557). This enabled the shipowner to reduce freight rates or go longer distances without refuelling or set aside more space for cargo carrying or any suitable combination of these three variables.

The technological interactions of wood, sail, steam and iron were complex but it was apparent by the middle of the nineteenth century that the full benefits of steam and iron could only be achieved together. While less than ten per cent of British vessels were built of iron before 1850, nearly two-thirds of steam vessels were so built (Slaven, 1980, 113). The greater strength of iron meant vessels could be built with thinner sides which made available up to 35 per cent more cargo weight and 20–50 per cent more cargo space (Pollard and Robertson, 13–14). The introduction of steel in the 1870s facilitated further weight reductions. Iron's superior strength was particularly relevant to steam vessels because engine vibrations could tear a wooden vessel apart. Iron vessels could be built much longer than the maximum of about 300 feet for wood and their length to width ratio could be increased without the danger of breaking their backs. This improved access to the cargo and reduced the water resistance, enabling them to travel more quickly. Iron was also safer from fire and more weather-resistant. However, iron hulls caused some cargoes to sweat and therefore ventilation had to be improved. The magnetic reaction of compasses to iron was also the cause of several maritime disasters before contemporaries identified and solved the problem.

Britain dominated the use of metal in shipbuilding. Clydeside and the north-east of England, helped by their developed metallurgical industries, became the major regional centres of iron shipbuilding in the second half of the nineteenth century. In the late eighteenth century copper was used for sheathing to preserve the ship's hull from marine life. It was common among Liverpool vessels voyaging in the Atlantic, which was the main habitat of the teredo worm. Coppering was also adopted by many European navies in the later eighteenth century. Copper sheathing was expensive, risked galvanic action and made it difficult to lay the ship aground. Keir's bolt was introduced in 1779 as an alloy of copper, zinc and iron which over-came the problem of the rapid decay of iron fastenings (Harris, 1966). The use of iron plates in hull construction did not occur until the 1840s but thenceforth soon became the norm. By 1862 iron had surpassed wooden shipbuilding in Britain (Slaven, 1980, 113).

Until the last quarter of the nineteenth century many technological innovations benefited sail as well as steam. It was only in the 1880s, with the use of better machine tools, more efficient engines and improved mild steel, that steam gained appreciable advantages. By the third quarter of the nineteenth century a third of British sailing vessels were built of iron. Sailing vessels shared in such advances as sharper bows, greater length and the use of water ballast tanks together with organisational improvements such as quicker port turnaround and more sophisticated shipping management. Sailing vessels benefited from declining raw material costs including timber, hemp and sailcloth. Improved oceanography was of more value to sail than to steam. Ironically, steam tugs helped sailing vessels get to sea more quickly by combating adverse winds and tide while the distribution of coal to bunkering stations became the responsibility of sailing vessels. Diagonal planking and the use of iron straps permit-ted economies in the use of timber. Additionally, speed and the cargo capacity of sailing vessels were on the increase and manning levels in decline. In the 1860s and 1870s the 'clipper' vessel with its iron hull steel masts and rigging and labour-saving machinery were strong competition for steamships in the ocean trades and dominated the Australian wool trade up to the 1890s. In favourable weather they could reach 15 knots, compared with the 10 knots of many cargo steamers.

The increased productivity of sailing vessels and the incremental progress in steam technology has led some historians to argue that the transition from sail to steam was a slow and protracted process and that the average cost curve of steam did not fall appreciably below that of sail until the mid-1880s (Graham; North; Walton, 1970). Graham's original statement of the 'gradualist' position was supported by North who argued that falling freight rates in the first half of the nineteenth century reflected the rising productivity of the sailing ship.

Fletcher, Harley and Knauerhase, however, believe that the transition occurred fairly suddenly in the 1870s and early 1880s. Knauerhase attributes this to the introduction of the compound engine and reinforces his argument with evidence of falling freight rates and of productivity improvements (Knauerhase, 400). Fletcher, on the other hand, believes it was the catalytic effect of the construction of the Suez Canal in 1869 which made the transfer to steam 'sharp and decisive' (Fletcher, 1958, 563). Suez was unsuitable for sailing vessels which had to be towed for 100 miles. Only 238 of 5236 vessels passing through the canal between December 1869 and April 1875 were sail. Suez halved the distance between London and Bombay from 11 600 to 5800 miles and created a route with many intermediate commercial centres (Fletcher, 1958, 559). Not only did Suez offer steam a shorter route mileage, it gave steamships the option of fewer refuelling stops or devoting less onboard space to coal. It forced the clippers out of the China tea trade in search of other trades such as British coal exports and American corn and oil exports.

The balance of evidence points towards a gradualist interpretation. Figures for changes in fuel consumption and boiler pressures suggest an incremental process of development rather than Schumpeterian technological spurts. The supersession of sail was a gradual process beginning in the coasting and short sea trades and spreading into the medium and long hauls. While the original compound engine was important it was no more than part of a long chain of progress and was soon improved upon with the triple expansion engine. The impact of the Suez Canal was confined to a few routes, particularly the Chinese and Indian trades. Even the trade between Britain and

Australia rarely used the canal; by 1880 less than two per cent of its tonnage went through Suez (Fletcher, 1958, 564). Falling freight rates in the later 1870s were caused by a shipping depression rather than productivity growth. The depression caused a revival of sail as shipowners feared that the extra capital cost of steam would not be repaid by regular and remunerative employment. Some steamers were converted back to sail. Walton (1970) criticises Knauerhase's productivity estimates which are based upon average total port clearings per crewman and therefore only measures labour productivity. The rapid relative growth of steam on short hauls, where more port clearances were made, in the 1870s and 1880s will therefore exaggerate the transition to steam over this period using Knauerhase's method.

The introduction of a major new technology requires adaptation and change in the infrastructure. Steam vessels required a network of bunkering stations. The expense and scarcity of coal discouraged steam-shipping in non-mining regions. It required the re-training of seamen and suitably qualified engineers. Steam-shipping called forth a new generation of port facilities, tailored to their need for a rapid turnround. These developments inevitably took time and until they were completed steam could not operate efficiently over most routes. The unreliability and inefficiency of early engines discouraged early adoption. Shipbuilders converting to steam and metal had to reorganise their yard, its capital structure and often move location. Many sailing shipbuilders never made the transition which left early iron and steam construction in the hands of many with no previous experience. If the economics of steam-shipping justified its introduction, it might still be delayed by entrepreneurial conservatism: the greater cost of steamships discouraged owners who feared concentrating their capital into a few steamers rather than a larger sailing fleet. In some ports the development of the joint stock company helped to solve this problem but elsewhere investors clung to the partnership system well into the age of steam.

Nonetheless, by the mid-1870s steam dominated the carriage of mails, passengers and fine cargoes on all routes except Australia. Steam was particularly dominant among the major European liner companies such as Cunard, P&O, Royal Mail, Hamburg-Amerika, Norddeutscher Lloyd, Messageries Maritimes and Austrian Lloyd. Steam spread to many of the bulk trades in the last two decades of the nineteenth century with the rise of the tramp steamer. At the end of the century sail still found employment in some trades such as the export of Welsh slates, where loading and discharging the cargo was a protracted process and speed was not of the essence; in these circumstances using a steamer might incur substantial demurrage charges. Sailing schooners were used in trades requiring the carriage of only small volumes or where the ports possessed only limited facilities. The Iberian fruit, the Newfoundland cured fish, the Chilean nitrate, the Quebec timber and the Newcastle (New South Wales) coal trades and some coasting voyages continued to employ sail at the end of the nineteenth and sometimes well into the twentieth century. Liverpool shipowners Brocklebanks sent sailing vessels to Antigua (rum), Calcutta (jute) and Chinchas (guano) before finally withdrawing from sail in 1901. Duncan Dunbar maintained a sailing fleet of around 40 000 tons concentrated in the liquor export trade (Fayle, 1933, 258–9). The huge growth of North American grain exports to Europe in the last quarter of the nineteenth century provided employment for European sailing vessels. Sail was often favoured in seasonal trades because its hold was considered to be the cheapest warehouse in the world (Wigram and Samuda).

During the 1880s steam tonnage surpassed sail in the British mercantile marine, at least a decade ahead of most other countries. By 1900 Finland, Greece, Italy and Norway still owned more sail than steam shipping. However, steam was more productive than sail. Historians have often worked on the assumption that steam was three times as productive as sail. Using this idea of 'effective tonnage', steam carried more than half the trade of all major European shipping nations except Finland by 1900. It is difficult to generalise about the relative productivity of sail and steam which changed gradually during the nineteenth century. Only by the later years of the century were steamers three times as productive as sail in most trades. Lower factor costs for sail enabled the shipowners of some nations to achieve comparable performance with steam. Calculations of the profitability of Norwegian shipping in 1875, 1880, 1885, 1890, 1895, 1900 and 1905 reveal that only in 1890 and 1895 were steam profits higher than sail (Gjolberg, 141). The later transition to steam of the Scandinavian fleets is therefore seen as a rational decision rather than the product of economic backwardness or entrepreneurial conservatism.

As late as 1914 only 18 per cent of the Finnish fleet was steam compared with 94 per cent in the United Kingdom, 83 per cent in Germany, 75 per cent in Scandinavia and 64 per cent in France. Most Finnish trade was in cheap, bulky goods more suited to sail. More-

over, a heavy volume imbalance in favour of exports made it difficult
for steam to be sufficiently productive with only one-way freighting.
Labour and timber were also cheap in Finland and low-priced
second-hand sailing vessels could be purchased from British owners
converting their fleets to steam. All of this has led Kaukiainen to
conclude that 'the opportunity cost of steam was relatively high, and
therefore the second best technology was more competitive than in
the leading west European countries' (1980, 184).

Adoption rates for steam varied regionally in Norway. Thirty-four
per cent of Bergen shipping was steam by 1881 compared with only
four or five per cent at Christiania, Stavanger and most of the smaller
ports (Nordvik, 125). This technological lead by the major port was
also reflected in Sweden and Denmark where Stockholm and Copenhagen were 58 and 34 per cent steam respectively in 1881, comfort-
ably above the national average (Nordvik, 125). The greater circle of
potential investors in major ports may help to explain their earlier
movement to sail. On the other hand, Liverpool's share of steam-
shipping (36 per cent) was surprisingly below the average for Britain
(41 per cent) in 1880 although London (52 per cent) was significantly
above it (Cottrell, 141–2). The speed of steam was more important
for Bergen vessels in the fish and fruit trades than for the timber trade
vessels of many other ports. Liverpool was the centre of the transatlantic bulk trades of timber and cotton and many cheap softwood
vessels were bought from North America.

Technological change in shipbuilding was also reflected in greater
ship specialisation. In the early nineteenth century the most popular
form of vessel was the multi-purpose cargo carrier which could be
switched between trades according to their fluctuating fortunes. In the
second half of the nineteenth century this role was played by the
tramp steamer which sailed from port to port in search of remunerative freights. A range of tramps including 'flush-deckers', 'well
deckers' and 'turret-deckers' were built. These designs left more
space for the cargo than single-deck vessels. Their strength enabled
the construction of larger and more economic vessels, and they used
less steel in construction which reduced the deadweight. Liners were
built for particular types of deployment. They were developed initially in the mail and passenger trades where speed was important
and thenceforth became commonplace in many trades, maintaining a
regular service between named ports and accepting small consignments of a wide range of goods. Many cargo liners were of the
'intermediary' class because they travelled at lower speeds in order to

economise on fuel. The distinction between tramp and liner, however, was as much one of commercial organisation as technical design.

In the 1870s Charles Tellier experimented with the application of refrigeration to ships. Ferdinand Carré perfected an ammonia-compression refrigeration machine and in 1877 the vessel *Paraguay* brought frozen mutton to Le Havre from San Nicholas. British firms followed shortly and by 1914 meat, dairy products and fruit were all being carried in 'reefers'. Specialist vessels were developed for the copper and iron ore trades to reduce the unloading time. Vessels were built in which ore was carried in sloping-sided bins or hoppers built into the ship and equipped with suitable outlets. Discharge was by means of electrical cranes powered by a generator in the engine room.

The growing demand for oil and its products in the later nineteenth century led to the growth of another specialist vessel, the tanker, because of the geographical concentration of oil sources and the problems of its transportation. The earliest shipments from the 1860s were carried in barrels and tinplate boxes which was expensive and a waste of cargo space as much broken stowage resulted. Leakage was also frequent which increased the risks of explosion. Nobel's *Zoroaster* in 1778 and Armstrong and Mitchell's *Glückhauf* in 1886 were among the earliest tankers built. For the tanker the wall of the vessel was also that of a cargo tank. She was designed to carry oil in bulk and generated large savings in stowage and loading times. One contemporary calculated a saving on the delivered cost of about £1 per ton.[1] Several other problems had to be overcome most notably the tendency for oil to change volume at different temperatures and the need to control the stability of liquid cargoes in heavy seas. The design of tanks therefore had to allow for some expansion of the cargo while the construction of a series of transverse bulkheads and a centre line bulkhead subdivided the cargo sufficiently to minimise instability. Subdivision also enabled the tanker to carry several grades of oil.

Shipbuilding, like shipowning, was concentrated in northern and western Europe in the eighteenth and nineteenth centuries where the bulk trades of coal and timber assured a high demand for ships and provided raw materials for shipbuilding. Few figures for comparative European shipbuilding exist but there seems little reason to doubt Britain's dominance. Sheltered ports on large, navigable rivers such as the Thames, Tyne and Clyde with long shorelines provided the ideal location for shipbuilding. Capital abundance and a highly skilled labour force were further benefits for British shipbuilding together with the large and growing home market as Britain was the leading shipowning nation.

At the end of the eighteenth century, British shipbuilding output was greater than that of most European countries a century later. The French Wars served as a major stimulus to European shipbuilding. The increased demand for merchant transports and naval vessels together with a supply limitation caused by convoy delays and the temporary inactivity of captured vessels rapidly filled up order books. As a capital goods industry, shipbuilding was influenced by the 'accelerator' effect whereby a relatively small change in the demand for shipping services would have a greater impact on the demand for new ships. After 1815 the end of the convoy system and the reduction in transport service work sent the accelerator into reverse and the demand for new vessels collapsed. Shipbuilding stagnated throughout Europe and the position was aggravated by the tendency of some builders to continue operating in the hope that things would soon improve. Baltic timber duties, cheap North American vessels and the legacy of the tonnage laws of 1773–5 all hindered the development of British shipbuilding in the first half of the nineteenth century. Traditional centres of the industry on the Thames and along the Yorkshire coast were severely affected. On the north-east coast, however, there were signs of buoyancy. Output at Sunderland grew rapidly throughout the 1820s and 1830s making it Europe's leading shipbuilding port. The low regional cost of labour and land helped Sunderland builders undercut their rivals but at least as important was the growth of the coal export trade from the area. This provided shipowners with an outward cargo for vessels importing timber from the Baltic, British North America and other areas. The result was lower freight rates to Sunderland and cheaper timber for shipbuilding.

British output as a whole moved sharply upwards in the second half of the century helped by the growth of domestic shipowning and substantial overseas sales. New and second-hand vessels were sold in many countries particularly Austria-Hungary, Belgium, Italy, Spain, Norway, Germany, France, Russia, Netherlands, Japan, Sweden and Greece. In some periods British shipbuilders built more than half of the fleets of Belgium, Italy, Austria-Hungary, France, Russia, Spain and the Netherlands. The proportion of British output sold abroad rose from 12 to 30 per cent between 1869/83 and 1904/8 (Pollard and

Robertson, 37; Slaven, 1982, 41). The active second-hand market, particularly to Norway, enabled British shipowners continually to update their fleet by placing new orders with local builders. By the 1890s British output had reached a million tons per annum and her control of the industry is indicated by the fact that eighty per cent of world tonnage was being built in Britain.

The second half of the nineteenth century had been the heyday for British shipbuilders; helped by Britain's powerful heavy industries they introduced new techniques ahead of their rivals which allowed yards and even ports to specialise and increase their expertise and efficiency. This counted for much at a time when more specialised vessels were being developed. The north-east emerged as a centre of tramp production while Clydeside became renowned for its liners, Barrow and Birkenhead for its warships and Dundee, Leith and Aberdeen for fishing vessels. Doxfords of Sunderland were particularly renowned for their construction of turret-decker tramps. From the late nineteenth century, British shipbuilding output grew little and her share in the world total dropped progressively to only 32 per cent by the early 1920s. Competition from industrialising Germany, the replacement of coal by oil and the impact of the First World War all helped to undermine British dominance.

Table 4.1   United Kingdom and World Shipbuilding, 1892–1923
(annual averages, 000 tons)

	UK	World	UK as % of world
1892–1895	986	1 232	80
1896–1900	1 262	1 844	68
1901–1905	1 394	2 354	59
1906–1910	1 300	2 218	59
1911–1914	1 790	2 935	61
1915–1918	943	2 255	42
1919–1923	1 378	4 288	32

Sources: Pollard and Robertson, 249; Fayle, 416.

In many respects coal was the linchpin of Britain's maritime dominance in the nineteenth century: it provided an outbound cargo for British vessels which enabled shipowners to offer competitive return freights while also serving as a low factor cost in Britain's development of steam technology. By the end of the nineteenth century, improvements in fuel efficiency, the development of coal resources by other countries and the rise of oil as a substitute were undermining British coal. The First World War forced importers to look for alternative coal supplies and encouraged the use of oil-powered shipping. The share of world shipping powered by oil rose from three to 25 per cent between 1914 and 1922 (Fletcher, 1975, 8). The ability of oil-powered engines to gain full power quickly and maintain it made them particularly appealing to the military navies along with passenger liners and packets. Before 1914 the navies of Italy, France, Germany and Rumania had begun to use oil and this trend was sharply reinforced by the war. British shipbuilders were slow to move towards the building of motorships. In the same way that North American and Scandinavian shipowners and shipbuilders clung to wooden technology because of regional cost advantages so the British stayed later with steam. Between 1920 and 1939 only 28 per cent of new British tonnage was motor-powered compared with a figure of 42 per cent for the rest of the world (Slaven, 1982, 44).

British deficiency lay not only in the construction of oil-powered vessels but also in the provision of oil tankers. While building some of the earliest tankers in the 1880s, Britain dropped behind during and after the war. In 1914 Britain owned half of the world tanker fleet but by 1939 this figure had dropped to a quarter (Sturmey, 74). British oil developers tended to preserve their capital for exploration by leasing foreign-owned tonnage rather than buying new British tankers.

The relative decline of several other British industries in the late nineteenth century has frequently been attributed to under-investment and insufficient attention to the training of labour and management.[2] Unfavourable comparisons have been drawn with German experience. German shipyards possessed highly trained technicians, designers and managers and were well-equipped with electricity and other forms of capital investment. Pollard, however, argues that shipbuilding was notorious for output fluctuations and so it was preferable to have a large workforce which could be laid off during a downturn than be burdened with the continuous cost of fixed capital (1957). In the regular downturns of the industry the more highly capitalised shipbuilding industries of Germany and America were unable to match British prices. In Sweden the large, highly capitalised Motala shipyards experienced problems in the downturn of the 1880s leading to bankruptcy by 1890. In Britain greater workforce intensity facilitated an increased division of labour with accompanying efficiency gains and the development of a large pool of skilled labour. Labour-intensive methods were used in France where average output fluctuations were three times as great as in England. However, insufficient and unstable supplies of skilled labour and low production levels made labour specialisation unsuitable. Instead, a policy of labour flexibility encouraged workers to develop a broad range of skills so that they could be transferred between tasks as conditions dictated. The inability to specialise skills or production prevented French builders from matching British costs (Lorenz).

Robertson defends the lower commitment to theoretical training in Britain by pointing out that it avoided higher schooling costs and that 'on-the-job' training produced a more efficient workforce in what was essentially a handicraft industry. This viewpoint probably underestimates the extent to which shipbuilding had become an applied science by the later nineteenth century and the role of scientific theory in British shipbuilding. The establishment of the Institute of Naval Architecture in 1857 and the subsequent creation of chairs of Naval Architecture at the universities of Liverpool, Newcastle and Glasgow bear witness to the progress being made in Britain. Denny's of Dumbarton took a scientific approach and were innovative in the fields of naval architecture and marine engineering. They were not entirely typical of British shipbuilders many of whom built tramps of a simple design whilst German builders concentrated upon the more technically demanding liners.

During the war British merchant shipbuilding was under the control of, first, the Shipping Controller and later the Admiralty. Both bodies emphasised expansion of the fleet rather than updating its technology. In other European countries, especially neutral Scandinavia, there were more wartime opportunities to build motorships. In 1915 the British Ship Transfer Restriction Act prohibited the sale of vessels to anyone not qualified to own a British registered vessel. This prevented British shipowners from continuing their pre-war policy of offloading second-hand vessels to foreign owners and buying new ones themselves. Britain, who had gone into the war with the most advanced merchant fleet, emerged from it with a technologically deficient one.

A temporary boom ensued between 1919 and 1920 as owners attempted to replace losses and wartime shipbuilding programmes reached fruition. A temporary shortage of shipping could also be traced to the port congestion caused by decontrol. Within a year or two the ports were no longer congested and wartime shortfalls had been made good. Shipping handed over from Germany as a result of the Versailles Treaty and the slump in freight rates also contributed to the collapse of shipbuilding demand. Conditions were exacerbated in Britain by the decline of her trade and shipping. In the 1920s at least a half of British shipbuilding berths lay idle, which pushed up the unit cost of output and led to a growing gap between British and European ship prices. The proportion of new British vessels sold abroad fell from 25–30 per cent before 1914 to around 17 per cent between the wars (Slaven, 1982, 39).

The main European challenge to British hegemony before 1914 came from Germany. German shipbuilding developed slowly before the last quarter of the nineteenth century. German shipowners ordered from more cost-effective British shipyards. State support for shipping developed at the time of the formation of the German Reich. Warship yards were established at Kiel and Wilhelmshaven in 1869 and a decade later the shake-up of tariff policy provided for the importation of shipbuilding materials free of duty. In 1885 Norddeutscher Lloyd ordered six new liners built in Germany as part of its mail contract with the government. Thenceforth, the rapid growth of Norddeutscher Lloyd, Hamburg-Amerika and other German liner companies together with the expansion of the German navy provided plenty of orders for German shipyards. Rapid German industrialisation particularly in the heavy industries facilitated import substitution in shipbuilding materials. In 1883 only Howaldt shipyard in Kiel was known to buy German steel. By the following decade major iron and steel producers such as Krupps provided a good domestic supply. Similar to the experience of many other German industries, a process of vertical integration often followed; in 1896, for example, Krupps bought the Germania shipyard (Leckebusch).

The number of German shipyards grew from eight to 35 between 1881 and 1901 and the output of new tonnage expanded from 83 000 to 371 000 tons between 1892–5 and 1911–14 (Pollard and Robertson, 39, 249). This was significantly faster growth than Britain's at the end of the nineteenth century but Germany's total output remained much smaller and was concentrated on liner production as German builders responded to the needs of its major liner companies. In contrast to Britain, Germany exported only a small proportion of her output because her prices were too high to be competitive.

France was the main European competitor for British shipbuilding in the 1860s and 1870s but her vessels were never price-competitive.

Table 4.2 Output of Major European Shipbuilding Countries, 1892–1914
(annual averages, 000 tons)

	UK	Germany	Netherlands	France	Norway	Italy	Spain	Denmark
1892–1895	986	83	10	21	18	9	–	9*
1896–1900	1 262	163	26	74	23	33	–	–
1901–1905	1 394	215	52	123	44	50	3†	14‡
1906–1910	1 300	218	65	61	48	31	–	–
1911–1914	1 790	371	104	132	48	34	14§	–

Notes: *1889–99   ‡1900–08
       †1899–1908 §1909–18

Sources: Pollard and Robertson, 249; Gomez-Mendoza, 1988, 24; Fayle, 1927, 416; Hornby and Nilson, 122.

Table 4.3   European Shipbuilding in 1913

	Ships	Tons (000)
United Kingdom	688	1932
Germany	162	465
France	89	176
Netherlands	95	104
Austria	17	62
Norway	74	51
Italy	38	50
Denmark	31	41
Belgium	54	30
Sweden	18	29

Source: Lloyd's Register.

In the later nineteenth century French builders suffered from insufficient and irregular demand as the home market expanded slowly. France's share of world tonnage fell from 5.4 per cent in 1870 to 3.9 per cent in 1900 and her shipbuilding output stagnated in a similar fashion (Lorenz, 604). This made it difficult for French yards to specialise or expand to gain economies of scale. As a result most French yards were small scale with high overheads and obsolescent equipment. The lack of specialisation is indicated by the range of output of the Penhoët yards: passenger liners, naval cruisers, battleships, tug boats, cargo and fishing vessels.

French governments began to intervene in shipbuilding towards the end of the nineteenth century. A law of 1881 offered some import protection to French builders: bounties were paid to shipbuilders and subsidies to shipowners buying French. A half subsidy was paid to shipowners buying foreign, as part of a programme to stimulate shipowning. It was only when this half subsidy was removed in 1893 that French builders began to dominate the domestic market. In 1902 the tonnage of sailing vessels to which government support applied was limited because the policy was perpetuating an obsolescent fleet. These policies together with the pre-war shipping boom facilitated an expansion of French shipbuilding. In the two decades before 1914 output doubled, existing yards expanded and new ones were established such as the Chantiers de France at Dunkirk, the Ateliers et Chantiers de Provence and the Chantiers de Construction Maritime at Nantes.

Dutch shipbuilding stagnated for much of the eighteenth and

nineteenth centuries in the wake of the country's declining trade and shipping and the failure to replace empirical methods with scientific practices common in France and England. One historian believes that the collective action of the ship's carpenters impeded industrial innovation but this view overstates the influence of the guilds; without them Dutch shipbuilding would still have been uncompetitive (R.W. Unger). Several government incentives were offered including a subsidy on ships for export in 1814 but development remained slow in the wake of low domestic demand and British competition. Friesland contained important centres of shipbuilding, especially at Groningen, but the absence of a local iron industry accounted for their relative decline after about 1870. Shipbuilding, however, expanded rapidly from 4000 tons in 1880 to about 100 000 tons by the eve of the First World War (Milward and Saul, 1977, 209). This expansion was concentrated upon Amsterdam and Rotterdam aided by the growth of trade and shipping there. Rotterdam's role as a place of cargo transshipment from ocean vessels to river boats enabled it to supply many Rhine barges and tugs. Plates and sections could be imported cheaply along the Rhine from the Ruhr. The revival of Dutch shipbuilding was supported by an advanced marine engineering industry led by Nederland Fabriek van Werktuigen Spoorwegmaterieel.

Dutch shipbuilders in the late nineteenth century concentrated upon specialist vessels such as barges, tugs and salvage vessels. This practice was followed by several other countries aware that it attracted less competition from British yards. European industrialisation and the invention of the Bessemer process of steel production provided many new opportunities for Swedish shipping and shipbuilding. Swedish iron ore was used in domestic shipbuilding and exported in specialist ore vessels built in Sweden. Swedish builders completed many vessels for the growing ore trades particularly smaller ones suitable for trading at minor British ports. Sweden also pioneered tanker design helped by orders from the Nobels who owned part of the Baku oilfields. About one-half of Swedish tanker production supplied Russian needs until 1904 when Russia began to produce her own vessels. Swedish builders also specialised in repair work. Despite government assistance, such as an import duty on ships in 1888, and an inflow of capital from expanding cities, particularly Gothenburg, most yards remained small and unable to gain the economies of scale of British and German shipbuilders.

Norway's traditional wooden shipbuilding industry was located along the southern coast, among the fjords of western Norway and in major coastal towns such as Stavanger and Bergen. The industry benefited from low raw material costs and cheap, seasonal labour from the surrounding countryside. The advantage of low cost materials was lost with the use of iron and steam while seasonal labour proved inappropriate for the continuous processes of the metal and engineering industries. The rapid transition to steam and steel in some countries (Britain and Germany) and the shift away from shipping by some others (America and Canada) in the late nineteenth century brought a large volume of second-hand shipping onto the market together with a high demand for tramping in the cross-trades. This was good news for Norwegian shipowners but bad for shipbuilders. Even new vessels were often bought abroad. In boom periods such as 1889–92, British order books were full and Norwegian owners turned to domestic suppliers such as Martens, Olsen & Co. of Bergen and Nylands Mekaniske Verksted of Oslo. The growth of Norwegian steam shipping from the 1890s provided a further stimulus but most Norwegian builders, like the Swedish, concentrated upon specialist vessels including fruit vessels for Bergen shipowners in the American fruit trade, whale catchers and special tramps for the timber trade and herring fishery.

Italian shipbuilding benefited from subsidies, such as those embodied in the law of 1885, and a reduction in import duties on raw materials. The industry also received substantial injections of British capital such as that by Maudsley and Armstrong in the Ansaldo yard and Thornycroft's contribution to the Pattison yard. Progress remained patchy, however, and by 1913 only a third of domestic demand was taken up by Italian shipbuilders (Milward and Saul, 1977, 260). Spanish shipbuilding also experienced a mixture of British investment and government encouragement. Shipbuilding was slow to develop in Spain. Retarded economic development and the loss of American colonies kept the level of demand low and prevented builders expanding in order to gain economies of scale. Most Spanish trade was carried in foreign built and owned vessels. The country was poorly endowed with timber supplies and failed to take best advantage of its iron ore resources in the later years of the nineteenth century. As a result its construction costs remained 30 per cent greater than Britain's and even 20 per cent above Italy's (Gomez-Mendoza, 1988, 27). Spanish yards concentrated upon the construction of small wooden sailing vessels of around 20 tons for coasting and fishing. No iron steamers were built until the 1870s. Between 1855 and 1864 the government paid a bounty of 30 pesetas per ton to encourage domestic shipbuilders. The size of this subsidy was subsequently increased, though with the stipulation that vessels had to be of at least 400 tons and must make an initial voyage to America or Asia. Shipbuilding materials were exempted from import duties though it took months or even years to reclaim the duty (Gomez-Mendoza, 1988, 25). These measures were ill-conceived and ineffective.

In the quarter-century before 1914 Spain's shipbuilding received some stimulus from the growth of trade, particularly mineral exports. While providing a high demand for shipping space and a return cargo for Spanish imports, the ore trade, and the construction of specialist vessels for it, fell mainly into the hands of foreigners. The naval expansion from the 1880s was a more effective stimulant. Government policy, as embodied in the Squadron Act of 1887, gave orders to domestic builders wherever possible. Domestic construction of a range of naval vessels including gunboats and corvettes led to the expansion of yards and the establishment of new ones. A further Squadron Act in 1908 together with an 'Act for the protection and encouragement of the maritime industries and communications' were passed under the lobbying influence of the Liga Marítima Española and the need to replace fleets obliterated at the end of the nineteenth century. Naval orders were won by a Spanish-British consortium, la Sociedad Española de Construcciones Navales. Under this agreement Spanish shipbuilding benefited from British technical expertise particularly in management skills and by gaining rights to the Parsons turbine patent. Spanish warship demand facilitated expansion and modernisation of shipbuilding but production costs remained too high to compete with foreign shipbuilders. Moreover, high opportunity costs suggest it may have been more economically effective for the navy to have purchased more cheaply abroad and redirected the resources to other Spanish industries. In shipbuilding, as in railways, Spain paid a high price for development.

SHIPOWNING

Between 1780 and the First World War the volume of European registered merchant shipping grew from less than 3.5 million tons to around 24 million tons. Random short term factors stimulated or depressed shipping throughout the period such as war, migration waves, harvest levels and government policy. The main long term

Table 4.4 Registration of European Merchant Shipping, 1780–1920
(000 net British tons; percentage of European total in parentheses)
Notes to table: see page 71

Country	1780	1800 Sail	1800 Steam	1800 Total	1820 Sail	1820 Steam	1820 Total	1840 Sail	1840 Steam	1840 Total	1860 Sail	1860 Steam	1860 Total
Austria-Hungary	84	–	–	–	–	–	–	197	2	199	321	21	342[1] (4)
Belgium	–	–	–	–	–	–	–	22	1	23	29	4	33 (0.3)
Denmark	386[3]	–	–	–	–	–	–	–	–	69	135	4	139 (1)
Finland	–	–	–	–	–	–	–	120[4]	0	120	169	1	170 (2)
France	729	–	–	–	–	–	–	653	10	663	928	68	996 (10)
Germany	123[5]	–	–	–	–	–	–	–	–	352[6]	754	23	777 (8)
Greece	–	–	–	–	–	–	–	111	0	111	263	0	263 (3)
Hungary	–	–	–	–	–	–	–	–	–	–	–	–	–

Italy	235[9]	–	–	–	–	–	–	–	644	10	654[10] (7)
Netherlands	398	–	–	–	–	–	–	–	485	11	496 (5)
Norway	386[3]	121	–	125	–	–	205	–	–	–	532 (5)
Portugal	85	–	–	–	–	–	–	–	–	–	– (5)
Russia	39	–	–	–	–	–	–	–	–	–	173[12] (2)
Spain	150	–	–	–	–	–	–	–	400	15	415 (4)
Sweden	169[13]	88	3	94	–	–	159[14]	–	–	–	281 (3)
United Kingdom	882	1 699	2 436	2 439	2 680	88	2 768	–	4 204	454	4 658 (47)
Total	3 350[15]	–	–	–	–	–	–	–	–	–	9 929

continued

Table 4.4 continued

Country	1880			1900			1920		
	Sail	Steam	Total	Sail	Steam	Total	Sail	Steam	Total
Austria-Hungary	198	64	262[2] (2)	54	191	245 (1)	–	–	–
Belgium	10	65	75 (0.5)	1	113	114 (0.6)	7	337	344 (2)
Denmark	198	52	250 (2)	147	247	394 (2)	101	392	493 (2)
Finland	262	10	272 (2)	287	54	341 (2)	380	108	488 (2)
France	642	278	920 (7)	510	528	1 038 (6)	433	1 085	1 518 (7)
Germany	927	177	1 104 (8)	584	1 319	1 903 (10)	288	1 546	1 834[7] (8)
Greece	–	–	–	176	143	319 (2)	138	494	632 (3)
Hungary	67	0	67[8] (0.5)	13	56	69 (0.4)	–	–	–
Italy	922	77	999 (7)	568	377	945 (5)	191	1 589	1 780[11] (8)
Netherlands	264	64	328 (2)	78	268	346 (2)	24	969	993 (4)

Norway	1 461	58	1 519 (11)	1 003	505	1 508 (8)	204	1 199	1 403 (6)
Portugal	–	–	–	–	–	–	–	–	236 (1)
Russia	379	89	468 (3)	269	364	633 (3)	–	–	510 (2)
Spain	326	234	560 (4)	51	735	786 (4)	83	875	958 (4)
Sweden	462	81	543 (4)	289	325	614 (3)	121	712	833 (4)
United Kingdom	3 851	2 724	6 575 (47)	2 096	7 208	9 304 (50)	584	10 777	11 361 (49)
Total			13 942			18 559			23 383

Notes: Motor vessels are included under steam tonnage, they were of little importance before the 1920s. Totals are given when only minor omissions exist.

1. 1861; 2. Venetia is excluded after 1866 and Hungary from 1870; 3. Denmark and Norway; 4. 1842; 5. Includes Hanseatic towns and Prussia; 6. 1838; 7. 1923; 8. 1881; 9. Includes Kingdom of Two Sicilies, Venice and Genoa; 10. 1862; 11. 1924; 12. 1859; 13. 1785; 14. Figures before 1830 relate only to the main ports; 15. Also includes Danzig (29 000 tons) and Ragusa (41 000 tons).

Sources: Mitchell, 1975, 613–33; R. Romano, 'Per una valutazione della flotta mercantile europea alla fine del secolo xviii', *Studi in Onore de Amintore Fanfani,* 5, 1962; Statement of Trade and Navigation, *British Parliamentary Papers.*

source of growth, however, was the increased demand for shipping generated by the industrialisation and accompanying international specialisation of the European economies. Improvements in the organisation of shipowning, together with technological developments, enabled the supply of shipping to grow at a slower rate than demand and therefore mitigated the bottlenecks associated with rapid expansion such as insufficient funding or port congestion.

Britain was the leading shipowning nation throughout the period. Her share of European shipowning grew from a quarter in the late eighteenth century to a half a hundred years later. British owners were the main beneficiaries of the French Wars; many entrepreneurs were attracted into the industry by the lure of high profits causing registered tonnage to nearly double. This expansion contributed to the prolonged shipping depression of the 1820s and 1830s when the industry suffered from chronic oversupply, poor trading opportunities and the fears surrounding the erosion of Britain's Navigation Laws. One shipowner noted, 'a man who has a vessel of 200 tons to depend upon and nothing else is gradually going to ruin'.[3] Thereafter, British shipowning grew consistently up to the First World War, interrupted only by temporary reversals and aided by the benefits of steam and metal and the many opportunities associated with the expansion of the international economy. Such was the strength of demand that the abolition of Britain's Navigation Laws, freeing many of her trades to foreign shipping, did nothing to dampen the shipping expansion.

France was the only serious challenger to British hegemony in the late eighteenth century with a fifth share of the European fleet but her mercantile marine grew slowly in the nineteenth century by the end of which she owned a mere six per cent of the total. Slow industrial growth, a greater concentration upon other areas of the economy and an ill-conceived state subsidy policy contributed to the relative retardation of her shipping industry. Dutch shipowning declined relatively from 12 to two per cent between 1780 and 1914 helped only by the recovery of Rotterdam and Amsterdam in the final few decades. In 1873 a transatlantic service from Rotterdam had been established by the Nederlandsche Amerikaansche Stoomvart Mij and in the following decades lines were established to trade with Australia, the West Indies and South America.

In contrast to Dutch and French experience the four per cent owned by the Hanseatic towns and Prussia at the end of the eighteenth century grew to 12 per cent for Germany as a whole by the eve of the Great War. Much of the progress took place in the final quarter of the nineteenth century and was aided by the country's rapid industrialisation with its heavy foreign trade orientation. This expansion was quite narrowly based upon two major ports, Hamburg and Bremen, and the operations of a small of number sizeable liner firms particularly Norddeutscher Lloyd and Hamburg-Amerika.

Denmark, Greece, Spain, Sweden, Italy and Norway offer pictures of greater stability with their shares maintaining at 1–2, 2–3, 3–4, 3–5, 5–7, and 7–11 per cent respectively. Some of these smaller shipping nations, particularly Greece and Norway, took advantage of the increased opportunities for tramp shipowning in the late nineteenth century. For Norway, in particular, the rise of tramping helped to offset her loss of relative cost advantages with the decline of the wooden sailing ship. Greek shipowners benefited from the country's emigrant trade from the 1890s. Danish shipowning similarly bene-fited from the emigrant trade together with their expanding trade in agricultural exports to Britain through the port of Esbjerg. The repeal of Spain's Navigation Acts in the late 1860s and the adoption of Figuerola's free trade policy weakened the position of Spanish owners whose share of the country's foreign trade fell from nearly a half in 1869 to only 18 per cent in 1882 (Gomez-Mendoza, 1988, 26). War at home and abroad also weakened Spanish shipping although this was more than offset by growth in the high-bulk ore trades and the opportunities for operating second-hand shipping. The success of Swedish shipowning was periodic, interspersed with depressed years. The main growth eras were in the second half of the 1850s, the early 1870s and 1900–13. In the first of these phases the boom in timber exports after Britain's revocation of the Baltic timber duties was the main stimulant while the second expansion was based upon the growth of the country's metallic ore exports and the third upon the general pre-war boom in shipping rates.

In the eighteenth century shipping was one of the major users of industrial capital along with coal, cotton and iron. Restrictions on the formation of joint stock companies presented problems in funding these industries. Nor did a network of financial institutions exist through which to channel investments. Shipping, however, attracted funds from a wide social, geographical and occupational cross-section of the population. Surviving shipping registers indicate that investors included widows, 'gentlemen', farmers, clergymen and solicitors none of whom possessed an obvious occupational interest in the shipping industry. In late eighteenth-century Newcastle, for example, shipping investors included widows, gentlemen, butchers, physicians, sugar refiners, wagonwrights, tilemakers and farmers (Ville, 1989). The experience of La Rochelle at the same period demonstrates the geographical spread of shipping investment particularly from other ports such as Nantes, Bordeaux, Le Havre and Marseilles. Investment was also attracted from inland areas such as Paris, Poitiers and Loudun as well as from foreign investors from London, Amsterdam and Hamburg. Shipping investment passed over national boundaries to avoid restrictive state legislation or to benefit from government subsidies. Foreign capital came into Britain to benefit from the Navigation Laws but moved out of it to overcome the monopolies granted to the chartered companies. A series of English mercantile and shipowning communities grew up along the Mediterranean to take advantage of unexploited trading opportunities. Lisbon was a particular stronghold for British shipowning where tonnage entrances and clearances were dominated by British shipping (Fisher, 1981, 34–5).

Since most businesses required little fixed capital and were managed by entrepreneurs reluctant to extend ownership or control, shipping provided one of the few outlets for the small investor. Shipping's notoriety for fluctuating fortunes made this a high risk investment to be set against the more constant returns in government stock in order to provide the investor with a mixed portfolio. Low share denominations served as a further encouragement to the small investor. For the purpose of ownership, vessels were often divided into sixty-four shares. An investor might purchase only one sixty-fourth which for small, old, coasting vessels could cost just a few pounds. In Norway vessels were sometimes divided into as many as 100 shares. Share owners were regarded as tenants in common which enabled them to buy or sell their share without reference to the other owners. Larger investors also tended to own small proportions of individual vessels. The absence of an effective system of marine insurance before the later eighteenth century encouraged fragmented ownership to spread risks.

In some agrarian communities the ownership and operation of vessels provided seasonal or part time work to supplement meagre earnings. In eighteenth-century Finland peasants supplemented their living by transporting and selling agricultural goods. In the southwest of the country peasants shipped foodstuffs and firewood to the Swedish capital of Stockholm. Peasant seafaring proved profitable and accounted for nearly half of the Finnish merchant fleet in the early nineteenth century (Kaukiainen, 1971). Thereafter, the growing professionalisation of shipping forced most of the peasantry to concentrate on one activity.

The market in ship shares operated through informal channels such as personal and business contacts, kinship, word of mouth and newspaper advertising. Interested investors could consult the ship's register to establish the name, address and occupation of the other owners. A merchant or some other individual connected with shipping might buy a vessel privately or at an auction and then resell shares to family, friends and partners. The informal nature of the ship market meant that most investors were drawn from the ship's home port although shares might also be sold at ports with which the vessel regularly traded. It also meant that, while shares were purchased by people from many walks of life, most shipping capital was owned by individuals connected with the shipping industry. Mastmakers, sailmakers, ship chandlers, blockmakers, ropemakers, boatbuilders and joiners invested widely in shipping. Besides benefiting from local connections, these tradesmen could assess the qualities of a vessel and keep in contact with the operations of the managing owner but the most important advantage was the business patronage it brought them. As one contemporary noted, 'almost every tradesman whose business was connected with shipping employed some part of his property in that line to extend his business'.[4] Similarly, a master mariner would hope to secure the command of a vessel in return for purchasing a few shares.

Most investors in eighteenth-century shipping played only a passive role in the business, leaving the day-to-day operations to the master or a managing owner. The fact that most investors came from the locality, were connected with the shipping industry and often knew the other investors gave them some reassurance regarding the management of the business. Although specific limited liability was not introduced until the nineteenth century, maritime law often restricted the extent of an investor's liabilities by creating a corporation based on the vessel and not on the individual. If the master was the manager the vessel was likely to be kept in the same trade, often coasting or other short hauls. The master was a major shareholder in many of the small Hamburg vessels which traded around the North Sea and in the Baltic. He rarely possessed the time or the knowledge to consider the relative merits of different trades. In the coasting trades, particularly coal, the cargo was often owned by the shipowner and sold on arrival which avoided searching for freights. The productivity of the vessel was thus restricted by limitations on managerial action. The master-owner structure worked best in depressions when masters took their vessels into various trades in search of employment and competed on more than equal terms with the sedentary specialist shipowner.

If the operations of the vessel were the responsibility of a shore-based managing owner this left more scope for policy variations such as changing the vessel's deployment or arranging different freights. The actions of the managing owner, however, were restricted. Policy changes might require the consent of other owners thereby preventing early, effective action. Managing owners often operated a number of vessels for different groups of owners and therefore their time would be limited and their loyalties stretched. The opportunity to run these vessels under similar policies and as part of the same business organisation rarely existed. In the eighteenth century there were few integrated shipping businesses where a fleet was run under a coordinated policy and reinforced by shore-based assets. Usually the vessel was the only significant form of fixed capital in a shipping enterprise and it was rare even for a reserve or contingency fund to exist from which abnormal expenditure or the cost of fitting out could be withdrawn. The 'adventure' system was more common whereby the particular costs of a voyage were raised from the shareholders before its commencement. Sometimes the whole cost structure endured for only the period of the voyage after which everything, including the vessel, was sold. In France vessels were often managed by *armateurs* who might own up to a half of the shares in a vessel and sell the rest. Shares were issued to cover the working capital of the individual voyage and were then redeemed once the profit and loss had been settled with the vessel remaining as the only capital asset of the business.

Merchant firms often owned several vessels as an adjunct to their main business interests. This form of vertical integration offered merchants some security against fluctuating markets and sometimes yielded operating economies. The extent of merchant shipowning varied from trade to trade and was particularly common amongst mine owners and merchants in the coal trade where a low value sturdy commodity presented few problems of transport and where a constant demand for shipment ensured a vessel could normally find full employment in that one trade. Since shipping management played a supporting role in most merchant firms it was simplest to keep vessels in the same trade. Shipowning was most common among merchants in major ports such as London, Hamburg and Gothenburg where many large mercantile firms existed.

The largest vessel-owning organisations in the eighteenth century were the chartered companies. These companies, mostly formed in the seventeenth or early eighteenth centuries, had been granted a royal charter of monopoly over a particular trade. They were most common in long-haul trades, such as to Africa, China and the East Indies, through politically dangerous areas where the length of the journey and the cost of armaments required high capital costs. The royal charter granted to the English East India Company in 1600 prohibited other English mercantile or shipping firms from trading to the East Indies. The Dutch East India Company was established in 1602 by a charter from the States-General which granted it exclusive Dutch trade and shipping rights east of the Cape of Good Hope and west of the Magellan Straits. East India Companies were formed in various other European countries including Sweden from 1731, Denmark from the early seventeenth century, the Austrian Netherlands from 1722 and Prussia from 1751–2. The structure of these enterprises reflected the semi-permanent nature of shipping capital in the eighteenth century. For most companies the charter was issued for a fixed period of time, maybe 10, 20 or 40 years. Before 1753 the Swedish Ostindiska Kompaniet had charters of only 15 or 20 years and had to raise operating costs by the voyage. The Danish Asiatisk Kompagnie operated with charters of around 40 years and a structure of permanent possessions in Europe and Asia. Its working capital, however, still had to be raised for each voyage. More common, though, was the public company with a permanent capital upon which the directors could draw to finance outfitting, repairs and other incidental costs.

The specialised needs of the chartered companies such as large well-armed vessels up to 1400 tons and an onshore defence militia encouraged vertical integration so that all their requirements were internally generated. The French Compagnie des Indes built its own vessels at its shipyard at Lorient and the Danish Asiatisk Kompagnie established its own shipyards at Copenhagen in 1732. The Swedish Ostindiska Kompaniet, though, purchased its ships from private shipyards. The English East India Company, finding the costs of such a large industrial structure increasingly burdensome, began to break up the organisation in the mid-seventeenth century. In 1639 it sold off its shipyards after an inquiry had revealed high costs and surplus capacity and subsequently also began to lease vessels from other shipowners rather than maintain its own fleet.

The chartered companies were already on the wane by the later eighteenth century in spite of periodic reorganisations to improve efficiency by ending the adventure system and decentralising an overcapitalised structure. Fragmenting the capital structure could bring perils as the English East India Company discovered when its decision to hire rather than own vessels made it over-reliant upon a small group of London shipowners who were able to charge very high freight rates. Some of these owners were Thames shipbuilders who owned the company's former yards and were best placed to offer the type of shipping required. Increased competition from private ship-owners operating more efficiently and able to raise more capital than hitherto and the reduced risks with the growth of marine insurance led to the demise of most of the chartered companies by the end of the eighteenth century. By that time English shipowners were cir-cumventing the English East India Company's monopoly by sailing under the Danish flag and delivering in Copenhagen where the route had been thrown open to private traders in 1772. In England the monopoly was finally halted in 1813 and English merchants returned to their national flag.

Thus, it seems, few shipping investors in the mid-eighteenth century were shipowners *per se*, that is, individuals who owned and managed their own fleet on a full-time basis. Most shipping investors were passive or mainly concerned with merchanting, while most managing owners operated vessels which were largely owned by other people. Towards the end of the eighteenth century, however, there began to emerge a new breed of professional shipowners who owned and operated their own fleets. This was part of a process of occupational specialisation which also produced shipping agents and brokers and may be explained by the huge growth of overseas trade associated with European industrialisation. In the first half of the nineteenth century the professional specialist shipowner became more important, gradually pushing out the merchant shipowner, the managing owner and the small investor. By the eighteen fifties shipping capital was increasingly concentrated into the hands of a limited number of professional shipowners.

The growth of marine insurance in the eighteenth century encour-aged the development of specialist shipowning. By the end of the century a majority of shipping was insured. Freights were sometimes insured on long hauls where they represented six months' or a year's earnings. The shipowner no longer had to spread his interests thinly among many vessels to guard against loss but could concentrate upon a limited number of insured ships and so develop a fleet over which he was the principal if not sole owner, free to implement his own policies. Marine insurance produced a wealth of maritime intelligence as insurers kept a check upon the condition and location of individual ships. Lloyd's List, established in 1734, served as a major source of information on shipping movements for aspiring shipowners. Centres of maritime insurance were developing in many European countries in the eighteenth century including Britain, Holland, Denmark, France and Prussia.

London was the principal centre for marine insurance initially through the monopoly on marine insurance given to the London Assurance and the Royal Exchange companies in 1720 and by the end of the century through the dominance which Lloyd's exercised as a central meeting point for private underwriters. While Lloyd's and the insurance companies insured vessels by policy, which was normally for the duration of a voyage, mutual insurance clubs insured a vessel for a year at a time. Clubs consisted of a series of shipowners, normally from the same port, who mutually insured one another's vessels by paying a premium each year according to the total claims. Clubs were particularly useful in small and medium-sized ports which lacked large insurance companies. Many were to be found in the north-east ports of Britain. French ports made less use of the mutual insurance principle. In La Rochelle an insurance company was established in 1751 but lacked the resources to cover the port's shipping capital and so insurance was negotiated with companies at other ports. Under both systems vessels were checked for their seaworthiness and the nature of their deployment. Under policy insurance vessels were charged more if they were in a poor condition or a risky trade. The clubs simply excluded poor quality vessels and prohibited trading in dangerous seas. The clubs tended to be cheaper but the companies and underwriters offered greater flexibility of cover.

Periods of war presented opportunities and challenges for marine insurance: high premiums attracted new entrants but survival and success depended upon a high degree of professionalism. Insurance rates doubled or trebled during the French Wars. In 1787 a vessel returning from Lisbon to London was charged a premium of two per cent but with the proviso that it would rise to ten per cent if war broke out (Ville, 1987, 130). Against this must be set the risk of substantial claims. At Lloyd's the experience of the French Wars led to a series of reforms in the institution. The list of subscribers was limited to merchants, bankers, traders, insurance brokers and under-writers. As a result of heavy claims in 1810 and suspicion of fraudu-lence, Lloyd's improved its marine intelligence particularly with the establishment of its agents in many more ports and by working closely with the Admiralty in order to enforce convoy discipline. Lower premiums were offered to British shipowners whose vessels sailed in convoy though this was rarely the case in France. The growing efficiency of Lloyd's was an important factor in British military success and enabled premiums to be offered which were on average five or ten per cent lower than in France, Britain's main military and maritime rival (Clark, 194).

The wars of the second half of the eighteenth century encouraged the development of professional shipowning. High wartime profits from increased freight rates encouraged merchants and other entre-preneurs to concentrate upon shipowning. Marine insurance reduced some of the risks of wartime shipowning. Many owners hired vessels to the government as transports for months or even years at a time. Transport owners were compensated for the cost of vessels captured by the enemy. Owners thus became accustomed to only shipping and not merchanting goods while the little day-to-day effort required of transport owners left them free to develop shipowning skills and to break into other trades which were higher risk in nature and required more effort. The rapidly changing fortunes of different trades in wartime required an active and responsive shipowner to take best advantage of this situation. Older forms of shipping management operated by masters, merchants and managing owners were largely unsuitable. Another possibility for the enterprising owner in wartime was the acquisition of prizes[5] as cheap vessels. Prizes could be bought at auctions and restored as merchant vessels at comparatively little cost.

The growth of shipping agents and brokers was part of the process of occupational specialisation but also contributed to the rise of shipowning. Port agents conducted the firm's business on a local level which left the shipowner free to develop overall policy and move in a series of different trades. It also weakened the master-owner struc-ture since much of the commercial responsibility which had devolved upon the captain after the decline of the supercargo now passed to the agent. The shipbroker played a vital middleman role between shipowner and merchant, relieving the shipowner of much of the burden of seeking out freights. The expansion of the telegraph system in the 1870s and 1880s enabled shipowners to gain rapid information regarding markets and freights. This created further opportunities for the professional, sedentary shipowner particularly in the tramp trades. It reinforced the declining commercial responsibilities of the master and attracted into shipping management entrepreneurs with a background in business administration rather than onboard employment.

We know disappointingly little about the pioneer, professional shipowners before about 1830, particularly as to their origins, extent and policies. Many probably came from among the ranks of merchants, shipbrokers and maritime tradesmen; men who had some knowledge of the shipping industry and probably owned several vessels as an extension of their main business activity. Rathbone's of Liverpool and Thomson's of Leith began as merchants before concentrating upon shipowning. Experienced master mariners often moved into professional shipowning, particularly when they were too old to go to sea. Shipbuilders were ideally placed to respond to the wartime boom by concentrating upon shipowning.

While the precise numbers are unknown there were significantly more professional shipowners by the middle of the nineteenth century than there had been in the last quarter of the previous one. The transition varied from country to country and port to port and appears to have taken place earliest in Britain under the stimulus of early industrialisation, a large overseas trade sector and careful wartime policies which included effective convoys and competitive insurance rates. In Sweden, on the other hand, national trade was insufficient to encourage widespread professional shipowning until the rise of the tramp steamer caused many owners to diversify into the cross-trades. The specialist shipowner appeared earlier in the larger ports where shipping demand was higher and there existed a large body of enterprising merchants from which shipowners would be drawn. In Britain, the concentration of shipping capital into the hands of professional shipowners occurred earliest in major ports like London and Liverpool. Newcastle and Sunderland were also major ports but the transition was delayed because many colliery owners preferred shipping coal in their own vessels to freighting.

Detailed evidence has come to light for one early English shipowning firm. Michael Henley & Son were shipowners in London between 1775 and 1830. Michael Henley began in business as a Thames waterman and then as a coal merchant before investing in a few ships in the 1770s in which to carry coal into the port. Henley's soon began to realise the opportunities for shipowning, particularly in wartime, and dropped merchanting and other interests to concentrate upon shipowning. The firm was highly successful, building up a large and profitable fleet of 6000 tons which made a fortune for Henley's (Ville, 1987).

Henley's are indicative of the managerial advantages connected with the professional shipowner. They were sole owners of most of their fleet which enabled them to respond swiftly to new opportunities without recourse to other owners. The constantly changing economic conditions of wartime dictated a rapid response. Henley's were quick to take advantage of opportunities in the transport service after 1793 and to deploy vessels in the timber trade with British North America after the introduction of duties on Baltic timber from 1809. It also enabled them to operate the business as a single entity and so benefit from various economies of scale. It was worth their while to build up a reserve stock of ship stores; they could find good masters and offer them regular work, employ agents and compete for major government contracts requiring the participation of a group of vessels. They built up the capital structure of the business to include a range of shore-based assets such as warehouses, a bakehouse, a counting house, and several wharves all of which served the needs of the business. With effective masters in charge of their vessels, aided by local agents, Henley's sought regular and profitable deployment for their ships at the evolving London freight market. In essence Henley's ran a highly efficient, integrated business which was indicative of a major organisational advance in the shipping industry enabling it to cope effectively with the huge increase in demand associated with industrialisation.

The Henley experience also confirms the continued fragility of the private shipownership structure. For some entrepreneurs the move into shipowning was a response to changing market conditions which might be reversed if the opportunities for shipowning became less favourable. The Lyle shipping firm began as coopers in Greenock in the late eighteenth century before a large fleet was established sixty or seventy years later. In the 1870s and 1880s they ran down their shipping interests to concentrate upon sugar refining before returning to shipping once more in the pre-1914 boom. Henley's struggled in the difficult years for shipping after 1815 but their decline was mainly due to the lack of interest shown in the business by the only grandson of its founder. Reluctance to spread ownership and control outside the family circle made the continued success of the private shipowning business highly reliant upon the interest and abilities of successive generations. In this case the grandson, Joseph Warner Henley, was more interested in buying social elevation than maintaining the business.

The introduction of the joint stock company and the principle of limited liability in the nineteenth century removed some of the dependence upon the individual. Most of the early joint stock shipping companies were associated with steam rather than sail. The high capital cost and unreliability of early steam-shipping discouraged the professional shipowner from abandoning a reliable fleet of maybe 20 sailing vessels for a handful of expensive and untried steamers. The General Steam Navigation Company was formed in London in 1824 and operated in the river, coasting and near-Continental trades. It was one of the earliest steamship companies and was financed by public subscription. It struggled to remain in profit and only survived by a combination of full utilisation, careful cost control and collusive rate-fixing with competitors (Palmer, 1982 (1)).

The association of joint stock companies with steam-shipping was not, however, an inevitable and consistent development. By the second half of the nineteenth century technological improvements in steam and the use of iron in construction began to bring down the cost of steam-shipping and enabled it to operate effectively over a widening number of routes. The availability of mortgages enabled private shipowners to finance expansion out of operating profits. Significantly, mortgages were most often offered on whole ships rather than individual shares. Finland was one of several countries in which the government provided low or interest-free loans to individuals and companies buying new vessels. In such circumstances private shipowners began to see the advantages of converting to steam. Cottrell's study of Liverpool, for example, reveals that as late as 1871 joint stock companies accounted for only 40 per cent of the port's steam tonnage (145). It was not until the end of the decade that the rise of the single-ship company encouraged most Liverpool steamship owners to convert to joint stock status.

Bergen was the first Norwegian port to convert to steam on a large scale but retained the private ownership structure later than the predominantly sailing fleet of Oslo. In Bergen sufficient finance could still be raised in traditional ways from among the wealthy maritime community and from abroad by foreign capital seeking a 'flag of convenience'. The growing opportunities for tramp shipping in the cross-trades encouraged private shipowning while the reliance on second-hand British steam-shipping kept down capital costs. Conversely, Oslo used the legal security offered by the joint stock company to attract new investors into shipping.

In Sweden greater reliance upon institutional forms of investment encouraged a heavier orientation towards public companies. Private finance flowed into manufacturing industry where the returns were considered more reliable and frequently higher. However, the extension of limited liability was delayed by a law of 1848 which required the crown to authorise every application of which only one was approved before 1863. In Finland private capital was reluctant to support an industry which was declining and was technologically backward compared with most other countries. When steam finally arrived at the turn of the twentieth century it was dominated by a few large joint stock companies particularly the Finnish Steamship Company (FAA) at Helsinki which owned nearly half of the country's steam fleet (Kaukiainen, 1980). In Germany the development of steam and joint stock companies went hand in hand. Most steamship companies were large-scale liner firms like Norddeutscher Lloyd and Hamburg-Amerika which required a great deal of capital to meet the cost of new high-quality liners and shore-based facilities.

It was thus, in tramp shipping, dominated by Britain and the Scandinavian countries, that the '64th' system of private ownership persisted longest; there were few overheads and the vessels in the firm were often old and small in size and number. By the 1880s, however, tramp owners were converting in large numbers to joint stock companies in order to take advantage of single-ship company status. Many owners found it safer to incorporate each vessel as an individual company with limited liability because it restricted collision insurance claims and facilitated the issue of low denomination shares to the small investor. The relative anonymity of these firms, exploited with dubious publicity, provided an ideal breeding ground for individuals intent on a quick fortune sometimes at the expense of the small investor. Evan Thomas Radcliffe, established in Cardiff in 1882, served as an umbrella for 31 single-ship companies. Evan Thomas had been a shipmaster and Henry Radcliffe a businessman and like most founders of single-ship companies they put up only a minimal amount of capital themselves. They acted as managers for the single-ship companies and drew their generous commission upon the gross freight earnings of each company (Geraint Jenkins).

By the end of the nineteenth century the joint stock company dominated the industry and, helped by the move to incorporation, the size of the average firm increased significantly. In the liner sector, in particular, there were many advantages to operating on a large scale. The development of fuel-efficient iron screw steamers and the assistance of government mail subsidies led to the expansion of the oceanic liner services. A large liner fleet could run to a regular timetable which connected with railway services and encouraged customer loyalty. Loyalty was also fostered by the lavish expenditure laid out on passenger liners in order to achieve high speed and luxury. The increasing size of vessels exercised a further expansionary pressure upon the companies. Average size trebled between 1848 and 1888 and this was followed by the construction of vessels much larger again in the years leading up to the Great War. The *Aquitania*, built in 1914, measured as large as 47 000 tons.

Among the pioneer large liner companies are to be found many famous British names including Cunard, Peninsular & Oriental, White Star, Leyland, Lamport & Holt, Booth and the Pacific Steam Navigation Company. By the last decade or so of the century British dominance was being challenged by the likes of Hamburg-Amerika, Norddeutscher Lloyd, Red Star and Holland-America. Hamburg-Amerika emerged as the largest shipping company in the world with an ocean-going fleet of 150 vessels in 1905 (Milward and Saul, 1977, 43). The trends towards concentration continued unabated. The domination by FAA in Finland has already been mentioned; in Denmark a half of the country's effective tonnage was owned by DFDS (Nordvik, 133). In Germany seven lines owned 60 per cent of national tonnage in 1905. In Britain the 'big five' (P & O, Royal Mail, Cunard, Ellerman and Furness Withy) owned 25 per cent although after the war they accounted for 75 per cent of the fleet (Aldcroft, 1974, 88; 1965–6, 21–2). Besides the technological explanations the growth of concentration was also the result of attempts to control the heightened level of competition which will be discussed later.

Expansion and the restriction of competition were also promoted by mergers, takeovers and controlling influences in the years prior to the First World War. Union and Castle merged in 1900, Blue Funnel and China Mutual two years later. The major German passenger lines controlled a number of other lines such as Austro-American while J. P. Morgan's International Mercantile Marine Company acquired many other shipping lines including the Belgian Red Star.

In spite of the growth of large shipping corporations, the opportunities for the individual shipowner remained good. Tramp shipping could still prove successful on the basis of a small operation. William Burrell and Walter Runciman were highly successful tramp owners. Many major shipping companies were controlled by leading shipping entrepreneurs who could make their fortunes within a corporate structure and influence closely the firm's performance. Aggressive policies could bring fortunes within the context of a profitable and expanding industry. The periodic shipping depressions gave the more wily individuals the chance to buy cheap vessels in anticipation of an upturn. The appointment of Owen Phillips as chairman of the Royal Mail Steam Packet in 1903 led to a reversal in the company's dwindling fortunes. Phillips raised money by calling in the balance of shares uncalled since shortly after the company's formation in 1839. He obtained a royal charter which allowed Royal Mail to hold interests in other companies and diversified into other areas of trade and shipping by means of a series of acquisitions. In order to retain personal control of the company he converted a large proportion of its capital into preference shares and debentures. Among other companies he acquired Elder Dempster, Pacific Steam Navigation and Union Castle to make him the leading British 'shipowner'. Phillips also organised cross-shareholding between the companies in the group in order to conceal the extent of his own interests and to inflate profits by paying dividends between companies. The war and subsequent revelations surrounding his business practices led to his downfall (Davies and Bourn).

Phillips was representative of a group of shipping magnates in the manner he pushed himself to the top by supplementing his own resources with public funds while taking care to ensure that he remained in overall control. Their background tended to be in business administration and clerical work. Alfred Jones worked his way up from clerk to take control of Elder Dempster while J. R. Ellerman came to shipping from accountancy when he secured control of the Leyland Line after the death of its founder in 1892. Some made their way into shipping from merchanting like many of the first generation of professional shipowners a century earlier. Thomas Wilson had traded in iron, Charles Booth in corn and Christopher Furness in provisions.

The onset of war in 1914 created boom conditions in the shipping industry and offered shipowners opportunities for great gain on a level similar to those afforded by the French Wars although circumstances were different in several important respects. Government regulation of the shipping industry was much greater and the opportunity for shipowners to operate cheaply-purchased prizes no longer existed. While wartime losses were naturally high, particularly after the introduction of submarine warfare, high freight rates gave the opportunity for large profits. Aggregate British tramp profits rose from £3.8 million in 1914 to £11 million in 1916 while in the liner trades £2.6 million was doubled to £5.3 million (Doughty, 19). The return on capital by British passenger liners has been calculated at 62 per cent for 1916 (Fayle, 1927, 182–3). In the Spanish shipping industry the profits of the leading six lines rose from 4.4 million pesetas in 1913 to 24.1 million in 1914 and 52.7 million in 1915 (R. J. Harrison, 93–4).

An indication of the rapid rise in freight rates can be given by the fact that British charter rates in July 1915 were already 230 per cent higher than in the previous December and by 1917 were 800 per cent higher.[6] Extensive requisitioning, however, meant that British shipowners were unable to take full advantage of the boom. From purely naval purposes to begin with, requisitioning was extended to include refrigerated holds in 1915 and later North Atlantic grain space. By 1917 there was a general requisition in Britain covering 96 per cent of cargo (Sturmey, 47). Requisitioned vessels were kept away from an owner's use for a long and undefined period and were paid at 'Blue Book' rates. Blue Book rates were established by a committee of shipowners in 1915 and were based upon 1914 levels with an increment added. Market rates, however, soon rose above the Blue Book rates which were not revised until 1918 after which they were still 200–300 per cent lower (Doughty, 28–9). While compensation was paid to owners of requisitioned vessels destroyed by the enemy, payment was delayed, which meant it was frequently insufficient to cover the full cost of replacement because of wartime inflation. One contemporary calculated that British shipowners lost £300 million per annum from not being able to operate in the open market.[7] Owners adopted various subterfuges to avoid requisitioning, such as keeping their vessels away from domestic ports. This was naturally easier for tramps than liners but they suffered heavy losses because they were slow-moving and ventured into dangerous trades. Passenger liners were among the earliest vessels to be requisitioned because they could find few customers in wartime.

There were other ways by which shipowners profited from war. Vessel prices rose and fluctuated wildly leaving room for speculation.

Glasgow shipowner William Burrell, for example, made a fortune by accurately anticipating changes in the ship market in order to buy vessels on a low market and sell them on a high one. On the other hand, shipping magnates Lords Kylsant (Owen Phillips) and Inchcape badly misjudged the post-war market when they agreed to buy all the merchant vessels owned by the government. The collapse of the shipping boom in 1920 left them with many depreciated pre-war vessels for which there was little work.

French and Italian shipowners benefited from a lack of wartime shipping controls and intergovernmental loans of ships from Britain. Shipowners from neutral countries such as Spain, Denmark, Norway, Sweden, Greece and The Netherlands were also able to take advantage of high market rates. There was plenty of work for Norwegian and Greek tramps while Dutch liners took over many of Britain's pre-war services. Neutral shipping losses were nonetheless high particularly at the hands of German submarines. The British government imposed an embargo on Swedish and Danish firms for trading with the enemy and was reluctant to sell bunker coal to vessels which were not trading to or from Britain.

The merger movement continued during the war as a means of replacing a fleet depleted by wartime losses and requisitioning in order to continue operating at a level appropriate for the firm's overheads. In 1916 Cunard acquired Commonwealth Dominion Line and Donaldson Line and purchased ships from Canadian Northern Steamships. The wartime losses amounted to over 12 million tons for the world fleet but as early as 1919 the 1914 figure had been attained once more (Fayle, 1933, 293). The balance, however, was changing, with the United States and Japan expanding output and ownership rapidly while Britain did not return to her pre-war tonnage figure until the 1920s. Some of the European allies were able to make good their wartime losses by seizing the fleets of the losers as part of the reparations payments. The fleets of Germany, Turkey and Austria–Hungary were all seized in this way. German shipowners had to give up all vessels over 1600 tons and half of the vessels in the 1000 to 1600 tons range. Including vessels under construction this amounted to 2.75 million tons leaving a merchant fleet of little more than half a million tons. German shipowners were paid compensation by their government but inflation eroded the real value of such sums (Sturmey, 44–6).

COMPETITION AND COLLUSION

The late nineteenth century witnessed growing economic competition between the major industrialising nations. British economic hegemony of the mid-nineteenth century was giving way to a pattern of several competing powers as industrialisation proceeded apace in Germany, the United States, Japan and, to a lesser extent, France, Italy, Belgium and The Netherlands. A common feature among most countries was the growing role of governments in this competition many of which pursued 'beggar my neighbour' policies to develop domestic industries at the expense of foreign ones by subsidies and import protection. The simultaneous trade depression in the later 1870s and 1880s and the flood of cheap agricultural imports from North America reinforced this trend. One of the most acute areas of international competition in the later years of the nineteenth century was the shipping industry. In the third quarter of the nineteenth century British maritime supremacy was based upon her domination of the new iron and steam technologies and control of many trade routes. As industrial development spread, countries such as Germany and Japan began to produce up-to-date and competitive shipping and operate more trade routes, while less wealthy, under-developed countries such as Norway and Greece began to compete on the basis of cheap second-hand steamers from Britain.

British success in the French Wars was followed by a long period of European peace up to the 1850s known as the 'Pax Britannica' during which British shipowners took advantage of their country's control of the seaways to expand existing and develop new trade routes particularly to Australia and South America. The only serious challenge to Britain came from the Americans whose neutrality during most of the French Wars had brought prosperity and expansion to shipping. This challenge persisted after 1815 particularly in the Mediterranean fruit trade and the transatlantic passenger and mail trades. In 1818 the Black Ball packets began to operate between New York and Liverpool followed by Red Star Line and Swallowtail Line in 1822. They competed upon the basis of the fast sailing qualities of their design and the cheapness of their American softwood construction.

While America was quick to develop steampowered river boats, she made little progress with ocean-going vessels. Britain's leadership in this field enabled her to challenge back on the North Atlantic route by the middle of the century. British companies also benefited from the payment of postal subventions by the government which, while not excessively generous, at least guaranteed them a regular income. Wilcox and Anderson were paid a subvention of £29 600 in 1837 to carry mails to Gibraltar which was extended to Alexandria in 1840 and led to the formation of Peninsular & Oriental. By 1842 P & O were carrying British mail on to Suez and India and soon afterwards to Penang, Singapore and Hong Kong. The opportunities presented by the mail subventions led to the formation of other major companies. The Royal Mail Steam Packet Company was established in 1839 for the carriage of mails to Havannah via the West Indies in return for an apparently generous subvention of £240 000. In the same year Samuel Cunard with George Burns and David McIver won the North Atlantic contract for the British and North American Royal Mail Steam Packet Company Limited which was the forerunner of the Cunard Company (Davies, 1978 (2), 183).

The American government offered support to some firms including the Collins Line which was in competition with Cunard on the North Atlantic route in the 1850s. Not all was competition, though, since the two companies entered into secret agreements to pool a proportion of the earnings. The Collins Line service, however, was discontinued in 1858; the company had laid too much stress upon the superior speed of its service which was only achieved at the price of greater fuel consumption and heavier shipping losses. This ill-conceived policy also brought several competing German lines to grief later in the century. Thenceforth the American challenge evaporated. They lacked the comparative cost advantages of British iron and steam shipping particularly when the development of the compound engine and suitable boilers increased steam's advantage on many routes. The Civil War certainly weakened the American challenge in the short run but it was principally the economic development westward across the United States in the second half of the century which turned American interest away from Atlantic trade and shipping.

By the 1870s British shipping dominated most of the major shipping routes of the world. Hamburg-Amerika, Norddeutscher Lloyd and the Netherlands Steamship Company had all been formed in the mid-1850s but their activities remained, as yet, small. In America only the Pacific Mail Steamship Company, operating on the San Francisco to Yokohama route, and the Guion Line in the North Atlantic were serious competition. In the 1880s European ship-owners began to challenge British hegemony in some of the liner trades. A Dutch company challenged Holt's domination of shipping in the Far East. French and Italian shipowners were also increasingly in evidence on major liner routes. Scandinavian, especially Norwegian, and Greek shipowners challenged Britain in the tramp sector.

The main challenge came from German shipping. By the early 1880s Hamburg-Amerika and Norddeutscher Lloyd carried 30 per cent of the westbound transatlantic passenger trade helped by the growing number of emigrants from central and eastern Europe and the formation of immigration control stations to channel emigrants through the north German ports (Aldcroft, 1974, 77). The number of major Hamburg shipping companies grew from four to ten in the decade from 1886 benefiting from Germany's growing importance as an exporting nation. By 1890 she was the leading exporter to Russia, Sweden, Denmark, Switzerland and Austria-Hungary and a series of bilateral trading agreements in the 1890s enabled further trade gains on Britain. Before 1914 Rickmers began a new service to Rumania, Hamburg-Amerika one between New York and the Near East, and Norddeutscher Lloyd a direct service to New Zealand.

German shipping benefited from the diversion of Rotterdam and Antwerp trade through her own northern ports secured by preferential railway rates. German shipowners handled an increasing volume of the entrepôt trade to Europe via Britain. An intelligence-gathering service helped them find the names and addresses of consignees of goods on British ships who were then canvassed to use German vessels. Some German shipowning firms were large and powerful corporations with a range of other interests including railways and banking. They muscled into British-dominated trades by aggressive policies, particularly ferocious rate-cutting, which forced British owners to concede to market-sharing agreements. An association of leading German shipowners (Rheederei-Vereinigung) formed in 1909 held a joint reserve pool of 23 000 tons which each member could use to conduct rate wars.

Most national governments offered support to their shipping industry against foreign competition. A variety of preference policies were adopted including cheaper internal rail rates and the refund of shipping duties. In Germany this took the form of preferential railway rates and the establishment of immigration control stations. The French government offered preferential rail tariffs to the ports for exports in French ships to French West Africa, South America, the Levant, the Far East and New York. Sweden, Denmark, Russia and Austria-Hungary all refunded the Suez Canal dues paid by national vessels. Britain possessed an entire system of preference derived from the seventeenth century known as the Navigation Laws. These excluded third-party shipping from most of Britain's foreign trade. The laws were relaxed in particular cases in the 1820s and entirely abolished in 1849. Postal subventions were adopted by many shipping nations. Direct subsidies on shipowning and shipbuilding were .offered in France, Italy, Finland, Austria-Hungary and The Netherlands. The Italian government began subsidising regular shipping services from 1877 and offered construction bounties from 1885. Dutch subsidies were deliberately aimed at encouraging services to Japan, China and South America. Government bounties were offered for particular steam services by Finnish shipping such as early winter traffic to Sweden and England. Finnish governments also built ice breakers to facilitate winter services and offered loans to shipowners to overcome the dearth of capital.

State intervention did little to strengthen the shipping industries of most nations. Policies were often ill-conceived, limited in their coverage and overwhelmed by more potent market trends and occasionally counterproductive. Britain remained by far the strongest shipping nation in spite of little state support for shipping. The abolition of the Navigation Laws proved a good thing for trade and shipping in Britain. The postal subvention was soon regarded as little more than fair pay. The growth of British trade and shipping in Latin America in the second half of the nineteenth century was due to improved trading opportunities in the region rather than subsidised mail services. Admiralty subventions were temporarily paid on a small number of vessels which were fast-sailing and could be fitted as armed merchant cruisers. This was dropped when it became clear that these vessels would meet this standard without Admiralty encouragement. British policy also addressed the issue of safety on board vessels. The Plimsoll Line, made mandatory in 1876, fixed the maximum depth of vessels in the water and was particularly aimed at the timber trade where deck cargoes often led to dangerous overloading. This measure gave a comparative advantage to shipowners from other countries such as Norway where no such regulations existed and encouraged some British owners to transfer their vessels to foreign registration in order to bypass legislation.

Nor did Britain's main rivals exhibit a high level of state support. In 1894 less than four per cent of net German tonnage received government subsidies (Meeker, 94). Firms which received government subsidies often had to buy domestically built vessels rather than more competitive British ones and had to ensure their suitability as military auxiliaries. This was the experience of Norddeutscher Lloyd which was paid subsidies for its services to the Far East and Australia. The subsidy paid to the German East Africa Company to conduct a regular service to the East African colonies failed to prevent it losing money. Preferential railway rates were largely restricted to trade with East Africa, the Levant, the Black Sea and southern Brazil where only a small proportion of consignments came from the German interior. The success of German shipping owed more to the impetus from industrialisation and aggressive rate-cutting policies than to state support. French subsidies were more generous but we saw earlier that they supported sail as well as steam and therefore slowed down technological change. Italian and Dutch subsidies had little effect upon their shipping industries.

Competition in the latter part of the nineteenth century existed between different modes of shipping as well as between the national industries. In the second half of the century the shipping industry was increasingly divided into tramp and liner operations and it was between these two different types of shipping that rivalry was often the most intense. The liner trades regularly between particular ports to a published timetable and at a fixed freight rate and carries a mix of different cargo consignments. It is often a comparatively new, fast and efficient vessel and to be effective is normally part of a large company. The firm requires a fleet of vessels to maintain regular sailings and a shore-based organisation to publicise sailings and organise the collection and distribution of consignments. In contrast the tramp is often a slow and old vessel which travels between any ports in search of a remunerative freight. It has no timetable nor regular route and is likely to be hired by an individual shipper by the voyage or the month to carry a single cargo. Its freight rate varies according to prevailing supply and demand conditions in the shipping industry. It requires few shore-based assets and therefore can operate individually or as part of a small shipping concern. While the liner offers certainty, reliability and speed, the tramp's competitive edge lies in its cheapness. In the bulk trades such as coal and metallic ores the tramp is often more effective because it offers cheapness while mail and passengers have normally been carried by liners because of their speed and regularity. Sometimes there was an overlap between the two sectors. In busy seasons some liner companies hired tramps to extend the frequency of their services while in bad times they sent some of their own vessels out tramping.

In the early nineteenth century there was no clear distinction between tramp and liner. 'Constant traders' normally sailed a designated route but were neither common carriers nor did they operate to a fixed timetable. Vessels sometimes tramped between ports in search of freights but as a temporary measure when no prearranged freight existed. Several factors contributed to the rise of tramp shipping in the second half of the century. Improved communications connected with the development of the telegraph kept the shipowner in immediate contact with freight markets throughout the world. He could therefore keep his vessel moving between one passage and another with a full payload rather than leave the master to go speculatively searching from port to port. It also enabled him to keep in regular and rapid contact with the master. The rapid expansion of international trade together with the ending of restrictive mercantilism provided greater opportunities for deployment in the cross-trades. The repeal of Britain's Navigation Laws in 1849 and the abolition of the Sound Tolls in 1857 provided fertile opportunities for the development of Scandinavian tramp shipping at a time when the movement away from wood and sail technologies and the insufficiency of domestic demand threatened their mercantile marines. Most tramp shipping was British and here its success had much to do with the growth of coal exports. Traditionally, Britain possessed an imbalance of trade volumes in favour of imports. The growth of Britain's coal exports resolved the imbalance in many cases and helped to make tramping economic by giving these vessels an initial outbound payload. The decline of Britain's coal exports after the First World War did much to undermine tramping.

Tramping benefited from the introduction of steam though it was less critical than for liners. Steam was late to enter the bulk trades in which tramps were common since its speed was not necessary and its freight rates were often higher to cover the capital costs. With the increased efficiency of steam in the last two decades of the nineteenth century it became more economic to use steam in the bulk trades and tramp owners could buy second-hand steamers. Steam enabled vessels to sail to a prearranged timetable which was the key feature distinguishing liners from the regular departures of the sailing packets in the first half of the century. Improving steam technology provided for fleets of liner vessels which were large, fast and economic. The growing reliability of steam also avoided much time being wasted on repairs.

In spite of their different types of shipping operation the tramp and the liner frequently came into competition with each other. The lower cost structures of tramps meant that in depressions they were a particular threat to the liner companies who required regular remunerative freights to cover their greater overheads. Their reputation for regularity and reliability was often insufficient to convince shippers during a trade depression when tramp rates were significantly lower. The tramp sector was also at least partially responsible for periods of over supply of tonnage caused by the mortgaging of vessels by tramp owners in order to finance the purchase of additional tonnage.

The existence of the tramp simply exacerbated an underlying problem for the liners of how to maintain a large highly-capitalised company during a depression. The response of the liner companies was to form a series of collusive agreements known as conferences or rings in order to mitigate competition and iron out the effects of trade fluctuations. The conferences were organised on the basis of individual trades rather than among groups of shipowners and were primarily concerned with regulating freight rates and market shares. The first major conference regulated the Calcutta trade from 1875 which was soon followed on many other routes including the China trade in 1879, Australia in 1884, South Africa in 1886, the River Plate and Brazil in 1895–6 and the west coast of South America in 1906. By then conferences covered most international trade routes. Coasting was excepted because railway competition made rate-fixing impossible. Conferences dealt mostly with manufactured and high value goods rather than the bulk trades which remained the preserve of the tramps. Conferences attempted to exclude non-members from a trade by various means, particularly the 'deferred rebate' weapon. The traditional payment of 'primage' by the merchant to the shipowner had developed into a means of securing the regular patronage of the merchant by refunding it.[8] Conference members took to deferring this rebate for six or twelve months. If during this time the merchant had shipped his goods with an owner outside of the conference the primage would not be repaid.

Some conferences were organised and held together by a single dominant company or an outstanding shipping entrepreneur. Prominent in the West Africa conference was Elder Dempster led by the dynamic Alfred Jones. Jones held the conference together fighting rivals with sudden rate cutting policies or by inducing them into the agreement. Donald Currie played a similar role for the South Africa conference pursuing highly restrictive policies and combining his Castle Line with the other major firm in the trade, Union Steamship

Company, in 1900. Albert Ballin was active in organising conference agreements in the highly competitive North Atlantic trade. An agreement in 1892 allotted market shares to his own Hamburg-Amerika along with Norddeutscher Lloyd, Holland-America and Red Star. By 1914 the conference had extended to 30 shipping lines and 12 separate agreements, epitomising the complexity which collusive policies could cause (Aldcroft, 1974, 79). Besides excluding tramp shipping, the conferences, many of whom were organised by British liner owners, were aimed against foreign, particularly German, rivals. A forty per cent rate reduction in the West Africa conference in 1907, for example, was aimed against German competition after the Woermann Line had achieved rapid penetration of the West African trade by increasing its deployed tonnage from 16 000 in 1892/3 to 72 000 in 1906/7 (Aldcroft, 1974, 90). Even where conference agreements included British and German lines there was constant friction leading to their periodic breakdown into rate wars. The Calcutta ring broke down between 1905 and 1907 regarding P & O's right to load at Antwerp.

Accusations of monopoly activities and price fixing were levelled against the conferences and led to the formation of a Royal Commission on Shipping Rings in Britain in 1906. Its report in 1909 concluded that the rings had not been essentially prejudicial but recommended that an association be formed in each trade so that shippers could bargain on an equal basis with shipowners and that tariff rates be published. In the absence of a specific historical study of the influence of the conference system, it would appear that they had a mixed impact. They enabled freight rates and sailings to be organised in a more systematic and coherent manner to the benefit of shippers and shipowners and provided management economies for individual shipping firms. While offering greater freight rate stability for the shipper, the reduction of competition which ensued most likely raised average freight rates above prevailing market levels.

DEPLOYMENT

The deployment of European shipping underwent regular changes between the eighteenth century and the First World War under the influence of shifting patterns of industrialisation, political alignment and government policy. Thus, the economic development of Latin America, the outbreak of the French Wars and the abolition of the slave trade all influenced deployment patterns. In general the deployment of European shipping had become much more geographically diverse by 1914 with less concentration upon European and Atlantic trades. The settlement and economic development of many areas outside Europe provided new opportunities while improvements in the technology and organisation of shipping meant that there were far more shipowners able and willing to send vessels to many parts of the world by 1914. The growing importance of long hauls and bulk trades such as coal and metallic ores increased the demand for shipping and provided many new opportunities for enterprising owners. Random factors could also affect the deployment of shipping in the short term such as the gold rushes in California in 1849 and Australia in 1851.

In the second half of the eighteenth century the dominant British fleet was to be found in most parts of Europe as well as in the growing transatlantic trades. Dutch, Danish, Swedish and German shipping was also prominent in Europe. Timber, iron, flax, hemp, naval stores, corn and oil seeds were all exported from the Baltic countries, largely in vessels from that area or belonging to Britain. Norway's share of the Baltic timber trade declined from a half to a quarter in the eighteenth century as Riga, Memel and Viborg came to rival Norwegian ports like Christiania. While Norway's coastal forests were being depleted, Memel was benefiting from cheap serf labour and vast unexploited forests (Astrom, 89). St Petersburg had the advantage of being able to offer a wide range of additional goods such as iron, linen, tallow and ravencloth to complete a full cargo. Pitch, tar and herring were shipped from Sweden. Before the development of the British coal export trade in the nineteenth century many vessels sailed northbound to the Baltic in ballast although some were involved in the entrepôt trade, re-exporting colonial produce from British and French ports. Norwegian and Swedish herring were exported around the Baltic and fish oil was shipped to Germany and western Europe. This trade fluctuated with the changing migration patterns of the herring. In 1747 the herring arrived in the bays along the Bohuslan coast of Sweden boosting the local herring industry at the same time as the Norwegian industry was in decline. In 1808, however, the herring left Sweden to return to Norway. The fisheries in turn generated shipments of salt from France and the Mediterranean. Sweden conducted trade with most of the Baltic powers particularly to the south where her exports of industrial goods and imports of foodstuffs complemented the needs of Poland, Russia and Prussia.

She also benefited from Finnish political dependency which required the latter to divert most of its trade through Swedish ports until the early nineteenth century.

British shipping also featured prominently in the Mediterranean. English exports of textiles and other manufactures were traded with fruit, oil, wine, cork and salt particularly in Spain and Portugal. British shipping was helped by settlements of British shipowners and merchants throughout the Mediterranean. In 1772/3 a half of the vessels entering Lisbon were English with many of them conducting the port's trade with the rest of the Mediterranean area (Fisher, 1981, 34–5). Some British shipowners conducted a cross-trade carrying wine and salt from Spain and Portugal to Newfoundland and returning with dried fish.

French shipping was more orientated towards long hauls and coasting than the European trades. Of 12 988 vessels which entered or cleared the Baltic in 1767/8 only 16 were French compared with 4601 Dutch and 3056 English together with lesser amounts of Swedish, Danish and German shipping. French competitiveness may have been damaged by manning regulations which often caused their crews to be up to twice the size of those on Dutch vessels (Clark, 34). Many of the French west coast ports such as La Rochelle, Bordeaux and Nantes grew up in the eighteenth century under the stimulus of the transatlantic colonial trades. La Rochelle vessels sailed primarily to Santo Domingo while those of Nantes, Le Havre, Marseilles, and Bordeaux were more frequently to be found at Martinique and Guadeloupe until after the American War of Independence when they voyaged increasingly to Santo Domingo. Vessels returned to France with tobacco, rice, sugar, coffee, rum, spices and cotton. The loss of their colonies in the West Indies at the end of the eighteenth century was a severe blow for French shipping only partly compensated by increased activity in the slave trade and new markets in the Indian Ocean. By 1814 St Lucia, Trinidad, Tobago, Martinique, Guadeloupe, St Thomas, St Eustatius and Curaçao, along with the mainland colonies of Surinam, Berbice, Demerara and Essequibo had all been captured by Britain. Together with existing colonies such as St Vincent, St Kitts and Jamaica they provided many new opportunities for British shipping in Central America. British shipping also ventured to Honduras to take advantage of the increased demand for mahogany.

In North America, loss of colonies also caused a dwindling of opportunities for French shipowners. Fishermen from St Malo, Dunkirk and Dieppe had been heavily involved in the Newfoundland fisheries but Newfoundland was lost in 1713. With each war the French position continued to slip; Louisbourg and Acadia were lost in 1745 and remaining French possessions in Canada were lost in 1763. St Pierre and Miquelon were returned to the French whose fishermen retained fishing rights on the Grand Banks supported by government subsidies from 1767. This was insufficient to prevent the continued decline of the French fishing fleet under the pressure of competition from New England fishermen. American independence damaged British deployment because the United States was no longer covered by Britain's Navigation Laws. Britain's role as a European entrepôt for American exports such as tobacco declined as other European nations were able to import directly. By 1792 Copenhagen had become a centre of discharge for American exports to northern Europe. North European shipping was also to be found in North America at the end of the eighteenth century. Exports of Russian iron, hemp, canvas and linen and Swedish iron were traded for American tobacco and rice. American shipping dominated the trade with Russia but the more powerful Swedish mercantile marine occupied a stronger position in trade with America. The French Wars and subsequent reciprocity treaties, between America and Sweden in 1818 and 1828 and between America and Russia in 1824 and 1833, encouraged the expansion of this trade. By the 1850s, however, America had become self-sufficient in iron production and north European shipowners were exploiting new opportunities presented by the abolition of Britain's Navigation Laws.

In the late eighteenth and early nineteenth centuries at least 150 vessels a year left English and Scottish ports for the Greenland and South Sea whaling (Fayle, 1933, 220–1, 223). German whalers operated in Pacific waters although Dutch attempts to establish a whaling industry based on the southern whaling failed in the face of American competition. German whaling declined in the 1860s as investors turned to transatlantic shipping discouraged by the need to tie up substantial amounts of capital for several years at a time in whaling ventures. The invention of the harpoon gun by Sven Foyn in 1865 had only a limited impact because demand for whale oil remained low. It was not until the early twentieth century that further technical developments and the wider use of whale oil in soap and margarine stimulated an expansion of the industry.

Trade eastwards from Europe in the eighteenth century was largely confined to the import of Chinese tea, silk and porcelain and south-east Asian and Indian spices, coffee, drugs and foodstuffs. This trade remained the preserve of the chartered companies for most of the century although during the temporary demise of the Compagnie des Indes between 1769 and 1783 private French shipowners operated this trade, sometimes combining it with slaving in East Africa. By the end of the eighteenth century eastern trade was being permanently opened up to private shipowners whose enterprise was to widen and expand it dramatically.

An area of deployment which was on the decline in the later eighteenth century was slaving. European shipowners sailed out to West Africa where they bought slaves and resold them to plantation owners throughout the American continent. French slavers sailed for Senegal and the area around the Congo river from whence they took slaves to the Antilles. Nantes was the foremost French slaving port with around 40 vessels a year in the trade in the 1780s. Bordeaux, Le Havre, La Rochelle, Dunkirk, Honfleur, St Malo and Bayonne were also involved in the trade (Clark, 32). The Dutch traded between the Gold Coast and the West Indies with major slaving depots situated at St Eustatius and Curaçao. Portuguese slavers traded between Angola and Brazil. The British slave trade was concentrated upon the ports of London, Liverpool and Bristol and went via British possessions in West Africa to the British West Indies. Some of these vessels may then have returned to Britain laden with colonial goods although Merritt's original explosion of the triangular trade theory remains valid. One major London shipowning firm of the period was heavily involved in the importation of West Indian products but never sailed in the slave trade and normally arranged freights in London before sailing directly to the Caribbean with only a partial cargo of manufactures or government equipment (Ville, 1987, 58). An alternative pattern displayed by the Portuguese was continuous trading between Angola and Brazil. Slaves were carried from Luanda to Pernambuco or Rio de Janeiro and vessels returned with alcohol, cloth, textiles and foodstuffs. Adverse wind and current conditions in the South Atlantic discouraged an early return to Portugal.

The British slave trade was abolished in 1807 for which varying explanations have been offered. The idea that the trade was abolished as its importance to Britain declined (Ragatz) has been disputed by Anstey(1975 (1)) who believes it was thriving. It was making an important contribution to Britain's trade and generating a profit of around 10 per cent which was higher than the French, Dutch or Danish slave trades. Anstey believes opposition from religious groups, particularly Evangelicals and Quakers, was highly influential upon public opinion and ultimately Parliament. The abolition of the slave trade created few problems for British shipowners who turned to the legitimate trade with western and southern Africa, new British possessions in the West Indies and South America and the emerging timber trade with British North America. Some continued to conduct an illicit slave trade.

British trade and shipping links with Africa expanded in the first half of the nineteenth century. Ships sailed to the Barbary States, the Guinea Coast, the Cape and other parts of Africa returning with imports of ivory, palm oil, gums, wine and fruit. However, there was no regular service until mid-century when the African Steamship Company and then the British and African Steamship Company began operating one. These early services facilitating cheaper carriage of letters, cargoes and passengers, helped to quicken the pace of economic development in the area which in turn encouraged more investment, trade and shipping. As part of German maritime expansion in the later part of the century the Woermann Line began regular services to Africa.

The Dutch abolished their slave trade in 1818 as part of an agreement with England which involved recognition of the new kingdom of The Netherlands. The withering away theory may be more relevant to the Dutch case where the Middelburgsche Commercie Compagnie returned minimal profit (W. S. Unger). The slowness with which the monopoly of the Dutch West India Company was abandoned delayed the introduction of private capital while the conflict with Britain in the 1780s did further damage to the trade. By 1825 the slave trade had also been abolished in Denmark, Sweden, France, Brazil and the United States although a small illicit trade persisted until many years later.

The other main area of deployment in the late eighteenth century was the coastal trade. Precise knowledge of coasting is difficult to establish because there were no customs records and often the trade was organised informally with small vessels loading and discharging cargoes on quaysides and miscellaneous landing sites, often little more than beaches. In 1768 a London directory listed 580 landing points for shipping in England and Wales (Armstrong and Bagwell, 143). Most coasting involved the carriage of essential bulk goods such as coal, corn and building materials. In addition, a wide range of imported goods such as tea, sugar and coffee were shipped coastwise from major ports in return for merchandise from the surrounding region. The value of coasting depended very much upon the geography and topography of a country. Britain, with a long coastline, plenty of good landing places and few areas of the country far from the sea or navigable rivers benefited substantially from coasting. Norway needed a healthy coastal trade to link her many islands. Vessels were sometimes transferred between coasting and foreign deployment. This was particularly the policy of the new professional shipowners pursuing active deployment policies and keen to keep their vessels busy. A short coastal voyage could fill in between longer overseas journeys particularly where the work was seasonal.

Coasting was the most cost-effective form of domestic communication for many regions before the introduction of the railway and therefore it experienced rapid growth and played an important role in the early phases of industrialisation, fostering inter-regional integration. British coastal shipping tonnage, according to one estimate, expanded from 155 000 tons in 1760 to 829 000 by 1830 and its share of total tonnage had grown (Armstrong and Bagwell, 144–9). While coasting failed to match the rapid growth of overseas deployment in the second half of the nineteenth century expansion was still significant. In Britain the volume of tonnage deployed in coasting grew by an average of 1.5 per cent per annum between 1837 and 1914 (Armstrong and Bagwell, 171). Nor was coasting largely eliminated by the railway. Armstrong has calculated that coasters made fewer journeys than railways in Britain by 1910 but completed a greater ton-miles aggregate (Armstrong and Bagwell, 173–4). Swedish coasting also grew strongly in the second half of the century at the time of the development of the railway system. Between 1873 and 1893 Swedish coastal shipping output grew at 2.7 per cent per annum compared with 5.7 per cent for railways (Krantz, 30). Sometimes railways and coasting complemented each other. Some of the earliest railways built on the north-east coast of Britain were designed to facilitate the coastal coal trade rather than compete with it. The suitability of railways or coasting also accorded to the type of cargo carried. The west coast railway in Sweden from Helsingborg to Gothenburg experienced strong competition from coasters in the movement of bulky building materials, such that coastal shipments grew by 70 per cent between 1873 and 1893 (Krantz, 34).

The largest coastal trade-flow in Britain and probably in Europe was the coal trade from Newcastle, Sunderland and Stockton which provided London and many other parts of the country with the essential fuel for industrial development. Hull, Boston, Harwich and

Colchester were the main grain shipment ports serving the East Anglian and Lincolnshire grain belt. Weymouth and Poole were outlets for Portland stone, while slates were shipped from Aberystwyth and Aberdovey. The passenger coastal trade has long been identified with the steam era, although many travelled by this form in the eighteenth century. In 1792, for example, 18 000 took the hoy to the Kent resorts (Armstrong and Bagwell, 162). Deployment to Ireland was part of the British coasting trade from 1823 and consisted mainly of the exchange of British manufactures, coal and colonial produce for Irish linens, butter and salted provisions.

Coasting was far more limited in Germany, given the short coastline. Moreover, the absence of deep draught facilities outside the major foreign trade ports meant coasters tended to be small inland river boats rather than larger vessels which mixed coasting and overseas deployment. This began to change in the nineteenth century as dredging improved coasting facilities on the north German coast and the development of Rhine barges of at least 1000 tonnes but of shallow draught provided a vessel suitable for a wider range of river, coastal and short sea deployment (Achilles). An active coastal trade in France supplied a similar range of essential products including grain and salt together with the redistribution of imported colonial goods such as sugar, indigo, coffee, cotton, furs and skins. Since most major French ports traded in these colonial goods their coastwise shipment tended to be over short distances to surrounding minor ports and settlements. In 1764/5 more than half the number of arrivals at La Rochelle had come from ports within a fifty-mile radius (Clark, 34).

The French Wars influenced deployment patterns both in the short and the long term. During wartime many trade routes were disrupted. Trade between warring states, particularly France and Britain, lapsed. Shipping movements in the Mediterranean declined as it became a centre of maritime warfare. In the first decade of the nineteenth century Napoleon's 'Continental Blockade' and British duties on Baltic timber greatly reduced shipping in the Baltic. Timber merchants turned to British North America as an alternative source. The timber duties remained until the middle of the century allowing the North American trade to grow and become a major area of activity for British shipping. Wartime military needs led to an expansion in merchant transports. They were sent to many areas, though especially the Mediterranean, for unspecified periods under dangerous conditions and carried a range of military needs including troops, ordnance, provisions and horses. Shipping movements slowed down in wartime as most vessels were obliged to sail in convoy which meant delays assembling and then sailing at the speed of the slower vessels. However, by creating an artificial shortage of shipping, convoys helped to push up freight rates and ensure vessels found regular deployment.

After 1815 the ending of the convoy system and the reduction in the demand for transports caused under-employment among shipping in spite of the reopening of some routes. The depression stretched throughout Europe with some vessels laid up for six months or more of the year. Owners sent vessels out tramping in search of freights but this proved a largely speculative and unprofitable enterprise. In the following decades new opportunities emerged particularly on the long hauls where the amount of shipping time required to move a given volume of goods was naturally greater.

One example of this trend was the growing communication with Latin America. Albion has suggested that, 'the crop of revolutions that freed Latin America shortly after 1800 at last created a maritime and commercial vacuum' (Albion, 1951, 361). This vacuum was exploited by the shipping industries of European nations including Britain, Germany, Scandinavia, France, Spain, Portugal and The Netherlands. Platt (1972) and R. G. Greenhill, though, argue that the main expansion occurred in the second half of the nineteenth century by which time improving political stability, a growing population and signs of economic development made the area far more attractive to European trade and shipping interests. The development of shipping links thus appears more as a response to economic growth than an initiator of it. Many of the earliest vessels to trade there regularly were supported by government mail subsidies suggesting that shipping services also contributed to economic growth in Latin America. The British liner companies, Royal Mail Steam Packet Company from 1839 and Pacific Steam Navigation Company from 1840, provided some of the earliest services. Royal Mail carried British mail to Mexico, Panama, Colombia, Venezuela and the West Indies and from 1851 also to Brazil and Argentina while Pacific Steam operated on the west coast. All things considered it appears fair to conclude that 'without British investment in shipping and ancillary services . . . economic growth in Latin America would probably have begun later and at a slower pace' (R. G. Greenhill, 265). Several German companies operated over similar routes particularly Norddeutscher Lloyd and Hamburg-Süd Amerika on the east coast and Kosmos on the west coast.

British shipping dominated the major trades to Latin America aided by her strong interlocking shore-based interests in merchanting and finance. By 1912 British shipping was responsible for 65 per cent of tonnage trading at Pernambuco, 61 per cent at Buenos Aires and 56 per cent at Bahia and Rio (Platt, 1972, 120). A greater proportion of German shipping headed towards the smaller countries such as Colombia, Dominican Republic, Chile, Venezuela, Bolivia and Uruguay. Some European shipping went to South America as part of a triangular trade in which they would then proceed to the United States to load a cargo such as grain or cotton for Europe. This was the practice of some Finnish shipowners.

Emigration and settlement created new or expanded existing shipping flows to other countries particularly the United States, Australia and New Zealand. The transatlantic migration provided outward payloads for vessels bringing timber, cotton or corn from North America. The potato famine caused many Irish to emigrate via Liverpool in the 1840s. Vessels in the tobacco trade from America to Bremen also began to carry migrants on the outward passage. The increased flow of migrants from central and eastern Europe in the later nineteenth century provided opportunities for lines to specialise in passenger and migration services. These included Austro-American from Trieste, Canada NLVD from Rotterdam and Belgian Red Star Line from Antwerp as well as the various services offered by Norddeutscher Lloyd and Hamburg-Amerika. The 'transportation' of British convicts to Australia at the end of the eighteenth-century continued into the nineteenth century with peaks in 1820, 1830–8 and 1841–4. This was shortly followed by generations of voluntary settlers there and, from the 1830s, to New Zealand. Before the development of staple Australian exports in wool from the 1840s and meat in the late nineteenth century, vessels used to call at other countries which had a surplus volume of exports with Britain. Teas and textiles were loaded in China, raw cotton in Bombay, coffee in Ceylon, sugar in Bengal, rice in Saigon and Bangkok and sugar in Mauritius. After 1815 opportunities closer to Australia begin to appear, such as coffee from Java and sugar from Manila. From the 1840s an export trade from the Pacific coast of America, particularly Chile and Peru, to Europe developed. Thus vessels began to return this way from Australia, helped by westerly winds, loading guano, copper ore and nitrates. Opportunities also developed for work in the local Asian cross-trades.

German shipping links with Australia developed in the 1840s. An agreement with Britain in 1841 allowed German shipping to trade with British colonies in German goods. Emigration, colonisation and whaling all attracted German shipping to Australia. In the following decade gold discoveries attracted around 5000 Germans to Australia most of them travelling out from Hamburg in the sailing ships of J. G. Goddefroy & Son (Harms, 12). Further emigration waves in the 1860s and 1870s benefited German shipping because of the Prussian government's refusal to allow its citizens to depart from British ports. A state subsidy of 1886 was given to Norddeutscher Lloyd to run a regular service from Bremen to Sydney via Antwerp, Adelaide and Melbourne. The German Reich sought an improved mail service which was not reliant upon Britain although imperialist motives and the desire to secure much needed industrial raw materials also played a part. The service, however, was a persistent money-loser and some migrant vessels found more success carrying coal on to China and then returning to Germany with tea or guano or returning directly with wool. Norddeutscher Lloyd also established a direct service with New Zealand in 1914.

The changing nature of economic development encouraged the growth of several trades. The increasing demand for steel and the possibilities for large-scale production following the invention of the Bessemer process in 1857 encouraged the development of the Spanish ore trade. The inability of Spanish industry to exploit indigenous sources of non-phosphoric ore led to their export in British vessels to supply the Welsh iron and steel industry. The expansion of the trade was facilitated by the removal of export duties on iron ore in 1862 and the establishment of the Orconera Iron Ore Company in 1873 by a consortium of British, German and Spanish businessmen. The trade grew rapidly from 26 tonnes in 1866 to 2391 in 1880 and 4373 by 1890 (Craig, 1978, 218).

The growing demand for iron and steel along with other aspects of the industrialisation process and the development of steam-shipping led to a substantial expansion in the overseas coal trade in the second half of the nineteenth century. Britain with her vast exploited coal resources dominated this trade, accounting for 70 per cent of sea-borne coal exports in 1912 (Palmer, 1979, 334). Europe took 75–86 per cent of British coal exports before 1914 particularly France, the Mediterranean, the Baltic and the Black Sea (Palmer, 1979, 335).

Smaller volumes went in a variety of oceanic trades. Less than half of British coal exported to Europe was carried in British bottoms (Palmer, 1979, 349). The rest was carried by vessels from the importing country or the tramp shipping of other nations particularly Norway. Outside Europe, however, most British coal was carried in British vessels. The establishment of preferential rail rates in Germany and the formation of the Westphalian Syndicate began to threaten British coal exports. At the same time the French market turned towards domestic sources and, beyond Europe, British coal faced challenges from Indian, Japanese, Australian and British Columbian suppliers.

The First World War disrupted deployment patterns cutting off some routes while encouraging others. Shipping demand was increased by the need to take circuitous routes around dangerous areas and as a result of the severing of near supply sources. Delays were caused by port congestion and convoy organisation. The need to pursue autarchic policies of import substitution and to avoid submarine attack reduced trade flows on many routes. This affected the shipping of warring nations more than neutrals and was particularly damaging for Britain with her large overseas trade sector. The collapse in the coal trade was most damaging accounting as it did for 51 per cent of Britain's trade volume in 1913. Only in the Ruhr crisis year, 1923, did coal exports return to their pre-war level. While finding employment for three million tons of British tramp shipping in 1913, by 1937 it only employed half of this volume (Sturmey, 53–4). The decline of British coal exports was most severe in the oceanic trades where British shipping was dominant. There was less decline on the shorter hauls where Greek and Norwegian shipping already had a comfortable proportion of British coal exports. British shipping also lost much of its stronghold in the cross-trades especially to the Japanese in the Far East and India and to the United States in the trade between North and South America. With the loss of the competitive edge given by coal exports, British shipping struggled to regain these trades after 1918.

The coasting trade declined dramatically during the First World War. In Britain, where coasting was particularly important, its tonnage declined to a half of its former level during the war (Aldcroft, 1963–4, 24). Coasters were frequently put under government requisition and the work transferred to the railways. Rail rates were carefully controlled by governments in wartime which meant it was often cheaper than by sea. Land transport was also less vulnerable to enemy attack. Similarly, the congestion of ports and their unsuitability for handling heavy military equipment favoured a transfer to the railways.

THE ECONOMIC EFFECTS OF THE SHIPPING INDUSTRY

Most maritime history has been written in isolation offering few comparisons with other industries and with scant regard to the overall process of economic development. We know little, therefore, of the contribution of the shipping industry to the industrialisation of the European economies in the eighteenth and nineteenth centuries. The contribution of shipping to industrialisation was much less dramatic than that of the railways. Its impact was neither as sudden nor as great yet for some countries it sustained a central and dynamic role throughout the period. Its importance varied significantly between countries; it was vital for Britain but of declining importance for France. For some of the under-developed Scandinavian economies, particularly Norway, it occupied a position arguably comparable to a Rostowian leading sector.

The productivity of shipping rose continually through the period. Several attempts have been made to calculate the rate of productivity growth. Walton studied American colonial shipping in the century to 1775 and estimated that its productivity grew by an average of 1.35 per cent per annum (1968). Ville's examination of the English coal trade, 1700–1850, produced a figure of 0.45 per cent (1986). Walton lays stress on risk reduction as the major source of productivity change. The decline of piracy and privateering, he argues, enabled lower levels of manning and armaments. Ville emphasises organisational advances associated with the growth of professional shipowning, a reduction in wintering and shorter turnround times. Productivity continued to grow in the second half of the nineteenth century although there is some disagreement as to whether previous to the 1880s this was primarily attibutable to the coming of steam and iron (Knauerhase) or infrastructure improvements which benefited both sail and steam (Walton, 1967).

Productivity growth enabled capital to be used more efficiently in the shipping industry. Since shipping was a heavy user of capital it enabled the industry to respond to the great increase in demand associated with industrialisation and internationalisation without causing capital shortages internally or in competing industries. The marginal efficiency of shipping capital, however, varied between nations. In Spain government determination to develop the inefficient ship-building industry at the end of the nineteenth century put a squeeze on limited capital resources.

Productivity improvements enabled a continual decline in freight rates. In the century between the end of the French Wars and the beginning of the First World War freight rates moved downwards, though there is some disagreement as to the precise timing of these movements, as we saw in an earlier section. One calculation, a deflated index of freights on board vessels travelling from America to Europe, estimated rates to have fallen from 100 in 1830 to 24 by 1910–14 (Milward and Saul, 1973, 221–2). This caused the freight factor to decline and thereby encouraged an extension of inter-national specialisation.[9] The result was a growth in the foreign trade ratio of many countries as world trade per capita grew at over 30 per cent per decade between 1850 and 1913 compared with a 20 per cent growth rate of domestic industrial production.[10] Western European nations were the main beneficiaries of the reductions in transport costs. They were the chief recipients of food and raw materials which, as bulky goods, gained the greatest benefit from the reductions in freight factors and enabled a favourable movement in the terms of trade. The rapid industrial development of these countries relied heavily upon imports of cheap raw materials to keep down manufac-turing prices and low food prices to stimulate industrial demand.

Productivity improvements enabled good profits to be made de-spite a secular decline in freight rates. During the French Wars profit levels had been high and throughout the course of the nineteenth century there were many opportunities for high peacetime profits. Nordvik's work on Stavanger shipowning in the 1870s shows average capital returns as high as 18 per cent (144–5). He also established that Bergen shipowners achieved greater returns than entrepreneurs in most other industries and from bank deposits. The fortunes of the shipping industry, though, were notoriously volatile. Profitability was low in the 1880s following the provision of too much easy credit which fuelled an overexpansion of the world fleet. In 1908 ship-owners throughout Europe and the world suffered losses as supply and demand were again unbalanced. It was the use to which shipping profits were put, rather than their absolute magnitude, which was of most importance. Reinvestment in local businesses in the port or the hinterland encouraged the development of particular regions. Many of the most rapidly growing areas in the eighteenth century surrounded the Atlantic-facing ports of France and Britain such as Liverpool, Bristol and Bordeaux. Shipping also demanded the goods and services of local industries and created new lines of enterprise such as marine insurance, shipbroking, maritime law and the development of commodity markets.

Shipping services created significant earnings-surpluses for some countries and deficits for others. This was particularly the case in the second half of the nineteenth century when the growth of tramping and the abolition of mercantilist legislation attracted increasing numbers of vessels into cross-trading. Britain as the largest shipping nation, including a large fleet of tramps, generated substantial invisible earnings which made a vital contribution towards balancing her international payments. In the second half of the nineteenth century shipping earnings took up one third of Britain's invisible income and represented five per cent of national income (Palmer, 1985, 89–91). Norway was also a major tramp shipping nation. Shipping earnings constituted 45 per cent of export values in a diminutive and underdeveloped economy. Moreover, it employed greater numbers than manufacturing industry up to 1890 and soaked up a great deal of seasonal unemployment among the peasantry (Milward and Saul, 1973, 524). It also linked up closely with the country's other major industries including timber and fishing. These linkages together with the industry's size and rapid growth suggests that it may be regarded as something of a leading sector of the Norwegian economy in the half century from 1840. Just before 1914 shipping contributed 25–30 million francs to Greece's balance of payments which was more than enough to pay for the total of grain imports (Milward and Saul, 1977, 434). For Spain, on the other hand, shipping produced a negative balance in international payments since much of her trade was carried in foreign bottoms. Shipbuilding involved international flows of earnings with Britain, again, benefiting from her role as the major and most efficient producer: up to 30 per cent of new British tonnage was exported. With the transition to steam Scandinavian countries relied heavily upon imports of British vessels, often second hand and offsetting, to some degree, their positive balance in shipping earnings.

The earnings of one particular trade have generated considerable controversy. Eric Williams, in a book entitled *Capitalism and Slavery*, argued that high profits of around 30 per cent, generated by the slave trade, were an important source of finance for Britain's industrialisation. In the slave trade the role of merchant and shipowner were normally vertically integrated. Williams's methods and conclusions have been widely disputed. Anderson and Richardson have contended that profits were much lower because of the high degree of competition which existed in the slave trade. The idea of perfect competition and low profits is supported by Thomas and Bean while Engerman argues that the output of the trade constituted little more than one per cent of national income. Finally, Anstey reassesses Williams's profits calculations to come up with a figure of around 10 per cent (1975 (2)). In support of Williams's original thesis Inikori argues that there was little competition in the slave trade; instead an oligopolistic market structure existed which yielded high profits. He goes on to criticise Anstey's profit calculations as underestimating the number of slaves loaded, their sale price and the value of the goods which slavers took back to England.

Darity has injected some common sense into the debate at a time when the 'numbers game' threatened to jettison it from historical reality. He criticises the assumption in the debate that the degree of competition and the level of profits were in inverse proportion. Williams's work, he continues, only covers an early phase of British industrialisation nor are high profits an accurate indication of the level of investment. The slave trade was abolished in 1807 when Britain was still principally an agricultural country. The impact of slave profits, like those of trade and shipping as a whole, were restricted to specific industries and areas. The profits of the British slave trade most likely found their way into the trade and shipping of major slaving ports like Bristol and Liverpool together with the hinterlands they served. If there is a causal relationship between the slave trade and British economic development it may be through the stimulus slavery gave to the American economy which in turn, helped by mercantilism, transmitted benefits to Britain.

Little attempt has been made to establish whether the shipbuilding industry caused the same degree of backward linkages as occurred in railway building. Shipbuilding was a major consumer of the products of the heavy industries in the late nineteenth century. At a time when railway demand for coal, iron, steel and engineering was past its peak the supply to shipbuilding was expanding. Shipbuilding and the heavy industries often worked in cooperation with each other on nearby sites, a relationship which sometimes led to interlocking ownership. The needs of the shipbuilding industry may also have spurred technological development in the heavy industries. In the late eighteenth century the problems of galvanic action in copper sheathed vessels stimulated the development of alloys. The galvanic action produced by iron bolts led to the development of Keir's bolt as an alloy of copper, zinc and iron. In the second half of the nineteenth century, the development of a widening range of specialist vessels imposed a whole new series of challenges upon engineers and architects. Little has been written about any of these matters. We need to know much more about the nature of the relationship between shipbuilding and the heavy industries particularly the extent of input–output ratios and the impact of technological change.

In contrast to the railways and the motor industry foreign investment was comparatively minimal. Attention has already been drawn to British investment in Spanish and Italian shipyards, English settlements in the Mediterranean and the use of flags of convenience but in total this represented only a small portion of the industry. Further research, however, may point to a good deal of concealed cross-ownership arising not only from mercantilist advantages but also from population movements within Europe. Foreign investment was probably more important in the development of non-European areas of the world; attention has already been drawn to West Africa and South America in this context. More and closer analysis is required to establish the role of shipping in opening up new economic regions of the world. The subsidised mail lines constituted a form of development by excess social overhead capital. Their importance in this role has been addressed for Latin America and Western Africa but elsewhere the subject has received little attention.

Notes

1. B. G. Nicol and J. Gravel, 'The use and transport of liquid fuel', *Trans. North East Coast Inst. of Engineers & Shipbuilders*, 3, 1886–7, 27.
2. In particular see two articles by D. H. Aldcroft, 'The Entrepreneur and the British Economy, 1870–1914', *Econ. Hist. Rev.*, 2nd ser., 17, 1964; 'Technical progress and British enterprise, 1875–1914', *Bus. Hist.*, 8, 1963.
3. *Select Committee on Manufactures, Commerce and Shipping*, British Parliamentary Papers VI, 1833, 339.
4. Anon, *The Late Measures of the Shipowners in the Coal Trade*, London, 1786, 15.
5. Enemy vessels captured in wartime.
6. J. A. Salter, *Allied Shipping Control*, Oxford, 1982, 45, 69.
7. J. J. Welsford in *Fairplay*, 8/3/1917, 421.
8. The origins of primage are obscure but probably it was originally a

payment of about 5 per cent of freight earnings to the master or owner for their careful attention to the cargo.

9. The 'freight factor' is the proportion which freight costs represent of total delivered price.

10. S. Kuznets, 'Quantitative aspects of the economic growth of nations', *Economic Development and Cultural Change* 15, 1967, 4.

5 The Railways

EARLY DEVELOPMENT

Whereas shipping, road and river transport stretched back many centuries, railways have a comparatively recent history. Their origins lay in two separate developments, the iron rail and the steam locomotive. The earliest railways, or wagonways, were simple wooden tracks which exploited the low frictional resistance of smooth surfaces. Several examples date back to at least the seventeenth century. In the eighteenth century wooden tracks were frequently used in lines connecting coal mines with riverside staiths. Coal was conveyed in trucks from the pithead to the riverside by the force of gravity. The empty trucks were then returned by a horse or stationary engine. Wooden tracks were gradually replaced by iron because of its greater durability and reduced friction. In 1821 John Birkinshaw patented the process of rolling wrought iron for rails which was more ductile than cast iron. Innovations in the steel industry in the second half of the nineteenth century, particularly the Bessemer process, enabled steel rails to replace iron. The application of steam power to railways in the nineteenth century also required the use of stronger, non-combustible metallic rails. Early experiments with steam for pumping in the seventeenth and eighteenth centuries led on to its use in transport once engineers learned to convert reciprocating into rotary motion. In 1804 Richard Trevithick developed a high pressure steam engine but it proved too heavy for railway tracks. The successful use of the steam locomotive had to await Stephenson's *Rocket* which in 1829 was chosen at the Rainhill Trials to operate between Liverpool and Manchester on the first steam-driven passenger railway in the world. Its tubular boiler and uncomplicated transmission system made it powerful but light.

CONSTRUCTION OF THE NETWORK

Britain led the world in the construction of a railway system. By 1850 nearly 10 000 km of railways had been built which was almost double her nearest rival, Germany, while France, in third place, had a network only half as large again. Belgium had begun to build a small

PLATE 66

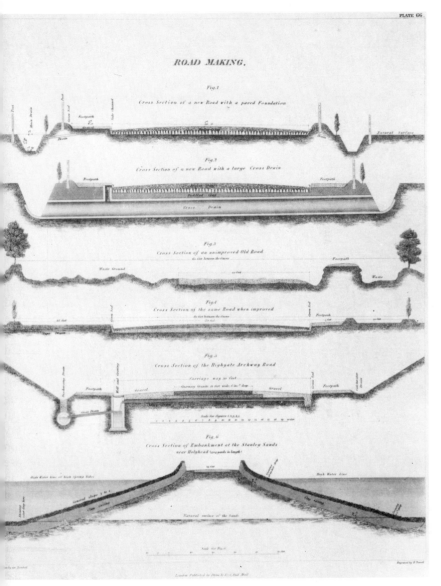

An illustration of road-making techniques by Thomas Telford, 1838.

2. A sedan chair.

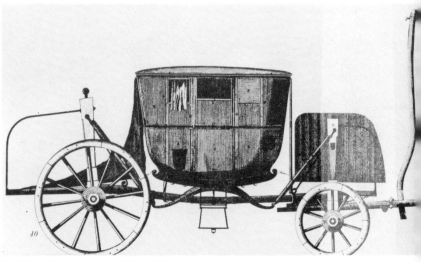

3. A French stage coach of the eighteenth century.

View of the Canal Imperial d'Aragon.

Coal barge on Leeds and Liverpool Canal.

6. Barton Swing Aqueduct under construction ca. 1891.

7. *SS Great Britain*, 1843.

8. Tug of war between a paddle steamer, HMS *Basilisk*, and a screw steamer, HMS *Niger*, 1849.

9. *Turbinia* alongside the *Mauretania*, 1906.

10. The opening of the Liverpool to Manchester Railway at Edge Hill in 1930.

11. Opening of Le Chemin de Fer du Nord, c. 1846.

12. The Engine House of the Great Western Railway at Swindon in 1830.

13. The last broad-gauge through-train leaving Paddington, 20 May 1892.

4. Cugnot's locomotive at Paris, 1770.

5. Two cars in the first Emancipation Run at Brighton, 1896.

16. Manchester tram, 1912.

Table 5.1 Growth of the European Railway System, 1830–1910 (km)

	Austria-Hungary	Belgium	Britain	Bulgaria	Denmark	Finland	France	Germany	Greece	Ireland	Italy
1830	–	–	157	–	–	–	31	–	–	–	–
1840	144	334	2 390	–	–	–	410	469	–	21	20
1850	1 357	854	9 797	–	30	–	2 915	5 856	–	865	620
1860	2 927	1 729	14 603	–	109	–	9 167	11 089	–	2 195	2 404
1870	6 112	2 897	21 558*	224	770	483	15 544	18 876	12	3 201*	6 429
1880	11 429	4 117	25 060	224	1 584	852	23 089	33 838	12	3 816	9 290
1890	15 273	4 526	27 827	803	2 005	1 895	33 280	42 869	697	4 496	13 629
1900	19 229	4 562	30 079	1 566	2 914	2 650	38 109	51 678	1 033	5 125	16 429
1910	22 642	4 679	32 184	1 897	3 445	3 356	40 484	61 209	1 573	5 476	18 090

	Netherlands	Norway	Portugal	Romania	Russia	Serbia	Spain	Sweden	Switzerland
1830	–	–	–	–	–	–	–	–	–
1840	17	–	–	–	–	–	–	–	–
1850	176	–	–	–	501	–	28	–	25
1860	335	68	67	–	1 626	–	1 649	527	1 053
1870	1 419	359	714	248	10 731	–	5 295	1 727	1 421
1880	1 841	1 057	1 144	921	22 865	–	7 490	5 876	2 571
1890	2 610	1 562	1 932	2 424	30 596	540	10 002	8 018	3 243
1900	2 771	1 981	2 168	3 100	53 234	571	13 214	11 303	3 867
1910	3 190	2 976	2 448	3 437	66 581	892	14 684	13 829	4 463

* 1871.

Source: Mitchell, 1975, 581–4.

but effective network. The belated construction of railways in Spain, Italy and Russia reflected the economic backwardness of these countries who possessed neither the capital and expertise to build a system nor the trade for it to carry. For other countries, such as Denmark, Norway and Switzerland, smallness or the nature of the terrain prevented the construction of a major network. By 1914 most European rail systems had been completed. Major networks had been built in Austria-Hungary, France, Germany, Italy, Spain, Sweden and the United Kingdom. Belgium built the densest network relative to land mass, followed by Germany, Switzerland, United Kingdom, Netherlands and Denmark (Milward and Saul, 1977, 541).

The network pattern varied between countries. The major routes were normally built first because of their greater economic importance and profitability. State supervision of construction or operation was not uncommon because of the political and military importance of these lines. Secondary lines came later, were less profitable and more likely to be found in private hands. France, Britain and Spain all built radial networks in which most major lines emanated from the capital. The German system took a multinodal form possessing several central points. Belgium developed a transit network catering for through traffic from north to south and east to west. This created a cross centred initially on Malines but later on Brussels and Namur. The Italian system followed the contours of the peninsula with an intensive local network around the industrialising Po Valley region. The Russian network was composed of several patterns imposed upon each other: a radial system operated around Moscow, other nodal points included St Petersburg and Warsaw whilst major east-west lines followed the American transcontinental configuration.

Both size and density mask many important considerations in comparing the effectiveness of the different networks. Britain's railways, in the early years at least, suffered from excessive duplication and fragmentation as many companies competed for different lines with scant regard for uniformity or standardisation of timetables, gauge size or rolling stock. These problems eased with the introduction of the clearing house in 1842 and the amalgamation of many companies in the 1850s and 1860s. In France, despite more careful planning, a network emerged which over-emphasised Paris to the detriment of many of the regions. Spain's network bypassed several economically important areas and towns as a result of the influence of foreign investors whose interests sometimes clashed with those of the national economy. In Germany the problem centred around the determined particularism of individual states which infrequently worked together to build cross-state connections, concentrating instead upon railways which diverted trade away from other states.

In terms of usage, the United Kingdom, Belgium and Germany carried the most freight per capita and Switzerland, the United Kingdom, Belgium and Germany the most passengers per capita (Milward and Saul, 1977, 541). This would suggest that the railways of Belgium and the United Kingdom were among the most effective in Europe though it tells us nothing about the length of journeys or the freight and passenger rates.

Table 5.2   Output of European Railway Services, 1910

Country	Freight traffic*	Passenger traffic[†]
Austria-Hungary	15 152	7 522
Belgium	5 729[‡]	4 306
Britain	516 053[§]	1 276[¶]
Bulgaria	196	210
Denmark	465	917
Finland	462	555
France	21 500	16 800
Germany	56 400	35 700
Greece	45	181
Hungary	8 095	4 404
Ireland	6 630[§]	31[¶]
Italy	6 185	4 448
Netherlands	1 422	1 368
Norway	294	335
Portugal	4 845[§]	15[¶]
Romania	8 244[§]	10[¶]
Russia	66	23
Spain	3 179[‡]	49[¶]
Sweden	2 663	1 573
Switzerland	1 249	2 307

Notes: * million ton/km
[†] million passenger km
[‡] 1913
[§] 000 tons
[¶] million passengers

Source: Mitchell, 1975, 591–612.

The Liverpool to Manchester line set the scene for rapid development of the railway map of Britain. It showed the ability of civil engineers to overcome major geological obstacles like Chat Moss, it witnessed the application of steam power along the whole length of the line, the company ran services itself and it proved a financial success, yielding good profits over many years (Richards). Many of the major trunk routes were completed in the 1830s and 1840s. The Grand Junction linked the Liverpool–Manchester to Birmingham in 1837 and the latter was connected to London in the following year. England and Scotland were linked by lines running along the east and west coasts while the Holyhead line improved communications with Wales and from thence to Ireland. Railways also penetrated south-west England and East Anglia.

The early railways encountered opposition from vested interests and from those who believed they posed an environmental hazard. Canal owners, coaching firms, wagonmasters, innkeepers and turnpike trustees all saw their livelihood threatened by the railway. Since railways required statutory sanction through a private Act, Parliament became a battleground between opposing interests. The superior wealth of the railway companies enabled them to build up a substantial basis of support in Parliament and thereby secure the passage of numerous railway Acts. Some vested interests were bought out by the railway companies, others adapted: coach makers turned to the manufacture of railway rolling stock while hauliers changed from long to short distance to pick up the increased demand for 'feeder' transport around railway terminals. Many landowners and farmers viewed the railways as an encroachment upon the rural scene, fearing the smoke and noise would reduce animal and crop yields but their alarmist views soon woke up to the inflation of land prices and the market advantages wrought by the railways.

After 1850 the rate of railway construction slowed down and concentrated upon secondary, branch and commuter lines to fill in the detail of the network. Several longer lines in less populous areas were completed in Scotland and Wales. The railway continued to throw up important engineering achievements such as the Severn Tunnel (1886), the Tay (1878 and 1887) and Forth Bridges (1890). The amalgamation movement helped to rationalise the system though at the end of the century there were still in excess of one hundred companies including many small ones, some of whom were controlled by the four largest (London and North-Western Railway, Great Eastern, Midland, and Great Western). These giants themselves were the consequence of repeated amalgamations (Cain, 1972, 623).

Railway construction in France was somewhat later and slower than in Britain, the main period of development dating from the late 1840s to the end of the century. Many trunk lines were built in the 1840s and 1850s with the branch and secondary lines being completed in the subsequent decades. France, like Britain, had primitive industrial precursors of the railway in the eighteenth century but it was not until 1832 that the St Étienne to Lyons line opened as the first locomotive service. Like the Liverpool–Manchester it was built as an industrial line but found great popularity as a passenger service. Five years later the Paris–St Germain railway appeared as the first intentional passenger service (B. M. Ratcliffe, 1971–2). Its success stimulated further construction. The project was the brainchild of the Pereire brothers whose connections with the Bourse, journalism and the government overcame opposition from landowners, road hauliers and river carriers and made them important figures in the early development of French railways. Railways also found support among the St Simonians, like Michel Chevalier, who viewed the great arteries of transport as an essential part of development.

Governments played a more central role in the planning and construction of the railways in France than Britain. Intervention in road and waterway construction had created a precedent. A national rail system was set out in the railway law of 1842 which mapped out the network. The Legrand plan, devised by the Director-General of the Corps des Ponts et Chaussées, consisted of a series of main lines radiating from Paris which came to be dominated by six major companies, Ouest, Nord, Est, Paris-Orléans, Paris–Lyons–Marseilles, and Midi. Operation of the system lay with the private companies, but the Ministry of Public Works took responsibility for overall planning. The government bought the land and its engineers built the major civil engineering works such as the road bed, bridges, tunnels and cuttings. The rights to complete the railway (rails, stations and rolling stock) and then operate it over a fixed number of years, known as concessions, were sold to industrial syndicates under competitive tender. Essentially, the railways were the property of the government and were leased on terms of forty years or more to private companies.

Enthusiasm for concessions began to diminish in the later 1840s when it became clear that government projections of costs and revenue were inaccurate. The length of concessions was extended to over ninety years. The Franqueville Conventions of 1857–9 encouraged companies to use the profits from the main lines to finance branch construction. Mergers were encouraged in order to create companies strong enough to support branch lines. A law of 1865 allowed prefects to allocate concessions in their *département* to encourage local groups to set up lines in competition with the major companies. These incentives had little effect and by the end of the 1870s many areas remained unconnected to the railway network. The Freyçinet Plan of 1879 provided for the expenditure of 3500 million francs over twelve years for the construction of minor lines. The government by this measure turned back to supporting the major companies, offering guaranteed dividends on shares. As a result, the system grew from 23 000 to 38 000 km in the last two decades of the nineteenth century.

Government intervention in French railway construction avoided the capital waste of duplication or the lack of uniformity experienced in Britain. However, their bureaucratic methods may have discouraged private industry until it became clear that the concession principle effectively handed out operating monopolies. Even at this stage delays and conflict between the government and the companies emerged over the plans and the terms of the concessions which at first were quite harsh. The government's engineers, while capable technicians, understood or cared little about financial and industrial matters.

Germany had its equivalent of the Pereire brothers; influential individuals who were determined to win support for the construction of a system of railways. Friedrich List held weight in business, political and media circles. List had visited England and the United States and was convinced of the value of the railway. He made regular contributions to the Augsburg *Allgemeine Zeitung* in support of the railway. He advocated transnational lines in Europe and suggested that governments act as guarantors on railway shares in order to attract investors. He was also a strong advocate of railway construction within Saxony, giving his weight to the Leipzig to Dresden line which was completed as early as 1839 (Henderson).

German railway construction began a little later than French, with the completion of the short Nuremburg to Fürth line in 1835. The 1840s witnessed the completion of more than 5000 km of track, a construction rate double that of France. A series of important east-west and north-south lines had been built linking major cities such as Munich and Augsburg in 1840, Berlin and Hamburg in 1846 and Cologne and Münden in the following year. Growth continued apace in the 1850s with the size of the network doubling. In the 1860s and 1870s emphasis turned to the building of secondary and branch lines.

The momentum was maintained up to the First World War with the expansion of commuter and suburban services. Unlike the case in France, there were few problems attracting interest in the smaller lines. This gave Germany, by 1911, a rail network whose size was unsurpassed in Europe and whose density was only exceeded by that of Belgium.

In spite of this achievement significant problems existed with the German network. Lines were built by different institutions and individuals with little thought for coherency or planning. Different gauges and truck sizes existed. The wider gauge of Baden's railways did not conform with practice elsewhere in the country until 1853. The Union of German Railway Administrations was established at Hamburg in 1847 to try and combat some of these problems of fragmentation. It compiled valuable annual reports on the performances of its members, organised a system of through trains between different networks and harmonised tariffs and tickets. The shortcoming of the Administration was the southern states' refusal to join for fear of Prussian domination. Nor were many of the states outside the Zollverein integrated into the railway system until the later nineteenth century.

German state governments were closely involved in the planning, construction and financing of railways. Even in traditional agrarian states, such as Prussia, where the consequences of railway construction were regarded with some suspicion, regulation was deemed necessary to control the pace of development. Most states responded to requests by railway promoters for land expropriation by extending existing legislation for roads and waterways. The Prussian Railway Act of 1838 established the state's right to supervise the founding, financing and operation of new railway companies. The Act dealt with such areas as expropriation, tariff rates and competition, the linking of lines and nationalisation. The companies were also obliged to carry mail free of charge. Negotiations over these regulations could be complex and drawn out, thereby delaying or discouraging construction. Bongaerts, however, believes this forced companies to think through their proposals more carefully and reject non-viable schemes.

Prior to 1871 state governments competed with each other by building lines confined to the limits of the state and attracting trade away from neighbouring areas. After unification, Bismarck's administration struggled to integrate the different state railways into a single uniform network. The Imperial Railroad Office was established in 1873 as a central controlling agency but remained impotent to the determined autonomy of many states. Old interstate rivalries re-emerged particularly in the 'railway wars' between Prussia and Saxony with fears that Prussian railway projects were a threat to the trade of Leipzig (Gisevius). Such considerations lend weight to Fremdling's (1980) revision of traditional historiography which had emphasised the positive role of the state in the emergence of the railway system. In contrast he believes that central intervention hindered railway development especially as a result of the particularism of state governments.

Individual entrepreneurs made an important contribution to German railway construction as owners of large industrial empires which stood to benefit from improved transport facilities. Ludolf Camphausen (1803–90) was one of the earliest German railway entrepreneurs, building lines principally in the Rhinelands. His other commercial interests included corn, oil and banking, besides which he also fulfilled the roles of economist and politician, leading the Liberal Ministry in Prussia in 1848 (Hartsough). Bethel Henry Strousberg (1823–84) was the largest and wealthiest of the German railway builders in the 1860s and 1870s and became known in Germany as the 'Railway King'. Benefiting from first-hand experience in England he integrated railways with his interests in mining, smelting and heavy machinery. In total he built about 2500 km of railways with a capital of 600 million marks which included lines in Hungary, Russia and Romania. He refused to delegate decision-making within his business empire which left him making unscientific, intuitive decisions and brought him to bankruptcy in the early 1870s (Redlich). The joint stock companies appear to have been more effective in the promotion of German railways. They had a more rational perspective of the position of railways in the economy and often benefited from the support of knowledgeable local government officials on their Board.

In mid-nineteenth-century Belgium writers like Perrot argued that their newly independent nation should build a national railway network. Railways, it was believed, would promote not only internal trade but also the cross-national links important for manufacturers in a small country. There was a determination to attract continental trade through Belgium rather than Holland. Since Holland benefited from Rotterdam's position at the head of the Rhine, Belgium concentrated on diverting trade via Antwerp by building a rail link to the upper Rhine at Cologne in 1843. With strategic considerations in

mind and the need to negotiate with other states in the construction
of some railways, government ownership of the main routes became
an imperative. Secondary lines were considered domestic concerns
which could be left to private initiative.

The railway law of 1834 set out the early lines which consisted of a
cross intersecting at Malines and stretching out towards England,
France, the German states and the North Sea via Ostend, Mons,
Liège and Antwerp respectively. The routes to England, France and
Prussia were completed as early as 1838, 1842 and 1843. Thus it is not
surprising to find one historian observing that 'in no other European
country did railway building have such specific and such well thought
out aims before 1850' (Milward and Saul, 1973, 442). In the following
decades private companies set to the task of building many secondary
lines. Between 1843 and 1870 around fifty companies built 2500 km of
track (Laffut, 1983, 205). In the later decades the state returned to a
more positive role in railway planning and construction. At the same
time, government legislation offered inducements to attract further
private railway building which produced many light, cheaply built
railways designed for workmen and agricultural produce. Thus two
distinct systems emerged: the major one, owned by the state, was
extensive and carefully planned and included many important trunk
routes to and beyond the country's border; the smaller system was
privately owned, intensive, poorly planned and consisted of mainly
secondary lines, often badly constructed of only a single track and
with less frequent points of access than the state system.

Blessed with an excellent system of inland waterways and hindered
by a hesitant entrepreneurial class, the Dutch were very slow to build
a railway system. Rotterdam's commercial interests strongly opposed
railways which they viewed as a threat to the port's prosperity
(Hartgerink-Koomans, 1958). Even when the Antwerp–Cologne line
threatened to divert continental trade through Belgium there was no
acceleration of development. Hartgerink-Koomans (1956) emphasises the spirit of enterprise among local contractors in the north-east
provinces but their efforts had produced less than 200 km of line by
1850 in contrast to the 850 km in Belgium. Moreover, they missed the
opportunity to link Dutch ports by rail with the Rhineland before the
Germans began building alternative routes to Hamburg and Bremen.
Amsterdam and Haarlem were linked in 1839, a line which was later
to take in The Hague, Rotterdam and Utrecht and go on to the
German border.

In the 1860s the state intervened to hasten the construction of a system. It met the cost of construction and sold operating concessions to private firms. The continued hesitance of Dutch capital is seen from the manner in which many of the construction contracts went to French firms. By 1910 3000 km of railways had been built but the tardiness of construction had helped strengthen the position of competitive Belgian and German interests. On the other hand, it had become one of the densest networks in Europe and helped to revive Dutch ports.

Swiss railway construction began in the 1850s and reached peaks in the 1870s and shortly before the first World War. Construction was delayed by a combination of factors. There was a low demand for the carriage of heavy, bulky goods like coal and iron which had stimulated railway building in Belgium. The Alps and the Dinaric Mountains acted as natural obstacles against connections with other national networks. The first Alpine tunnel was not built until 1871 when the Mont-Cenis line connected Modane in the French Alps with the Dora Riparia in Piedmont. In 1882 a line was completed running along the Reuss valley from Lake Lucerne towards the Saint Gotthard massif, linking the Rhinelands with the Italian Plains. There was an initial government reluctance to assist the development of the network though from 1848 the Federal government adopted a supervisory role but left the construction and operation to private companies until 1898. It commissioned a report from two British engineers who advised only a small network and to avoid attempting an Alpine crossing. Swiss enterpreneurs rejected these proposals which created further delays. Nonetheless, by the First World War its network of 4500 km was the third most dense in Europe and was comparatively well used.

The Spanish railway system was built in the second half of the nineteenth century, with construction peaking in the decade after 1856 and the two decades from the mid-1870s. The first period arose out of the incentives offered to foreign investors in the 1855 railway law (tariff concessions, subsidies and favourable company status) and was concentrated on the construction of main lines. Lines were built to connect Madrid with the French border and the coast. In 1864 Madrid was linked with Paris. Two major railway companies played an important part in developing the network, the Compañía de los Ferrocarriles del Norte de España (Norte) and the Compañía de los Ferrocarriles de Madrid a Zaragoza y Alicante (MZA). Between them they expanded to carry over 70 per cent of Spain's rail freight (Gomez-Mendoza, 1983, 154). A slowdown in the rate of construction from the mid-1860s reflected an economic downturn and disappointment at the performance of Spain's railways. The Andaluces company was created in 1879 through a series of amalgamations. This was the third major company and arose out of a general rationalisation drive in an attempt to reduce costs and revive traffic. Although construction rates rose in the following decades and branch lines were built, the equipment used on them was generally poor, the track cheap and often only single and the trains slow. Major towns and industrial areas were often bypassed because construction subsidies were based upon mileage.

Many lines were built in the early years by foreign interests and served their needs rather than those of the Spanish economy. Railways, it is also alleged, were built by exploitative contractors who left the system with high fixed costs and low traffic volumes. Recent historiography, however, has revised the image of 'hit and run' construction and profiteering arguing instead that most interests operated the lines they built and sought long term returns (Artola). Falling railway investment and depreciating capital stock at the end of the century was due less to neglect than to a desire to keep down costs. Simultaneously, the agrarian depression reduced demand from the main rail user. With demand reviving in the years leading up to the First World War, the railways went through a period of capital renovation.

Portugal had built only a small density system of less than 3000 km by 1913. The main period of construction was between 1860 and 1890 and the final half a dozen years before the First World War. It comprised in the main of a north-south line parallel to the coast from which branches penetrated eastwards in to the interior and to link up with the Spanish network. With such a long seabord in relation to its size railways were naturally regarded as of lesser importance. That they were poorly used in the interior as well can be attributed largely to the inconsistency of gauge sizes and the backwardness of the economy.

Italy, like Spain, built railways late in comparison with west European countries but early in relation to her own economic development. The first Italian railway came as early as 1839 with the link between Naples and Portici. Most were local short lines though the Milan to Venice link was completed in 1857. Construction continued at a slow pace until the 1860s. Less than 2000 km had been completed by the time of the unification of Italy and these were mostly concentrated in Piedmont, Lombardy, Veneto and Tuscany. Some nascent industrial areas, such as around the Po Valley, were linked to the ports. The fact that one half of the pre-unification lines were built in Piedmont owed much to Cavour's enthusiastic support. As early as the 1840s he pushed for the construction of a state-owned trunk line and offered inducements to foreign and domestic enterpreneurs. One historian has gone as far as to suggest that one of the principal motives behind unification was his desire to build a national railway system (Cameron). Although lacking individuals of the stature of the Pereires or List, men like Rodolfo Castinelli, inspector of waterways and roads for the Grand Duchy of Tuscany, envisaged an Italian rail network serving Europe as a whole, acting as a bridge for traffic from England and northern Europe bound eastwards through the Suez Canal (Landi).

Unification transcended the particularism of state governments and encouraged the promotion of a national network. Main lines were built connecting Rome and Naples (1863), Bologna and Florence (1864) and the latter to Rome (1866). Trans-peninsular lines connected Rome with the Adriatic in 1866 and Naples with the Adriatic in 1870. North-south lines running along both coasts completed the country's main line network. Bologna was connected to Ancona by 1861 and extended to Lecce five years later. On the Ionian coast progress was slower through more difficult terrain, delaying completion until 1874–5. Construction also advanced on Sardinia and Sicily. Progress slowed in the 1870s following the financial crashes of 1867. A return to more rapid progress in the 1880s and the early 1890s reflected the commitment of Leftist governments to public expenditure and enabled many minor lines to be completed. A further period of railway development occurred in the years following nationalisation in 1905 (Ferrovie dello Stato) though this mainly took the form of replacing and updating technologically obsolescent capital.

Italy drew heavily upon foreign investment and know-how to build her railways but the main stimuli for railway development came from domestic political sources: unification in the 1860s, the return of the Left in the 1870s and the decision to nationalise in 1905. After unification, the system was rationalised into first five (1865) and then four (1885) regional groups. By the First World War Italy had a system twice as dense as that of Spain and spanning most of the important industrial areas, the ports and the major cities. On the deficit side, the network was under-utilised because of high freight rates and costs and the low demand in a backward economy. Only in the more heavily populated and highly industrialised area of the Po Valley were railways more successful.

Austria-Hungary, like other backward countries, viewed railway construction as a panacea for under-development. Thus, many of the early lines were state-built including the earliest in 1832 between Linz and Budweis to convey state monopoly salt to Hamburg via the Elbe. Although one of the first substantial railway lines on the European continent, it remained horse-drawn for several decades. Emperor Francis opposed railway construction fearing it would cause social disruption. His opposition stood in the way of Rothschild initiatives to link Vienna with the coalfields of Moravia and Silesia and with the salt deposits of Galicia. 'Not until he was safely interred in the soil could the Rothschilds commence excavating it for large scale railway networks' (Trebilcock, 351). When railway building recommenced in the 1840s the state played a leading role building two-thirds of the lines. Military feeder lines connected with the borders of Saxony, Bavaria and Italy while several private lines were built to link to the main European network, especially the Nordbahn which connected Vienna to the German network through Silesia.

Construction peaks were reached in the 1850s and 1867–73 but this time the private sector was dominant because the state had begun to sell off its lines and auction concession rights over new lines to the private sector in order to raise money. By the time the boom ended with the Vienna stock market crash in 1873 all the main towns of Austria-Hungary, except those on the Dalmatian coast, were linked with Budapest, Vienna and the European network. Aware of the benefits that railways were bringing to the economy, the government returned to railway financing in 1875 to sustain the momentum of activity. State credit was made available to construct the Arlberg line and the Bohemian transversal railway.

The railway network was too heavily concentrated on Vienna and Budapest, being built on the 'star' system with the capital cities at the centre. Insufficient planning and frequent policy changes by the government discouraged investors while private firms manifested corruption and inefficiency. Nor were the lines equitably distributed, their density being much greater in Bohemia than Dalmatia.

Railway construction came later to the Balkan countries than elsewhere in Europe as a result of the area's economic and political backwardness. The political legacy of Turkish feudalism persisted while subsistent agriculture and few mineral resources meant the demand for transport was low. Most railway building took place between the 1880s and 1912. There was not a single line in the area until a British company linked Cernavodă with Constanta in Romania in 1860 to avoid travelling through the Danube delta. Two other important lines were built in the 1860s, Ruse to Varna and Bucharest to Giurgiu. These early lines grew out of the consequences of the Crimean War which increased western interests in the area and made Turkey realise the importance of economic modernisation. As late as 1883 Serbia had no railways and barely 1000 km by the First World War in spite of various schemes such as a link to the Adriatic in order to lessen her political dependence upon Austria. Most Romanian railways were built after 1875 when the state took over responsibility for their construction. A state railway company (Caile Ferate Romane) was formed in 1880 and within a decade had control of most of the system. Railway building took off in Bulgaria after nationalisation in 1884. In Serbia railways were nationalised in 1889 but there was little acceleration in activity until shortly before 1914.

In 1869 Baron Hirsch, a Bavarian financier, obtained a concession from the Imperial Ottoman Government for the construction and operation of a railway to connect Vienna and Constantinople and thereby link Turkey with the main European network. Hirsch was related by birth and marriage to many of the leading German and Austrian banking families and became a leading figure in the flotation and direction of railway, industrial, banking and insurance companies. He had reached Sofia when the Balkan War of 1875–6 left the Turks surrendering land to Serbia in the path of the railway. The line was completed under Austrian leadership in 1888 (Grunwald).

The small Greek system began with the short link between Athens and Piraeus in 1869 and was added to in the 1880s by links from the capital to the Peloponnese and Thessaly, helped by the latter's acquisition from the Ottomans. In general, though, the geology of Greece, small compact regions, separated by mountains and coasts, militated against a national rail network.

The late arrival of the railways in Scandinavia had more to do with their limited value for small waterborne economies. Only Denmark had any railways before 1850, principally the link from Copenhagen to Korsør. A number of major lines were built in the last two decades of the century including links to the growing port of Esbjerg. Railway building began in the 1860s in Norway with several short lines in the vicinity of Christiania. The system grew slowly up to the First World War. Norway, along with Finland whose network was similarly sparse, shared a geography and geology more suited to coastal shipping. A commission of 1875 recommended the construction of main routes in Norway but this did little to hasten the rate of construction; the Bergen to Oslo line, for example, was not completed until 1907 nor was there a line from Oslo to Stavanger by 1914.

A more comprehensive system was built in Sweden, four times the size of those of Denmark and Norway. Though less geographically dense than Denmark's rail system, Sweden built more lines per capita than anywhere else in Europe. A system was first planned in the 1850s with the state taking charge of the main routes and the secondary lines remaining in the private domain. A central role for the state was viewed as necessary to avoid the undue influence of foreign investors which, it was believed, had hampered the development of some economies. However, an economic and political backlash against the state in the late 1860s led to private builders playing a major role in the following decade. Construction reached a peak in the 1870s and 1890s, helped by a good credit system, low tariffs, low taxes and a liberal attitude to company formation, to bring a total network of 14 000 km by 1913. Stockholm, Gothenburg and Malmö were linked and connections were made into Norway at Oslo and, later, into Finland via the Gulf of Bothnia. Lines were also built connecting the iron-mining districts of Bergslagen and Kiruna with the ports of Gothenberg and Narvik.

In Russia socio-political as well as economic considerations delayed construction. In contrast to most of western Europe, the landed interest retained the reins of political power for most of the nineteenth century. They feared that the railways and accompanying industrialisation would unleash challenging social forces. Toĺ, the Director of Transport in the 1830s, was firmly opposed to the development of a railway network whilst Kankrin, Minister of Finance, 1823–44, believed that the railways would foster, 'rampant social equality, uncontrollable mobility and the concentration of large numbers of potential insurgents in inconvenient places' (Trebilcock, 223). Very few railways were built in Russia before 1860. Exceptionally, the St Petersburg to Moscow line, completed in 1852, was built by conscripted serfs and its motivation was largely political and military rather than economic. Attitudes began to change in the second half of the nineteenth century as the government began to appreciate the international political implications of economic backwardness. The link between economic strength and military might displayed by her German neighbour was all too clear.

In the first half of the 1860s construction rates remained low as the

Russian economy laboured under the impact of the raw cotton famine brought on by the American Civil War and the workforce struggled to adapt to the aftermath of the serf emancipation. As the Russian economy prospered in the late 1860s and early 1870s construction moved ahead. Many lines rediated from Moscow, connecting to the central grain producing region and the northern ports such as Riga. Following a plateau for about ten years, a rising trend of railway building emerged once more from the mid 1880s much of which was aimed at connecting different regions of Russia. The first major railway into the Urals was completed in 1878 and was connected to Moscow in 1892. Other lines linked Moscow with the middle and lower Volga, the southern steppes and the south-west. As in the earlier period many lines were designed to encourage the internal and external grain trade, though increasing attention was paid to the needs of manufacturing industry. The Baku–Batum railway of 1883 connected the main oil producing area on the Caspian Sea to the Black Sea and thereby facilitated a huge growth in oil exports. In 1885 the Ekaterine railway served as a major stimulus to the development of the iron and steel industry by joining up the coal region of the Donetz basin with sources of iron ore in the Ukraine. As a result the Donetz was to become the major supplier of rails to Russian railways.

Construction peaked in the 1890s encouraged by European prosperity and the positive industrialisation policies of Witte who built 25 000 km of lines. These included the vast Trans-Siberian railway completed in 1901 as part of his policy of opening up the Siberian economy. The subsequent slowing down resulted from the completion of the major lines and the reaction against Witte's style of policy.

Lines built in their Polish territories reflected Russian strategic considerations. Warsaw was connected to St Petersburg in 1862. In order to avoid reliance upon the German Baltic ports a line was built from Warsaw via Czestochowa in 1848 in order to channel Russian trade through the Adriatic. The rapidly expanding textile town of Łódź, however, was not connected to the rail system until 1866.

FINANCE AND INVESTMENT

Railway construction and operation required vast expenditure, particularly in overcoming natural obstacles and in the employment of locomotives and rolling stock. The completion of some railways represented considerable engineering achievements for the nine-teenth century. The drainage of marshes, the construction of viaducts and the digging of tunnels were completed almost entirely by manual labour. The engineering problems varied from the mountains of Austria to the marshlands of Russia and the intersecting waterways of the Netherlands. Moreover, there was a determination in some countries, particularly Britain, to build in a grandiose manner which meant large and ornate buildings using expensive materials. Even before construction began, a railway project could sustain consider-able costs in planning and securing political support and legal status. Thus, financing the railways was a major problem and even the best engineers grossly underestimated costs. Stephenson, for example, underestimated the cost of building the London to Birmingham by more than 700 per cent. It was only in Britain with her dynamic entrepreneurial class that finance came entirely from private sources. In continental Europe, governments contributed towards the cost to a greater or lesser extent, aware of strategic considerations and the political implications of economic backwardness. In the lesser-developed countries, convinced of the economic expediency of pos-sessing a rail network but possessed of sparse financial resources, overseas investors and governments helped to bear some of the expenditure in return for political and trading payoffs.

In Britain the repeal of the 'Bubble' Act in 1825, which had restricted joint stock company formation since 1719, broadened considerably the field of investors. The flotation of shares with low denominations of only £5 or £10 also served to attract the small investor. New lines were promoted vigorously with considerable publicity emphasising the high profits of early lines like the Liver-pool–Manchester whose shares were returning ten per cent per annum and had doubled in face value within a few years (Donaghy, 226, 230). Peaks of railway investment in Britain occurred in boom years in the late 1830s, mid 1840s and mid 1860s when employment and incomes were buoyant throughout the economy. These peaks turned into speculative manias as investors became carried along on a tide of euphoria, persuaded by unscrupulous promoters that high returns were guaranteed. Few railways fulfilled the profit hopes of the Liverpool–Manchester; many made little or no profit, some were never built. The poor financial performance of some lines became legendary; the Manchester, Sheffield and Lincolnshire (MSL), for example, became known as the 'Money, Sunk and Lost'. Investment was at first localised, emanating from tradesmen in towns which were to have been connected by the railway. By the 1840s, investors were attracted from many parts of the country as a national investment market in railways began to emerge (Pollins, 1971; Reed) although the Lancashire and Yorkshire Railway continued to attract mainly local investment (Broadbridge, 1955–6, 1970). As a result of the railway mania, provincial stock exchanges were created, for example at Liverpool and Manchester in 1836 and Glasgow, Edinburgh and Leeds in 1844–5.

With labour and material costs rising and investors being discouraged by poor performances many projects were in serious trouble as early as the 1840s. Shareholders were refusing to meet payments on call leaving the company to resort to loans. The upshot of this was the increased use of debenture stock (loan capital) in place of equity shares (risk capital), leaving the investor with a guaranteed annual return as part of the company's normal costs. Railway companies also turned increasingly to contractors to build the line. They would take over much of the financial responsibility during construction such as arranging land purchase, paying engineers and solicitors and guaranteeing interest on stocks as well as purchasing some shares themselves and accepting payment partly in this form (Pollins, 1957–8).

Many of the successful English railway contractors, such as Brassey, Peto and Betts, used their know-how and capital in the construction of railway systems throughout the world. English and Scottish mercantile houses trading with India campaigned for the construction of railways there in the 1840s. The Indian government was keen to build railways in order to increase trade, improve social conditions and encourage further investment from overseas. In 1849 the Indian government and the promoters agreed terms for several lines which were to be financed, built and operated privately but the government would indemnify shareholders in years when profits fell below five per cent. By 1902 a network of 25 000 miles had been built at a cost of £236 million borne largely by British investors but incurring frequent losses sustained by the Indian government (Thorner, 391–2). Britain also invested heavily in the construction of railways on the American continent. By 1913 around three-quarters of the Argentinian network was owned and managed by British firms and individuals (Jenks, 1951, 375, 384). British finance was heavily involved in United States railways, particularly after 1869 when their shares became a specialist part of the London stock exchange and played a critical part in sustaining the pace of building. Finance mostly came from small investors who took no part in management of the railways (Jenks,

1951, 375–9). Hand in hand with British overseas investment went British overseas trade. In the years between 1847 and 1880, up to 50 per cent of rail production in the United Kingdom was exported to the United States (Hidy, 34).

More common than the British system of private financing was a joint system of public and private responsibility. The French government bore the cost of the civil engineering works in railway building and sold the rights over completion and operation to companies or syndicates. The principal members of these syndicates were Parisian and Swiss bankers, large freight firms and English capitalists. The Compagnie du Chemin de Fer du Nord was founded in 1845 between Rothschilds, Barings, Hottinguer, Lafitte, Blount and other Parisian bankers. Rothschilds, in particular, supported the operations of many of the larger French railway companies including Nord, Est and Paris-Lyons-Marseilles as well as financing construction in many other countries including Italy and the Balkans. As in Britain, share denominations were purposely pitched low to attract the small investor and there was a significantly greater resort to the safety of the bond market. By 1880 eighty per cent of French railway capital took the form of bonds compared with twenty-five per cent in England (Caron, 1983, 29). Bonds were brought to the public's attention by heavy publicity; they were even sold at railway stations. Holders of railway securities were given further reassurances by the state's policy of guaranteeing a minimum rate of return on their investments (*garantie d'intérêt*).

There seems little doubt that 'the massive issues of railway securities over the second half of the nineteenth century dominated and widened the market for paper securities in France right up to 1900' (Caron, 1983, 30). Given the insufficiency of local sources of industrial wealth, only the short early railways such as Lyons to St Étienne were built by local concessions. The problems of industrial financing in France derived from the tendency of peasants to hoard their savings and for the middle class to invest in property and government securities. The Pereire brothers, with their customary foresight, established the Crédit Mobilier in 1852 as an institution designed to channel private savings into industrial investment by selling low denomination shares to the public. The idea arose out of the need to raise money for railway projects and most of their early work was in this direction. The Crédit Mobilier failed in 1867 when investors began to question the profitability of railway investments. Despite its ephemerality, the Crédit Mobilier broke down the traditional division between personal and investment banking and made an important contribution not only to French railway financing but also to that of many other countries in which it invested. Its methods were soon followed by institutions in many other countries including Austria, Spain, Italy and the Netherlands. In the 1860s, helped by reforms in joint stock company legislation, local institutions specialising in transport finance emerged in many provincial French towns including Lyons, Marseilles and Lille.

The German system was constructed relatively cheaply and there existed a great abundance of personal savings within the states. The domination of the capital market by government bonds, mortgage bank debt notes and life assurance annuities, all safe and reliable investments, meant there was a need for a higher risk alternative. This was provided by railway investments; by 1842 railway shares and options were being traded on the Berliner Börse. Options gave the investor the chance to defer a decision on purchase or payment and therefore helped to attract interest from the lower classes. Businessmen and engineers were important in financing and sometimes formed 'railway promotion clubs' (Bongaerts). The financial contributions of major entrepreneurs like Camphausen and Strousberg were important but involved notorious fraudulent activities. The so-called 'Strousberg system' occurred when railway corporations created finance and construction commissions which, though legally independent, were in the hands of the promoters. Money was 'creamed off' to the commissions by charging the railway company inflated building costs and transferring stock at below par value (Redlich).

German state governments followed the pattern of guaranteeing shareholders a minimum interest payment for an initial period. The degree of central financing varied: in Hanover, Brunswick, Baden and Württemberg the railways were state owned while in Prussia and Saxony they were privately owned although the state still exercised a regulatory hand. Junker-dominated Prussian governments opposed state ownership of the railways since it would necessitate calling the Diet of Estates in order to raise money which might increase bourgeois pressure for constitutional reforms. The extent of central financing also varied over time; from the mid-1870s state governments began to buy up many railways so that by the eve of the First World War only six per cent of lines remained in private hands. As with the salt trade and the post office, governments conceived of railways as a means of raising revenues. The Royal Hanoverian

Railway Company yielded nearly five per cent of that state's budget in the middle of the nineteenth century (Bongaerts, 343). Bismarck's desire to bring the German rail system under Reich control was probably born less of a belief in unification and rationalisation than of a desire to use the profits in his budget.

Up to 1843 the state financed all the Belgian lines, aware of the strategic and cross-national considerations for a small economy. Thenceforth, private enterprise figured prominently. Concessions were awarded to individual firms and groups including English railway promoters, French companies and Belgian capitalists. Belgian governments took care to ensure that no foreign influences became too powerful, intervening, for example, to restrain the expansionism of the French Compagnie du Nord. Frequently, finance was raised through the sale of shares and bonds by limited liability companies (*sociétés anonymes*) and through the backing of the banks. By the 1860s some companies were experiencing financial difficulties which led the banks who had supported them to spearhead a movement towards rationalisation and concentration. After about 1870, the state returned to large-scale railway financing, building new lines in unpromising areas with low traffic volumes and buying back unprofitable lines from private firms to save them from closure and encouraging further private finance. In 1884 the Société Nationale des Chemins de Fer Vicinaux was formed; financed by the state, the provinces and the communes it built many new lines.

Sweden also relied heavily on overseas finance after an initial sale of bonds on the domestic market in 1854 fell flat with only 279 000 of a three million kronor loan finding subscribers. In the 1840s Count Adolf von Rosen, an enthusiastic supporter of railway development, argued that sources of international investment could be tapped with the state offering guaranteed minimum returns. However, investment was rejected in favour of loans which gave the government greater freedom of action away from the influence of foreign interests. It also avoided the capital shortage and high interest rates which heavy reliance upon domestic finance implied. In 1858 a 20 million kronor loan was arranged with four German financiers. By 1914 514 out of 689 million kronor of national debt was attributable to railway loans most of which was owed to foreigners (Hedin, 6). Sweden had had no long-term national debt since just after the Napoleonic Wars, which made financing a problem in the 1850s through lack of experience in government and international uncertainty about Sweden's credit rating. The early loans came principally from northern Germany where the creditworthiness of the Swedish government was known (Söderlund, 43–4). By the 1880s most finance came from France who could offer lower interests rates of four as against five or six per cent in Germany and England (Hedin, 7). The state, as well as constructing railways itself, gave loans or occasionally grants, to private firms towards the cost of railway building. Grants were given where a railway offered political and strategic benefits such as the Karlskrona–Vaxjo. The Riksdag, however, rejected the view that the state should pay for around a quarter of the cost of private construction and ramained with the loans policy up to 1914 (Hedin, 13).

Most private lines were built by limited liability companies whose share capital derived mainly from within Sweden either from individual investors or from municipal and county councils. The Bergslagen Railroad Company, whose line cost more than three times that of any other Swedish railway, drew heavily upon the private investors and the City authority of Gothenburg. The line connected the port with Sweden's mining and industrial heartland. Once more bonds were of great importance to railway financing and, in turn, represented 80 per cent of the national bond market in the 1870s (Hedin, 15).

For the less developed countries, financing railway construction was made more problematic by subsistence activity, the absence of a cash-nexus economy and low levels of personal wealth. Governments of Italy in the 1860s and 1870s, and of Russia in the following two decades, attempted to squeeze the peasant surplus with high taxes, but low yields made this an ineffective source of finance. Thus the governments of Spain, Italy and Russia turned to foreign investors to finance railway construction, backed by state guarantees of minimum investment returns. Helped by international institutional growth and a mania for railways they were able to raise huge sums in this manner. Lack of creditworthiness made a loans policy more difficult.

The Russians were most successful at attracting foreign investment, reflecting investor confidence in the government's commitment to rapid industrialisation. Integrated industrialisation policies had been carefully thought out: railway development and tariff subsidy meant increased exports, balance of payments surpluses and therefore a gold-backed currency which gave reassurance to foreign investors. Foreign finance peaked in the 1890s helped by Witte's determination to see these policies through and his direct intervention in French finance markets, publicising the alleged profitability of Russian firms. In return for their capital, however, the French wanted to secure Russian military and political support against Germany. Thus, in the decade following the Franco–Russian alliance of 1891, Witte's policy of building 'economic' railways conflicted with the French desire for military ones in Russia. Despite pressure from the Russian military, Witte largely had his way. The futility of the Orenburg–Tashkent line, completed in 1906 and aimed against British interests in Asia, confirmed the logic of Witte's stance. The subsequent drawing together of Britain, France and Russia made this line pointless. Despite more successful pressure for strategic lines in 1912, the French largely bore the financial burden of Russian railway building in return for little political gain (Collins).

In the first railway boom, of the late 1860s and early 1870s, the government sold concessions to private builders and guaranteed a minimum interest on the capital. These terms led to a speculative mania in railway promotion and so the conditions were tightened from the end of the 1860s: a scheme of priorities was established, interest guarantee was to be for only fifteen years and projects were to be looked at more critically by the ministries of Finance and of Ways and Communications. Zemstvos were given the right to promote railways of local benefit. They built some railways directly and sold the concession rights on others to private firms.

By the time of the second boom in the 1890s, foreign investment was responding to the industrialisation policies, private capital was abundant and the government, unhampered by war, could afford to finance some major lines. Existing companies competed for new concessions and often had to build some unprofitable lines as part of the bargain. From 1905 a further growth in private railway building emerged from government subsidies and incentives financed mainly by French and German banks.

Spanish railways relied heavily upon foreign investment. Historians have variously calculated foreign investment to have represented 40–67 per cent of total railway investment (Platt, 1984, 131; Gomez-Mendoza, 1980, 126). Foreign investors also showed an interest in the extractive industries but adopted something of a predator role, exporting necessary raw materials from the country with little consideration for domestic industry's long-term development. In Italy foreign investment was limited largely to government loans and railway shares, the latter helped by institutional growth and optimism concerning the impact of the railways. The inability of Spain and Italy to attract a broader base of foreign investment, probably due to the lack of coherent industrialisation policies, goes a long way to explaining the failure of their railway systems to inject the kind of economic stimulant that had been expected of them. Insufficient industrial investment and development outside the Po Valley meant there was little demand for rail transport.

French banks and companies were heavily committed to financing Italy's railways as they had been to her roads, administration and defence. French and Italian syndicates took over many of the trunk routes after unification. The Società Vittorio Emanuele, for example, built railways in Piedmont, Calabria and Sicily and Rothschild money went into many lines. English railway contractors, like Brassey, also featured heavily in Italian railway construction. Indeed, by 1862 foreign capital controlled all the lines in Lombardy, Veneto and central Italy so that only one major undertaking, the Società Italiana per le Strade Ferrate Meridionali, was under Italian ownership.

Investor confidence in Italian railways, however, soon faded as it became clear that most lines were unprofitable because of their low usage. In an attempt to encourage expansion of the network the government had offered kilometric guarantees of revenue on new lines. This linked the credit of the companies directly with that of the state so that when Italian government bonds fell on the Paris bourse during the war of 1866, railway bonds followed suit making it difficult for some firms to continue their building programmes. This experience and worsening political relations between the two countries led to some withdrawal of French investments in Italian railways. The gap was filled by increased German investments and greater government ownership leading finally to nationalisation in 1905. With the unprofitability of many Italian railways, the government met most of their cost through the investor guarantee on returns.

Spanish reliance on foreign investment was also threatened by the financial crash of the mid-1860s. French investors began to withdraw when they realised that even the major rail routes were not showing a profit. Responsibility again fell back upon the government. As part of recent revisions of Spanish historiography however, Artola has suggested that railways were a good investment for the state. He calculates that the government paid a quarter of the cost of railway construction up to 1890 (700 million pesetas) and recovered at least four times that investment in the course of seventy years (Gomez Mendoza, 1980, 126). The state also played an important role in assisting the companies when a falling exchange rate in the 1880s made it difficult to meet payments on bonds held overseas.

Whereas economic weaknesses are alleged to have encouraged predator foreign investors into Spanish and Italian railways, the Balkan countries were able to turn domestic political weaknesses and strategic importance to good effect. There has been a tendency to view railway construction in the Balkans largely in terms of economic imperialism by Germany and Austria-Hungary (Earle). German capital financed the Orient railway and an agreement between Germany and Austria-Hungary in 1903 provided for its continuation across Asia Minor. Balkan railways, however, were of little value to the great powers: less than three per cent of Germany's foreign trade was with the Balkans and much of this was carried on Hungarian railways. Instead, its value was as a strategic weapon to resist Serbian expansionism and to contain Turkey. Aware of such considerations, Balkan governments were able to play off foreign powers against each other in order to secure finance for the construction of railways in economically remote areas which would not attract private capital and were beyond the means of the state. The Bulgarian government in the 1880s was attempting to build lines running through Sofia and establish good links with the port of Burgas. The Austrians were opposed to such plans on strategic grounds, particularly of the threat they believed it represented to the Orient railway. When the Bulgarians sought French support, from the Crédit Lyonnais, Austria was persuaded to resume funding.

British capital and technology, however, was attracted to the area for economic reasons. The engineering and entrepreneurial family of Barkleys played a leading role in the construction of several lines in the 1860s, supported by contractors like Peto and Betts. In 1857 they agreed a concession with the Ottoman government for the Cernavodă–Constanta railway on very unfavourable terms because they believed the grain producing potential of the region promised annual net profits of up to 40 per cent. The line was financed largely by the promoters but in the building of the Ruse–Varna line a few years later they obtained support from Turkish and English investors (Jensen and Rosegger).

Austria drew upon French investment in the early years before political relations deteriorated and German later, but the need for external finance was reduced by the strength of the Viennese banks many of which emerged in the middle of the nineteenth century in response to the demand for railway funding including the large Kreditanstalt für Handel und Gewerbe established in 1855 (Blum).

The stock market crash of 1873 brought to an end the heavy financing of railways from the private sector. The state, which had largely financed railway construction before 1855, returned to fill the void. The railway programme of 1875 provided 23 million kronor of state credit for the construction of further railways and within a few years the state began buying back many private lines, particularly unprofitable ones, so that by 1913 it owned three-quarters of the system (Milward and Saul, 1977, 303).

The smaller systems built elsewhere in Europe posed fewer problems of finance. Dutch railways were financed by the state and local business interests together with supporting capital from France, Belgium and England. Swiss railways drew their finance largely from domestic entrepreneurs at first and later from the state and French bankers.

Railway investment dominated capital formation in many European countries in the second half of the nineteenth century. In Britain it constituted as much as a half of gross domestic fixed capital formation in the later 1840s.[1] The corresponding figure was 26 per cent (1875–9) for Germany (Fremdling, 1977, 585), 25–30 per cent (1896–1900) for Russia (Gatrell, 151) and 15 per cent (1875–84) for France (Caron, 1983, 37). In Spain the proportion was a remarkable 90 per cent (1856–64) (R. J. Harrison, 50). The implications of this predomination have caused confusion and contradiction among historians. Fremdling's identification of German railways as a Rostowian leading sector must be set beside Nadal and Tortella's pessimistic view of the impact of railways in Spain which, they believe, crowded out manufacturing investment. In Britain the magnitude of railway investment has been revised downwards and doubt thrown on the contention that it saved Britain from a serious investment shortfall in the 1830s and 1840s (Gourvish, 13–14). Caron maintains, however, that high investment rates made railways the 'engine of growth' in France, 1840–84.

The size of these investment rates would appear to lend weight to Rostow's idea of the railway as a leading sector. Indentifying dynamic growth through high investment rates is insufficient grounds, however, for denoting the railway a Rostowian leading sector; it must occupy an important position within the economy and possess those necessary linkages with other sectors. The linkages will be discussed later. Railways took up seven per cent of national income in Britain (1847), the same in France and 6.3 per cent in Sweden (Mitchell, 1964, 322; Hedin, 13). These constitute very high figures for investment rates in a single sector. In Germany, the railway's share of the capital stock rose from three per cent in the early 1850s to twelve per cent by the early 1880s by which time the railways had become both the most important and the fastest growing sector of the economy (Fremdling, 1977, 585). Fremdling, nonetheless, modifies the Rostowian approach by talking of a 'leading sector complex' consisting of railways and heavy industries in combination.

Spain had tried to induce industrialisation by providing social overhead capital and waiting for an entrepreneurial response; it did not come. Russia pursued a similar DBE policy but produced a more balanced form of development through railways, the heavy industries, protectionism and monetary stability. It was not so much that railway investment crowded out manufacturing in Spain but rather that the government only worked with a partial development policy. Since most Spanish railway investment came from the capital-rich countries, it seems unlikely that there was a trade-off between transport and manufacturing investment. The investment flowed into railways rather than industry because this is what the government encouraged and where the institutional channels existed. Gomez-Mendoza points out that given the depression of Spanish trade in the 1850s and the relative backwardness of the economy, foreign capital would not have penetrated Spain at all without the incentives of the 1855 Railway Law.

The problem of unbalanced investment in an undeveloped economy is also reflected in the Italian experience. Rather than consider the competition between railways and manufacturing industry for investment funds, Fenoaltea has accepted the predomination of railway capital as inevitable in the circumstances of mid-nineteenth-century Europe. Dismissing supply side constraints, he considers the degree to which railway investment induced manufacturing investment through its demands for the products of various industries. Fenoaltea concluded that, in terms of investment, the mature railway system had more to offer an economy's development than the waves of construction which preceded it. This questioned existing wisdom and hammered a further nail in the Rostowian coffin. There was no sudden impulsive leading sector which faded away after its initial stimulus had been imparted. Instead, the railways' importance grew as it matured. The Italian experience, however, differed significantly from that of many other countries: poor quality construction and geological problems made maintenance and improvement important considerations in Italy. Nationalisation in 1905 raised investment levels as the state set about modernising a system which had been neglected in recent years and gave orders to Italian firms. Improvements to the system in the late nineteenth century were often capital saving such as steel rails, electrical signals, lighting, gravity shunting operations and continuous brakes.

If Fenoaltea's conclusions cannot be accepted in full for other countries, there is nonetheless an increasing belief that railway investment came less in sudden waves of a few years at a time and was more incremental in nature. In Britain, the traditional emphasis upon the manias of the 1830s and 1840s now receives less attention. Reed doubts whether railway development was so influenced by the trade cycle and speculation and argues that railway building was more of a continuous and geographically rational process. A similar picture emerges in France and Germany where railway investment remained buoyant over three or four decades. Exclusive dependence upon private sector financing distinguished Britain's railways and so one might expect railway investment to have been more subject to cycles of economic activity than elsewhere. Though influenced by the level of economic activity, state investment was additionally contingent upon economic planning, the political climate and the government's political complexion.

The traditional argument held that there was a countercyclical relationship between railway development and the level of economic activity. Railways were planned during periods of boom when the outlook was good and there were many potential investors. Railway building was a lengthy process and therefore its investment had a long gestation period from planning to completion. Railways planned during a period of economic prosperity were often actually built several years later during a depression as the trade cycle moved inexorably from boom to slump. Railway investment stimulated economic activity during a depression and so reduced the amplitude of the trade cycle. In practice there are problems with this argument even for the private investors of Britain. Because of the inevitably speculative and even fraudulent character of many lines planned in a boom, only a fraction were actually built. Financing occurred throughout the period of construction, as shareholders were regularly called upon for part of their commitment. Thus investment was spread over phases of boom and slump. Often investors were unable to meet new calls in the middle of a depression, or the company, underestimating the cost, came to the shareholders for additional money. Nor is there any consistency in calculating the length of the gestation period,

Fremdling estimated it as eighteen months though much depended on the line. If railway building was countercyclical in Britain before 1850, as Gourvish maintains, it may be explained by the construction of many major lines. In the later years when many smaller lines were built, with a shorter gestation, or existing ones modified, there was less indication of an investment lag.

For France, Caron argues that 'fluctuations of investment by railway companies contributed to the amplitude of business cycles in the nineteenth century, particularly to the depression of 1847–52 and the boom of 1879–83' (Caron, 1983, 35). He identifies a railway investment cycle with peaks in 1847, 1856, 1862, 1884, 1900 and 1913. He then uses figures for railway construction to deduce a transport building cycle with peaks in 1847, 1856, 1862, 1884, 1900 and 1913 (Caron, 1983, 33–5). These figures coincide investment and construction peaks, suggesting that the French built their railways very quickly indeed! The investment peak years are often only marginally larger than neighbouring years. Building peaks might more accurately be interpreted as 1849, 1858, 1867, 1878, 1881, 1884, 1891 and 1902 indicating some evidence of a gestation period. Capital saving innovations and government intervention, particularly with the Freyçinet Plan, further complicate the picture. Essentially it is difficult to extract any clear or regular cycle in either investment or building, thus confirming the incremental nature of railway development.

Fremdling, (1977, 586) argues that 'as overall net investment declined in the late 1870s, railroad investment remained high, thus counteracting to some extent the unemployment-creating and growth-retarding effects of that decline'. Certainly railway investment reached a peak in the 1870s although *gewerbe* investment was also high in the first half of the decade. Of more importance than the timing of investment is the transport building cycle which shows expansion of a similar magnitude to previous and subsequent periods. Over the period as a whole, there is no consistent pro or counter cyclical trend in railway development. Fenoaltea, while continuing to play down the importance of the construction phase, concludes that 'railway investment somewhat amplified the largely synchronous cycle in industrial production' (Fenoaltea, 1983, 76) but presents no figures on investment nor alludes to a railway building or maintenance cycle.

Rather than try and relate railway development to an existing general cycle of economic activity it might be worthwhile to see how far railways created their own cycles. Given the huge importance of

railway building and investment, this sector may have created intervening cycles which complicated the assumed five- or ten-year
cyclical pattern. Italian railway nationalisation in 1905 created a
significant stimulus by releasing much private investment which found
its way into other and new fields such as hydroelectricity. The
Freyçinet Plan in France may have induced another out-of-pattern
cycle in France in the 1880s. Similar comments may be made of Spain
in the decade after the passage of the 1855 Railway Law. On a longer
term basis, it has been suggested that a railway Kondratiev cycle was
created in Germany in the third quarter of the century.

RAILWAYS AND INDUSTRIAL DEVELOPMENT

Railway building exerted a demand for the products of particular
industries most notably coal, iron and steel, engineering and building
materials. The extent of the impact depended upon the proportion of
that industry's output taken up by railway demand and the elasticity
of supply for those goods. If supply was relatively inelastic, the
railway stimulus could prove to be disadvantageous by creating
bottlenecks and price inflation. Alternatively, the benefits might be
lost to foreign producers with deflationary consequences for the
economy though much depended upon the government's tariff policy
and the exchange rate. Most countries relied initially upon Britain for
railway equipment, the subsequent rate of import substitution varied
significantly between countries.

Railway building exerted its greatest influence upon the iron industry. Mitchell calculated that 18 per cent of United Kingdom pig
output was consumed by the railways between 1844 and 1851 (1964,
325). Mitchell's contention that railway demand was of great importance to the iron industry in the middle and late 1840s has been
questioned by Hawke. Exports and technological advance, especially
Neilson's hot blast technique, have been seen as more significant
stimulants.[2] Much of the export demand for iron, however, was for
rails. On this basis, Gourvish (24) calculates that rails took up 39 per
cent of the output of the iron industry between 1844 and 1851 with a
smaller though still important figure of 22 per cent for 1856–70. The
stimulus appears to have been concentrated upon the iron industries
of South Wales, Cleveland and South Staffordshire. This is still an
under-estimation of the impact on the iron industry because it deals
only with the 'permanent way' (rails, chairs, bridges and so on) and

Table 5.3 Output of Major Industries Delivered to the Railways, 1830–1914 (%)

	Pig iron	Steel	Coal	Bricks	Wood	Engineering
England & Wales	39 (1844–51)	–	2–14 (1865)	30 (1840s)	–	20 (1830–50)
Spain	6.0 (1890–1914)	8.5 (1890–1914)	18–29 (1865–1914)	–	–	–
Germany	22–37 (1840–59)	–	3 (1860s)	–	–	–
France	–	12–18* (1845–85)	–	13–18[†] (1845–85)	1 (1875–84)	–
Italy	–	12–13[‡] (1861–1913)	–	16–23[§] (1861–1913)	–	5–11 (1861–1913)
Belgium	6 (1860–1913)	20–60[¶] (1890–1913)	10 (1913)	4–10 (1865–1913)	–	–
Russia	–	59* (1895–9)	–	–	–	–
Sweden	–	–	–	–	–	17–30 (1870s)

Notes: * Iron and steel;   [†] Building materials;   [‡] All ferrous materials;   [§] Construction materials;
[¶] Proportion of finished steel output used in rails and sleepers.

Sources: O'Brien, 1983, 16; Gatrell, 153; Holgersson and Nicander, 21; Laffut, 1983, 220–1; Gourvish, 24; Mitchell, 1964, 327–8.

not locomotives, rolling stock and related equipment which clearly demanded a great deal of iron.

The knock-on effect to coal meant that between six and ten per cent of coal output was used to produce iron for the railways in 1844–51 (Gourvish, 25). Historians have given little thought to the mature system's demand for coal which was probably greater than during its construction phase. In the late 1830s and 1840s railways took up about 20 per cent of the output of the engineering industry in the form of rolling stock and was largely responsible for the establishment of mechanical engineering. Many railway companies operated their own workshops and independent producers catered for overseas markets. Railways were also responsible for 25 to 30 per cent of brick production in the 1840s. In a general summing up, Gourvish correctly identifies the need for more attention to the impact of railways on coal, engineering, construction, the process of technological change and the level of exports. Greater attention is also required of the direct stimulus imparted to such industries by the completed network. Historians have looked at the mature system too much in terms of performance and organisation. Even if Fenoaltea exaggerates to suggest that the direct impact was greater at this stage, there remained an important direct stimulus through repair, improvement and, for coal at least, immediate consumption.

Whereas the collapse of building manias in Britain is seen as disturbing the iron companies who had originally benefited from the stimulus, in France historians have emphasised longer term benefits. Throughout the four decades after 1845, railway orders continued to take up between 12 and 18 per cent of the output of the iron industry. Railway output was particularly dominant in iron and steel products made by new processes which has led Caron to conclude that the perfecting of iron processes in the 1840s and 1850s, the diffusion of the Bessemer process in the 1860s and the Gilchrist Thomas method in the 1870s were all 'direct consequences of the pressure exerted by the railways on their suppliers' (Caron, 1983, 37). Rejecting Fogel's belief that railway innovations were 'restricted devices', Caron suggests that many important industrial innovations of the later nineteenth century, particularly in connection with steel and electricity, were a response to the problems railways had encountered. This may help to answer the railway and technology issue missing from British historiography. Whether the impact of railways on industrial technology was as great in Britain is open to some doubt; the conversion to steel rails, for example, was barely under way until the 1870s and therefore may have been of little importance in the adoption of the Bessemer process.

French railway companies were in a buyer's market with their suppliers which helped them force the pace of technological change and enabled them to secure good products at low prices through strong competition. Supply industries benefited from more rapid technological change and the greater efficiency which competition frequently bred. In addition, five-year railway contracts with the iron companies gave the latter some stability in their medium term planning. Against this, strong competition may have prevented individual firms from expanding sufficiently to achieve the large scale economies to be gained in the iron and steel industries. The criticism of smallness has been justifiably levelled against the French iron and steel industry.

Between 1845 and 1884, French railways took up 13–18 per cent of the output of building materials. High railway demand encouraged the development of standardised and easy to assemble iron bridges. Where French historiography is lacking is in the assessment of the direct impact of railway building on the coal industry. France, alone among the major economic powers, lacked exploited supplies of good coal and the demands of the railway, therefore, may have increased its import. England was the chief source of imported coal. With the reduction in duties on imports of English coal in 1853, 1861 and 1863, these imports rose from less than half a million tons in 1841–5 to 1.4 million in 1861–5 and three million by 1876–80; by the final date this represented 35 per cent of French imports (Caron, 1979, 99). It would be helpful to know the degree to which these rising imports were attributable to railway construction.

Though less quantified, railway demand stimulated the growth of mechanical engineering. Locomotives and rolling stock were provided by French manufactures from an early stage. These firms often grew out of companies in related fields who took advantage of the new opportunity. Iron foundries and forges were sometimes converted to locomotive production such as Gouin and Company which became the Société des Batignolles. Rolling stock producers often emerged from coach-building firms such as Desouches in Paris and Bonnefaud in Ivry.

In general French railways exerted a strong stimulus upon supply industries. The fact that the stimulus was received by nascent heavy industry in France rather than the more developed sectors of Britain and Belgium owed much to a tariff policy designed to keep out

Belgian rails and British locomotives. The German approach was somewhat different. Aware that the small and technologically backward German iron industry of the 1830s would have been quite incapable of producing rails and locomotives, initial railway supplies were met through imports. Although this had deflationary implications it enabled the Germans to surge ahead in building a railway system more cheaply and quickly than France with her tariffs.

The pace of import substitution enabled Germany to produce most of her railway materials before their volume became large enough to have seriously deleterious effects on the balance of trade. Zollverein tariff policy taxed imports of processed iron products while allowing pig iron imports duty free and thereby encouraged the domestic production of rails and rolling stock. As early as the 1840s iron processing plants were being established using British technology. Fremdling's excellent calculations demonstrate clearly the German success. Between 1843 and 1863 German industry's share of rails produced for Prussian railways rose from ten to 85 per cent and Britain's share slumped from 88 to 13 per cent. German industry produced just eight per cent of Prussia's locomotives in 1840 but 97 per cent by 1852. Over the same period Britain's share collapsed from 92 per cent to two per cent (Fremdling, 1983, 126, 128). In 1844, keen to further the process of import substitution and establish coke-using blast furnaces, the tariffs were revised to include a duty on pig iron. It was not until the following decade that domestic production of pig-iron rose significantly and even then highly competitive British pig continued to arrive in large amounts.

In the light of these facts it is not surprising to find that railways took up a large proportion of the output of the domestic iron industry. In the first half of the 1840s rails and rail fastenings took up 22 per cent of domestic iron production; a decade later this had risen to as high as 37 per cent. Even this large figure excludes railway iron demand for locomotives, wagons, buildings and bridges. Holtfrerich has calculated, somewhat optimistically, that railways took up as much as a half of the output of the iron industry in the early 1870s. The stimulus to expansion of the German iron industry thus seems to have been more significant than in France and possibly Britain. In contrast to Britain, Germany imported substantial amounts of pig iron over the middle decades of the nineteenth century and therefore the value-added benefits to German industry may have been less than in Britain. Although Germany did begin to export railway material later in the century it was never on the scale of Britain and the new effects on the Balance of Payments were probably negative. It is also worth remembering that railways supplied scrap to the iron industry and therefore the net flow was not as high as the figures suggest. However, the iron industry benefited from cheap scrap which reduced the reliance upon pig-iron imports.

Locomotive and rolling-stock production grew up around Berlin, as the centre of the rail system, in the 1840s. Borsig emerged as the main locomotive producer and Pflug as the principal maker of rolling stock. Borsig had established his engineering works as early as 1837 and, in contrast to the French, was trained in the engineering industry and had not begun in iron production or coach-making.

The huge railway demand for iron had knock-on effects for the coal industry. Given the large imports of pig-iron, the demand for coal may have been greater once import substitution had taken place and when the system was consuming coal directly in operation. The introduction of domestic coke blast furnaces in the 1850s coincided with the substantial growth in coal production particularly in the Ruhr. Holtfrerich has estimated that the railways took up one third of Ruhr coal production in the early 1870s although he may have overestimated the railways' importance by use of fixed input–output coefficients.

The centrality of railways to the industrialising German economy led Fremdling to conclude that 'the railway deserves to be labelled the hero of Germany's industrial revolution' (1983, 137). He argues that the strong interconnections between railways and heavy industry served as a 'leading sector complex' which propelled German industrialisation. He constructs a table of input–output relations between these industries. Unfortunately, there are many omissions from the table. Railways are shown as only offering output to coalmining and this was only significant from the 1860s. Similarly, railways only received significant inputs from iron processing, receipts from coal mining are minimal, and there are no figures for inputs from blast furnace production. The only other significant figures are some coal inputs into iron processing and substantial blast furnace inputs into iron processing both of which should come as no surprise! The most significant and interesting information in the table is the knowledge that 20 to 30 per cent of iron processing went into agriculture which appears to contradict his leading sector complex idea. Railway historians of other countries might think more carefully about the competing demands of agriculture for the products of the iron industry.

Import substitution of railway supplies was even more rapid in Belgium. Belgium was also to become a major exporter of railway equipment. The earliest rails and locomotives came from England but domestic production of both quickly commenced. In 1835 Seraing built the first locomotive in Belgium and within seven years was exporting 7000 tons of rails to Bavaria. By the end of 1839, 81 out of 123 locomotives operating on Belgian railways had been domestically built. By 1890 rails and sleepers represented 60 per cent of finished steel made in Belgium (Laffut, 1983, 209–12). The railways prompted organisational changes in the structure of the iron and steel and engineering industries. Originally founded as an iron works in the 1820s, Marcinelle was converted into the production of railway equipment and joint stock status was achieved in order to expand capacity. By 1845 it was producing 30 000 tons of rails (Milward and Saul, 1973, 444). The Providence ironworks converted to coke-smelting and much larger rolling mills were built at Couillet.

Laffut has calculated that the proportion of Belgian coal consumed by locomotives rose slowly to ten per cent by 1913 and concludes that 'the growth of the coal industry cannot be explained by the development of the railways' (Laffut, 1983, 213). His calculations exclude the large volume of coal consumed in the production of iron and steel for rails and locomotives and therefore may underrate the role of railways in the expansion of Belgian coal output from two to 14 million tons, 1830–70 (Mitchell, 1975, 360–2).

Between 1855 and 1872, all Spanish rails were imported, 62 per cent coming from Britain and 30 per cent from Belgium. From 1873 to 1890 only five per cent of rails came from Spanish industry as railway companies continued to take advantage of duty free imports. In fact with the replacement of iron by steel rails in this period the railway became a net supplier of pig-iron to the iron industry. In the 1890s the introduction of protection for the iron industry and a depreciating exchange rate enabled output to expand rapidly and by the following decade the domestic industry supplied 75 per cent of the demand for rails although this was only eight per cent of pig-iron and steel production (Gomez-Mendoza, 1983, 159). These low proportions suggest that the railway was of limited significance in the development of the iron industry. Thus it would appear unfair to blame ill-advised government policies, particularly on tariffs, for the absence of railway-led industrial development in the second half of the nineteenth century. A wide ranging industrialisation policy, similar to that in Russia, would have secured more balanced economic development in mid-century Spain. The iron industry was very small scale and backward in the 1850s and to have protected it with a tariff would simply have delayed, and increased the cost of, railway construction with little benefit for the iron industry. Gomez-Mendoza has calculated that to impose a prohibitive import duty on iron rails, to ensure domestic production, would have increased construction expenditure on permanent way material by around 32 per cent and have necessitated a twelve-fold expansion in capacity, 1855–64 (Gomez-Mendoza, 1983, 163). Nor is the railway stimulus to the heavy industries in France, Belgium and Germany simply explained by protectionism: finance was more readily available, entrepreneurs were more responsive to the new opportunities and the pre-rail heavy industries were more developed and in a position to expand.

Spanish coal imports increased for much of the second half of the nineteenth century. British coal was highly competitive because return cargoes of Spanish iron ore to Britain enabled lower freight rates to be charged. Thin, uneven seams made pithead prices higher in Spain and quality lower. Railway consumption of Spanish coal varied between regions and was greatest in mining areas and inland areas protected from imports by high overland carriage costs. Coastal lines mainly took British coal. In the mid-1890s Britain's share of the Spanish market fell with protectionism, falling exchange rates and improved organisation of the Spanish industry although 40 per cent of railway coal was still imported. The railway nonetheless consumed a quarter of Spanish coal output (Gomez-Mendoza, 1983, 159–60).

For Italy, Fenoaltea takes issue with Gerschenkron's contention that railways were a missed opportunity for Italian industrialisation in the second half of the nineteenth century. He argues that even with a systematic tariff policy, railways would have exerted insufficient stimulus upon industry to initiate a period of major economic development. Half of the cost of railway building was formed of basic construction work by manual labour. Quarrying and construction materials took up another 25 per cent, leaving only 17 per cent for mining and natural resources and eight per cent for engineering and metalworking. Moreover, it was the construction industries which were largely protected from foreign competition while imports of rails and rolling stock came in freely before the tariff-rises from the late 1870s. It was in the mature system that the heavy industries commonly associated with industrialising economies became more predominant: engineering and metalmaking took up 30 per cent of costs and mining 27 per cent (Fenoaltea, 1983, 66–7). Private and foreign-controlled concerns often looked abroad for industrial equipment: of 602 locomotives acquired by Alta Italia between 1861 and 1878, only 39 were built in Italy (Milward and Saul, 1977, 246). Only after nationalisation in 1905 did Italian industry gain the lion's share of industrial supplies to the railways. Exceptionally the steel industry experienced import substitution from the late nineteenth century. It was suggested earlier that Fenoaltea's elevation of the mature railway system may have reflected unique conditions in Italy. It may also be the case that more thought needs to be given to certain areas of the argument. The amount of scrap iron returned to the iron industry by railways requires consideration. Many improvements to the mature system were capital saving. Finally, average fuel consumption and its importance in operating costs were falling as a result of improved engine efficiency.

Russia faced the same problem as Spain and Italy: industrial backwardness made import substitution difficult. Most early locomotives were imported from Britain, France, Belgium, Germany and Austria along with mechanics to assemble and maintain them although the 1844 St Petersburg to Moscow line used Russian-built locomotives and rolling stock. What distinguished the Russian experience from that of Spain and Italy was the government's determination to encourage import substitution. The charters of many railway companies required a proportion of rails and rolling stock to come from domestic factories. At first this policy had little success because of lack of entrepreneurial response in the supply industries and the ability of railway companies to get round the clause aware that foreign equipment was both cheaper and of better quality. In the 1870s the incentives were increased: concessions were granted for the construction of rail-rolling plants though again the take-up rate was low. More successful were the subsidies to encourage factories to convert from iron to steel rail production. By 1898 there were 13 steel rail factories in Russia with an aggregate annual capacity of half a million tons. The state also founded a factory for the production of pig-iron for the railways (Westwood, 92).

Russian locomotive production was encouraged by tariff protection and generous government contracts to five designated suppliers. The government paid these firms high prices for locomotives and subsidised those produced for private railways. Output rose from 39 in 1870 to 251 locomotives in 1879. By the 1890s, of 5196 engines delivered to Russian railways, only 826 were imported. The direct feedbacks to the coal industry are less well known. Before import substitution gathered apace part of the stimulus went abroad. The continued use of wood fuel by locomotives to a late date (46 per cent in 1881) also suggests a minimal impact in the early years. As engines became more efficient, their average fuel consumption fell; thus between 1881 and 1890 fuel costs fell from ten to eight and a half per cent of operating costs (Westwood, 98).

The problems Russia experienced in encouraging domestic rail production reflected the stranglehold Britain, Germany and Belgium had in producing cheap iron rails with the assistance of coke-using blast furnaces. Bulgaria, Romania, Greece, Switzerland and Sweden all relied almost exclusively on imported rails, with detrimental consequences for the balance of payments. In the production of locomotives and rolling stock, however, even the more backward countries were able to achieve some import substitution. A more complex product, one which was expensive to export and was open to adaptation by engineering firms probably explains the difference. Though often, as in Moravia, foreign engineers were imported to provide the technological know-how. Exceptionally, in the Balkan countries hardly any locomotives or rolling stock were built. They imported locomotives from Austria, rolling stock from Belgium, France and Germany and rails from Britain. Although when the Barkleys built the Danube and the Black Sea line they established railway workshops and trained local men. For the Balkans railway building could become a liability, financed as it was by overseas loans and investments and exerting a strongly negative effect on the balance of payments. They gambled that a cheaper and more effective rail transport system would induce industrial development before their indebtedness became burdensome.

Sweden relied heavily on imported railway equipment more than half of which was imported during the production boom of the 1870s. This was twice the rate of penetration in the first decade of building up to 1866 (Holgersson and Nicander, 13–16). Sweden relied almost exclusively upon rail imports but was much stronger in the production of rolling stock. Seventeen per cent of the engineering industry's output fulfilled railway orders in the 1870s and in several years the figure was a high as 30 per cent. The effect was to encourage the growth of existing enterprises, such as Nydqvist and Holm, rather than attract new entrants into the industry. Since rolling stock was mostly built of wood, there was little knock-on effect to the iron and steel industry.

THE ECONOMIC EFFECTS OF RAILWAY TRANSPORT

Longer-term benefits were to be gained from the railways where they provided a cheaper, quicker, more regular and comprehensive service. In the early years, at least, their greater cost efficiency could not be automatically assumed especially where the motivation for building a railway was political or in the interests of foreign investors. The initial civil and mechanical engineering technology was primitive while fragmentation of the industry and inexperience operating large businesses also militated against early efficiency. Even where railways represented a significant improvement upon previous transport forms, its impact depended upon the elasticity of demand for rail transport. In Spain, for example, the railway undoubtedly improved the transport service considerably and yet to begin with this brought little benefit to Spanish industrial development because of the inability or unwillingness to exploit this new innovation. In some countries, however, geological considerations put a limit on the efficacy of pre-rail transport particularly where there were few navigable rivers and uneven terrain prevented the construction of canals.

The competitiveness of coastal shipping and a developed canal and road network suggested that the impact of railway services may have been limited in Britain. Although general figures are hard to come by it does seem that railways frequently offered lower rates and forced competitors to lower theirs. By 1845 railways had forced long-distance overland passenger fares down to nearly half their previous rate. A further 30–40 per cent fall had occurred by the late 1850s (Gourvish, 30). Nonetheless, road rates had already been declining in real terms in the later eighteenth century.

Thereafter there is less evidence of decline which may have been weakened by the buying out of many rivals, particularly canals, by the railway companies. Attempts were also made to buy out shipping lines although the coasting trade remained a formidable competitor for most of the nineteenth century. While the railways had initially forced down coastal shipping rates (Channon), later in the century it became coasting's turn to oppose railway monopoly. In Scotland railways were generally quicker and more regular but not always cheaper. Coastal shipping matched rail rates here until the rate changes of the 1890s and were sometimes preferred for their directness and proximity to town centres (Vamplew, 1971–2, 134). From the 1870s there was increasing resentment in business circles against high railway rates and a feeling that the system should serve the

Table 5.4   Freight and Passenger Rates on European Railways, 1830–1913

Country	Freight rate		Passenger rate	
Germany	1840	16.9		
	1880	4.4		
	1913	3.6		
	(pfennigs per ton/km)			
Britain	1830	1.67	1830	2.5
	1865	1.2	1870	1.5
	(pence per ton/mile)		(pence per mile)	
France	1870	6	1840	7
	1908	4	1913	3.4
	(centimes per ton/km)		(centimes per km)	
Belgium	1850	10.3	1845	5.25
	1913	3.6	1913	1.80
	(centimes per ton/km)		(centimes per km)	
Russia			1860	1.17
			1905	0.84
			(kopeks per km on)	
			long hauls)	

Sources: Fremdling, 1983, 132; Gourvish, 29–30; Caron, 1983, 45; Laffut, 1983, 215–16; Westwood, 58, 148.

national economic interest. The failure of the railways to respond to the compromise of the 1888 Railway and Canal Traffic Act led to a further measure in 1894 which curtailed their rates more seriously.

In spite of the fact that most early railways were built for the carriage of freight, particularly coal, the initial impact was strongest on passenger travel where rates fell further in the first few decades and receipts were greater until 1850 (Gourvish, 26). The introduction of steam locomotives, improvements in organisation derived from the creation of the railway clearing house, the elimination of the multi-user system and subsequent company amalgamations all made railways more serious competitors for canals and shipping and in-creased the volume of freight traffic.

It was not until the 1860s that rail traffic took up a significant share of the London coal trade. During the middle of the nineteenth century, productivity in the coasting trade was growing at least as quickly as in the railways. Nor was this due simply to the stimulus of rail competition since the improvement had begun at least a century earlier (Ville, 1986). The huge amount of capital and degree of business interest vested in the coastal coal trade made it inevitable that any transition to railways would be a lengthy process. The rapid growth in the demand for coal in the mid-nineteenth century also dulled competition between railways and shipping. Some railways were built to complement the coasting trade such as the Durham and Sunderland Railway (1836) which improved the supply of coal from outlying mines to the ports of the north-east.

In most cases railways reinforced existing settlement patterns and industrial locations in Britain rather than creating new ones. The exceptions include South Wales (anthracite and iron), South Yorkshire (coal) and Northamptonshire (iron ore). Towns like Middlesbrough and Barrow grew up largely as the consequence of railway communications while some settlements became purely railway towns (Crewe, Swindon) because of their centrality to the system. The process of suburbanisation, encouraged by the roads in the eighteenth century, was reinforced by the railways particularly where cheap workmen's trains were introduced as a result of parliamentary legislation. While Dyos was probably wrong to see the railways as critical in changing the anatomy of mid-Victorian towns they clearly made many people homeless; possibly 20 000 in the construction of Euston terminus (Dyos, 10–12). The structure of trade and the flow of traffic was affected: retailing was extended and new traffic in perishable goods such as meat, milk, fish and vegetables appeared. Communications such as the telegraph, postal services and newspapers were all improved.

Transport rates in France fell before and during the railway age. The decline was particularly sharp during the railway age and sufficient to exert a major influence on the development of the market. The cost per ton kilometre of freight fell from 23–28 centimes before the 1840s to six in the 1870s and four by 1908 (Caron, 1983, 45). Passenger fares fell from 11–16 centimes before the 1840s to seven by the 1840s, five by 1883 and three by 1913. Where road and rail came into competition the latter was clearly the winner. In the 1840s the railway could complete the journey between Vierzon and Orleans with a 36–60 per cent cost saving and 60–93 per cent time saving over road haulage, depending on whether ordinary, accelerated or express rate was used (Price, 1981, 21). The concessions system enabled the government to exert pressure for lower and more uniform rates and avoided the type of conflict with the industry that occurred in late nineteenth-century Britain. Tariffs varied between regions according to the nature of the rail network and the degree of market control exercised by the companies. Paris, at the centre of the network and with intense competition here, was clearly the major beneficiary. The early emergence of six dominant regional companies suggests that tariffs may have suffered from monopoly control in certain areas. On the Midi network, for example, rates were generally regarded as inflated by the company's control of the Canal du Midi which prevented alternative rail–canal competition. In most parts, however, a strong and independent waterway system served as important competition.

Productivity in railways grew steadily rather than dramatically by about two per cent per annum during 1851–73 and 1887–1914, coinciding with the decline in rates (Caron, 1983, 40). Between these dates productivity fell with the construction of secondary lines. As in Britain most of the early improvement was due to better utilisation and the latter to technological developments such as continuous brakes and steel rails. Although other transport modes made progress during this period they were unable to match the railway whose share of volumes moved rose from 11 per cent in 1851 to 73 per cent by 1913 (Caron, 1979, 32).

France was late to develop her domestic supplies of coal. Instead, she had to import it at great expense. Belgian pithead coal prices were eight francs per tonne in 1838; by the time coal reached the Haute-Marne, its furthest penetration into France, the price had risen to 88 francs in spite of waterway improvements (Price, 1981, 122). Thus many of the earliest railways were designed to reduce the cost of coal transport and to stimulate domestic production. Coal prices began to drop sharply, halving, for example, at Marseilles after rail links had been established. Coal output grew from three million tons in the early 1840s to 15 million three decades later (Price, 1981, 125). The coming of the railway to Dijon in 1851, for example, facilitated the use of coal both domestically and in a wide range of industries.

The impact of railways on the supply of food can be seen by the narrowing of price differentials between producing and consuming areas. Between 1859 and 1878 differences in corn prices between nine French regions fell from 4.6 francs to 1.7 francs. The decline did not begin with the railway era; between 1817 and 1847 the differential had already fallen from 45 to 20 francs in the light of improvements in the waterways and roads (Price, 1981, 72). Railways also mitigated the effects of harvest failures; better rail transport enabled the poor harvests of 1853 and 1855 to be replenished with imports totalling three or four times the maximum recorded figure prior to the advent of the railways. By 1861 two-thirds of total cereal consumption was transported by the six main railway companies. The near monopoly of agricultural producers in the vicinity of major towns and cities was broken by the railway. The supply area to Paris, for example, rose from 50 to 250 km although some perishable goods continued to travel poorly over long distances before the introduction of refrigeration in the 1890s (Price, 1981, 80). The line to Dijon improved the supply of fish and meat to the town while also providing a much wider market for local Burgundy wine (Laurent). Railways also increased the supply of fertilisers, particularly imports of Chilean nitrates and Peruvian guano which helped to bring into cultivation poor soils in Britanny, the Massif Central and the Vosges. Elsewhere railways influenced the development of the vineyards of Languedoc, stock-raising in Thierache and Charentes, fishing off Boulogne and, more generally, the production of sugar, oil, iron and steel in northern and eastern France and mechanical and food processing industries around Paris.

Retailing in France received a boost from the railways. Parisian department stores, such as Bon Marché (1855), Printemps (1865) and Galeries Lafayette (1895), resulted from the greater flow of freight and passengers which passed through the hub of the rail network. Cheap chain-stores likewise benefited: by 1914 Docks Remois and Comptoirs Français between them owned over 500 stores (Caron, 1979, 92). Government fiscal policy and the growth of specialist luxury and technical trades, however, prevented the entire elimination of the small shopkeepers.

Price has concluded that the railways transformed the nineteenth-century French economy out of its backward eighteenth-century structure. He concerns himself particularly with the price-reducing and market-widening effects it had on agriculture. Although clearly important to French economic development, especially agriculture, Price may have overstated the impact of the railways. One must remember that food supplies were already rising, their prices falling and transport costs lowering before the advent of the railways. French road haulage, like British coasting, was experiencing rising productivity before the railway age. His assessment of agriculture ignores developments in that sector independent of the railway including land clearance, drainage, liming and the general improvement of agrarian knowledge with the establishment of agricultural colleges, more scientific research and higher rural literacy rates.

Caron, while agreeing that the railways exerted a stronger economic impact in France than Britain, points to negative as well as positive aspects particularly the de-industrialisation it caused in some areas. In the 1840s and 1850s new and traditional structures existed alongside each other in a dualist economy. In the following decades, with demand growing more slowly and the competitive edge of railways increasing, inter-regional competition led to the decline of some markets, industries and areas. The ancient markets of Rouen and Mulhouse declined as did the textile industry of Limousin, metallurgy in Poitou and iron and steel in Berry.

Rail rates fell substantially in Belgium over the course of the second half of the nineteenth century: passenger fares from 5.25 to 1.80 centimes per kilometre and freight rates from 10.30 to 3.60 centimes per ton-kilometre. The government encouraged low rates and private companies offered special rates such as season tickets and lower charges for longer distances. With the demand for rail transport price-elastic these policies ensured a rapid growth in rail output of six and seven per cent per annum for freight and passenger traffic. Railways offered much the fastest service, reaching 60 km per hour in the 1830s compared with only 10 km for roads. Helped by the flat terrain, canals operated at a similar cost per ton mile to railways which was half that of road haulage, making them competitive in the carriage of heavy raw materials, where speed was less important (Laffut, 1983, 220).

The output of canals continued to grow through the second half of the nineteenth century by two to three per cent per annum helped by rising transport demand. In some areas the canals complemented the railway and so improved its effectiveness and contributed to the resultant increase in demand for transport services. Where the two networks came into competition, such as between Brussels and Antwerp, the canal sometimes survived by reducing its rates and concentrating on bulky goods. The construction of waterways, however, declined in the second half of the century and the density of goods traffic on the canals, though rising, was soon surpassed by that on the railways.

Laffut points out that freight traffic as a whole grew more rapidly than industrial production in the second half of the nineteenth century suggesting transport played an important role in widening markets and stimulating commercial exchange. In fact Belgian historians have written little about the impact of railway services upon the country's economic development. It seems likely that Belgium's early and dense network helped the development of her strong coal, iron and steel industries together with the growth of European transit trade through the country.

In Germany the state both encouraged rate reductions with special tariffs for particular cargoes and stood in the way of further general rate falls by refusing to pass on productivity gains. Rail freights fell from 17 pfennigs per ton/km in 1840 to four pfennigs in 1880 as a result of productivity gains. The rates were a substantial saving on the pre-rail carting rates of around 40 pfennigs (Fremdling, 1983, 132). In the subsequent period up to the First World War productivity continued to grow but the Prussian state, which owned much of the system, held on to the gains as a source of state revenue so that rates fell by less than one pfennig. So heavily did the Prussian state budget depend upon railway revenues as a substitute tax that between 1890 and 1904 their net contribution exceeded tax revenues. The Prussian state bank invested much of this railway surplus with the result that in deficit years it could effectively deficit finance by drawing on these reserves. This process was formalised in 1903 by the establishment of a special fund (*Ausgleichsfond*) by which railway surpluses could be transferred between good and bad years for budgetary purposes.

As in Britain, the early years were dominated by the carriage of low volumes of high value freight and the superiority of passenger revenues. By the 1870s, though, railway output began to grow significantly. Between 1830 and 1870 railway traffic grew much more quickly than other forms of transport. Already by the 1840s traffic on the Rhine was less than half that carried by railways and that on the Elbe had dropped to a third of its level of the previous decade. By the 1880s, as we saw in Chapter 3, river traffic began to revive and canal construction commenced on a large scale. Thenceforth to 1913 the output of the waterways grew at a similar rate to that of the railways, offering feasible competition in the carriage of the bulky products of the heavy industries.

Fremdling believes that the successful provision of extra transport by the railways encouraged industrial demand for transport as the market began to widen. Therefore the construction of canals became viable either in competition with railways or to complement them. Some railways were designed to connect with existing waterways. Steitz explains how the Cologne–Minden railway linked up the Rhine and Weser and thereby expanded the Ruhr coal market and, with the Cologne–Antwerp, circumvented Holland's control of the trade of the Rhine. Fremdling supports the importance of railways by arguing that the critical period was 1830–70 when railways were the dominant mode of transport and canal construction was not yet a viable alternative. It is true that this was the major period of price falls but, on the other hand, railway output in 1870 was less than 6000 million ton-kilometres and thus under ten per cent of the 1913 figure (Fremdling, 1983, 132).

Railways offered important market benefits to the coal industry. Before 1840 most German coal was sold only in the locality of its production because of the high cost of transport. Carting rates of 40 pfennigs per ton-kilometre meant that the price of coal would double within 14 kilometres overland. Even early rail rates caused its price to double every 38 to 50 km (Fremdling, 1983, 133). The result was that cheaper British coal dominated German markets because of its lower pithead price and reduced shipping rates from two-way trading in the North Sea and the Baltic. When British coal arrived at North German ports it could be moved to inland markets such as Berlin along the Rhine and the Elbe.

In the 1850s the reduced '*einpfennigtarif*' was introduced to enable Upper Silesian coal to compete with that of Britain on the Berlin market. The Upper Silesian Railway Company was obliged to maintain this rate under pressure from the Prussian Minister of Trade who had the right to run state trains on the network under the 1838 legislation. Railway companies were also encouraged to cut their rates through the realisation that demand was highly price-elastic. The consequence of the '*einpfennigtarif*' was dramatic: British coal's share of sales on the Berlin market collapsed from 100 per cent in 1846 to 21 per cent by 1865 (Fremdling, 1983, 135). In contrast, the Upper Silesian share rose from nothing in 1846 to 54 per cent in 1865. British coal remained more competitive in the coastal areas and continued to supply Hamburg, for example, up to the First World War. As well as changing the competitive balance in established coal markets the railways also opened up new inland markets particularly in the mountainous regions of middle and southern Germany where canal construction was not feasible. Railways similarly lowered the cost of coal and iron ore carried to iron foundries and engineering works.

The textile industry and trade of Berlin was a major beneficiary of the coming of the railway. Berlin's position at the centre of the railway system and the various benefits this brought to local industry served to create a wealthy industrial middle class. This brought with it a demand for high-value clothing such as shawls and frock-coats. Good rail links also widened the market for Berlin textiles reaching many German states but also competing with French styles in other European countries from The Netherlands to Poland. It also helped to break down localised styles and create standard fashions from which Berlin, as the centre of the rail network, stood to be the main supplier. Already by the 1840s large textile firms such as Herzog and Gerson were emerging, yielding large scale economies in the expanded market and by the following decade American sewing machines were widely used. The impact of railways on agricultural markets appears more limited. A study of the Prussian grain trade between 1821 and 1865 found little evidence of regional price convergence (Fremdling and Hohorst).

For Spain, Gomez-Mendoza has estimated that railways cut transport costs by a factor of nine and largely removed its seasonality (1983, 165). His conclusions reaffirm Ringrose's argument that the railways lifted the Spanish economy out of its eighteenth-century structure and brought industrialisation to the country. It has already been seen in Chapter 2 that the inadequacy of transport facilities acted as a bottleneck on Spanish economic development before 1850. With the coming of the railway, markets widened and increasing proportions of consumption were carried by rail. Between 1881 and 1913 the share of the domestic consumption of grain carried by rail increased from 25 to 47 per cent, that of flour from 16 to 34 per cent, of wine from 10 to 65 per cent (1886–1913) and of coal from 14 to 46 per cent (1882–1909) (Gomez-Mendoza, 1983, 165). Railways opened up new coalfields and extended the trade of the mines of central Spain.

Gomez-Mendoza rejects the idea that the benefits of the railway were negated by serving the interests of foreign investors. It is true that exports of metallic ores, in which foreign investment was heavy, rose sharply but it took up only a small proportion of railway transport, nor was mineral traffic always destined for the ports. This is not surprising since most ore deposits were to be found in the coastal regions. The growth of ore exports can be explained by rising world demand. By taking this line, however, Gomez-Mendoza is in danger of supporting the pessimists' argument that railways played little role in Spanish economic expansion in the later years of the century, which was based upon the foreign trade of the coastal cities backed by protectionism. With the construction of railways ahead of industrialisation, they relied heavily upon the transport of raw materials and agricultural produce. Metallic ores were of little importance to the railway while coal and grain suffered from increased import penetration from Britain and America respectively. In Barcelona, the proportion of wheat brought from other parts of Spain by rail fell from 60 to 11 per cent, 1884–6, as a result of American competition (R. J. Harrison, 33).

In Russia the government policy of guaranteeing minimum investor returns in private railway companies served to depress the level of rates as firms, regardless of losses, sought to preserve their market position by rate-cutting. Varying rates between companies made for a chaotic structure and left the shipper with little realistic idea of transportation costs over long distances. Therefore, in the 1880s the government rationalised the rate structure and fixed minimum rather than maximum rates in order to minimise the financial burden to the state. A carefully conceived tariff structure was introduced over the course of the next ten years which formed part of the state's industrialisation policy. Low rail-tariffs were offered on particular routes to encourage the export of grain, butter and sugar and thus build up positive trading balances and higher gold reserves with which to put the rouble on the gold standard. Lower unit rates were charged on long than on short hauls in order to encourage inter-regional trade and to promote the economic development of Siberia. Sometimes this worked in the opposite direction. In the textile industry it led to raw cotton being transported to factories in European Russia rather than being manufactured in Central Asia where it was grown. The Cheliabinsk basing point was effected to ensure that Siberian peasants exported their produce rather than selling it to the towns and cities of European Russia in competition with farmers from the region. Freight going through Cheliabinsk had to begin a new tariff rate at this point. Therefore, Siberian grain travelling west through Cheliabinsk was charged two short-haul tariffs rather than one long-haul which carried a lower unitary rate.

Several important studies have emphasised the impact of Russian railways upon market integration. Metzer looked at the inter-regional market for rye and wheat and discovered that 83 per cent of the decline in the price differential between Odessa and St Petersburg in the second half of the nineteenth century was due to 'railroad-induced decline in transportation costs' (1974, 548). He concluded that railways promoted regional specialisation, increased the proportion of output marketed and reduced uncertainty by better arbitrage. White goes further in arguing that railways also reduced periodic violent price fluctuations which minimised entrepreneurial risk and therefore encouraged subsistence farmers to produce for the market.

Kelly found similar railway-induced differential reductions for oil and grain in the two decades leading up to the First World War. Kelly, however, attributed this benefit to the government's effective subsidising of many tariffs rather than the innate economic advantages of the railway. This distinction may help us to understand why the railway's market benefits were more immediate in some countries than others. Russia and Germany benefited from the tariff manipulation of their governments, an area ignored by Spanish and Italian administrations.

Russian railways also differed from Spain's in terms of demand. While Spanish railways found insufficient freight to be economic and so ran half empty, Russian railways could not keep pace with demand. The result was considerable delays and very long delivery times which were costly in terms of the deterioration of goods and the tying up of inventory capital. In 1873 grain bound for export was piling up at Odessa and decaying for lack of sufficient transport. Similar problems were experienced in coal carriage along the Donetz railway. The state attempted to improve organisation; the establishment of through trains between the lines of different companies was made obligatory in 1879 and the Kharkov coal committee was to regulate coal movements. Delays remained into the twentieth century despite the establishment of the Central and Raion Committees to improve the planning and coordination of shipments. However, some of the major causes of inefficiency remained, notably under-investment and poor management together with extreme weather conditions and the seasonal concentration of agricultural produce.

The benefits of Russian railways were limited to particular products and areas. In the early years agricultural goods were mainly carried on the railways: grain took up 42 per cent of shipments in 1875 but only 20 per cent by 1897 as coal, oil and iron and steel began to figure more prominently (Westwood, 78). By 1913 coal, cereals and timber were the most important shipments in terms of weight. The geographical spread of freight movements was uneven, with a concentration in the mining and metallurgy regions of the south while Siberia and the Urals took only small proportions of railway traffic.

Railway services offered limited benefits to the Italian economy. Rail links from the Upper Po Valley to the sea helped the development of the industrial triangle of Turin, Milan and Genoa but elsewhere in the country the railway did little to unify the domestic market or change patterns of production. The system was significantly under-utilised and as late as 1911 nearly 30 per cent of railway traffic was imports of coal, cereal, phosphates, raw cotton and lumber (Fenoaltea, 1983, 77). Railways moved building materials, non-metallic ores and citrus fruit to the coast for export. Internal shipments were limited to a narrow range of basic commodities such as lime, cement and chemical fertilisers. The concentration of industry in the north-east and the development of vertically integrated plants suggested a limited need for transport. It might be argued, alternatively, that industry developed in this manner because of high transport costs. The low degree of inter-regional trade meant that many local traditional economies survived, particularly in the south where more modern centres were concentrated round the coast because transport costs were lower by sea.

The main problem of Italian railways was their high freight rates which were the consequence of public policies and high costs. The state regulated these rates and its right to a share in railway revenues encouraged it to set charges well in excess of marginal costs. In 1875, for example, operating revenues were typically 60 per cent above current costs. This gradually fell to 40 per cent by 1898 and 20 per cent by 1911 but was mainly due to rising costs rather than a more enlightened rate-policy. At the same time the state offered subsidies to companies prepared to build railways which led Fenoaltea to conclude that 'this policy of simultaneously encouraging the construction of railways and discouraging their use was self-contradictory and absurd' (1983, 87–8). If demand was reasonably elastic rate-reductions would have led to revenue gains and improved market integration. Nor was there much attempt to follow the Russian and German principle of offering discriminating rates on particular routes.

These high rates were set in excess of costs which themselves were two-thirds higher than in France and Germany. High fuel costs, difficult terrain, diseconomies, and low load factors all made for high costs. The need to import coal for use on the railways meant unit costs two or three times those of Germany. Irregular terrain meant a high incidence of curves and gradients and therefore high fuel consumption, slow speeds, double-headed trains and rapid capital depreciation. Poor utilisation meant that the burden of fixed costs, including administration, had to be borne by a low level of output. Low load factors resulted from uneven traffic movements; trains carrying bulk imports from the ports had few return cargoes. Moreover, passenger travel, notorious for low load factors, featured prominently.

Although political and military considerations strongly influenced the building of railways in the Balkan countries, economic benefits sometimes ensued. Jensen and Rosegger believe that the railways played an important part in the economic modernisation of the peninsula through market integration and the attraction of Western entrepreneurs. The growth of railway traffic in the Lower Danube Basin and the expansion of shipping, especially at the port of Constanta, opened up the area to western merchants seeking grain, cattle, tobacco, forest products and, later, petrol. The competition of rail helped to break the Austrian steamboat monopoly on the Danube and bring down rates. The Danube Commission was stimulated to improve the river's navigability for ocean-going vessels and therefore compete with the railway which had to tranship goods at coastal ports. Significantly, the 1857 concession for the building of the Danube and Black Sea railway included a stipulation that the promoters also had to finance improvements to the port of Constanta. As a result the port grew from a small settlement of 40 dwellings in 1856 to a population of 5000 by 1878 (Jensen and Rosegger, 125). The 1897 Sofia–Varna line facilitated grain exports through the ports of Varna and Ruse together with sales in the urban market of Sofia. Elsewhere agrarian localism was curtailed and specialist production for the market stimulated. The railway encouraged the establishment of various industrial and extractive enterprises. In Serbia the completion of the Paraćin to Zaječar railway in 1912 linked the valleys of Morava and Timok and helped the development of the rich copper mines of Bor and Vrska Cuka. Nonetheless, the peninsula remained the most backward area of Europe beyond the First World War. The benefits of the railways were sporadic and scattered rather than comprehensive and unifying of whole economies.

THE SOCIAL SAVING CONTROVERSY

One aspect of the economic impact of the railways has generated a remarkable and disproportionate amount of historical discussion. This concerns the benefits railways offered to economic growth as a superior form of transport to previous modes. If railways were cheaper, quicker and more regular than other forms of transport they would have enabled resource reallocation and a growth in national income. Historians and economists have attempted to calculate this railway 'social saving'. In order to do this a counterfactual model is

Table 5.5   Social Savings of Railway Freight Traffic, 1848–1912

Country	Years	SS as % of GNP
England and Wales	1865	4.1
England and Wales	1890	11.0
Russia	1907	4.6
France	1872	5.8
Germany	1890s	5.0
Spain	1878	11.9
Spain	1912	23.0
Belgium	1865	2.5
Belgium	1912	4.5
Netherlands	1848–53	0.1

Sources: O'Brien, 1983, 10; Hawke, 1970, 196; Metzer, 1976, 90; Caron, 1983, 44; Fremdling, 1983, 139; Gomez-Mendoza, 1983, 151, 154; Laffut, 1983, 221; De Vries, 214.

set up to establish what would have been the extra costs of carrying goods by other forms of transport if the railways did not exist. Hawke calculated how much it would have cost to carry all railway goods by other forms of transport in Britain in 1865 if the railways did not exist or were closed down during that year. He concluded that railway carriage of freight had caused a four per cent growth in national income.

The social saving concept can be used to measure the impact of any innovation upon economic growth. Its application in railway history came to prominence in America in the early 1960s at a time when the 'new economic history', with its stress upon economic theory and econometrics, was beginning to take root. Fogel, in an article of 1962 and a book published two years later entitled, *Railroads and American Economic Growth*, used the social saving concept to question the central importance of railways to American economic growth in the nineteenth century. Rostow had asserted that railways were 'historically the most powerful single initiator of take-offs' (1960, 302) while Jenks (1944) had emphasised railways' importance to American economic development. Fogel, together with Fishlow whose work on railways in the ante-bellum American economy appeared in 1965, calculated that railways achieved a saving in the region of four to six per cent of national income and concluded that the central role attributed to this innovation by previous generations of historians could, on closer inspection, no longer be justified (1964). American waterways, they argued, could have performed a similar service at comparable cost.

Fogel and Fishlow's work stimulated an intense debate among economic historians over the next decade and a half. McClelland and Schreiber, for example, challenged the figures he used for waterway rates. While Gunderson drew attention to the limited scope of the social saving idea and criticised it as 'a tool of only static analysis' (218). At length, in 1979, Fogel mounted a determined defence of his original methods and conclusions in a lengthy article in the *Journal of Economic History*. While defending himself against some of the more rash criticisms of the previous fifteen years he retreated significantly from the bold assertions of the early sixties. The social saving concept, he conceded, does not deal with the railways' impact on industrial location, technological change, industrial inputs or production. He admitted that waterway rates required further research and that the railways were indispensable in areas where waterways were not a feasible alternative.

The American debate encouraged European historians to reassess the impact of the railways in other countries and to apply the social saving methodology. The result has been a bewildering mix of methods, conclusions and interpretations. Hawke produced a social saving figure for England and Wales barely larger than Fogel and Fishlow's for the United States and yet chose to view this as a reaffirmation of the railways' importance. Gomez-Mendoza derived a much larger figure for Spain and yet remained highly sceptical about the interpretation of extant statistics (1983). White used the example of Russian grain movements in the 1870s to demonstrate the reasons why Fogel underestimated the true size of the social saving (1976).

The major criticisms of the social saving idea remain largely unrefuted. Both the methodology and the handling of evidence contain significant weaknesses. If railways had not been introduced other transport services would have developed in a different manner. The provision of services would have been greater in some areas where the demand for transport became more pressing. Elsewhere some canals or roads emerged only because of the opportunities presented by the railways. Industrial location would have developed differently according to the services waterways and roads could offer. Transport prices would also have been different without the railways; railway competition brought down freight rates on many of the roads and canals which survived into the later nineteenth century. In Britain it was seen that coasting rates came down sharply with the coming of the railway. On the other hand, the elimination of the canal in many areas prevented the increased efficiency which often accompanies the maturity of a technology. The analysis also assumes zero price-elasticity. If freight rates had been higher in the absence of railways, the demand for transport would certainly have fallen.

Even if it were possible to derive an accurate financial figure for social saving, its automatic expression as a proportionate saving in national income is open to doubt. As Fishlow concedes, the social saving concept cannot include the benefits of speed, seasonality and flexibility brought by the railway because these variables do not form part of national income calculations. The importance of these service improvements to European economies has already been emphasised. The social saving model seems incapable of absorbing many secondary or external effects of railway transport. Railways set off reverberating effects in at least several of the heavy industries and so further increased national income. Similarly, the cost savings, rather than boosting national income, could be lost overseas through increased import penetration. Much also depends upon what happened to those resources reallocated through more cost effective transport; the effect will be limited if former road carriers become unemployed as was the case in Spain.

Many of the statistical pitfalls behind the model are illustrated by attempts to calculate a social saving for Spanish railways. In 1878 in the absence of railways, waterways could serve as a substitute in only one per cent of journeys. Geology and climate militated against an inland waterways system in Spain. Coastal shipping could substitute for just nine per cent. Legal restrictions together with the poor state of Spanish harbours and the domination of foreign lines added to the natural limitations on the country's coastal trade. This left road haulage to substitute for 90 per cent of railway traffic. Road haulage in Spain lay with professional hauliers and part-time seasonal peasant carriers. Many carriers operated over short hauls so it is difficult to imagine how they would have substituted for the railways. Moreover, while many peasant carriers might have been able to take on the extra transport demand in winter, at harvest time there would have been a substantial opportunity cost of transferring labour from agriculture to transport in lost grain output. A further loss would have been in the agricultural output required to feed the additional draught animals. Gomez-Mendoza calculates that 30 per cent of wheat acreage would have been required for this purpose. He also suggests that it would have been more effective to have concentrated the extra transport demand into non-harvest periods as far as possible, though here there would be an extra cost of inventory stock. In general much depends upon how much of the extra demand is absorbed by the professional hauliers and by the peasant carriers. The complexities and alternative scenarios seem interminable and in the end Gomez-Mendoza settles uneasily for an intermediate solution which assumes that professional carriers take up the extra demand in the busy agricultural seasons and compete with the peasant carriers at other times (1983, 149–57).

Aldcroft (1971–2) has criticised Hawke's social saving calculation for Britain. Hawke does not examine the economic effects of faster rail travel, the carriage of mail and the impact of railways on urban and social development. He criticises Hawke's material as consisting of 'very slender evidence' and 'fragmentary scraps of data'. The assumption of constant costs over time and the difficulty of calculating marginal cost in the nineteenth century are also highlighted. The burden of such problems convinced Fenoaltea of the need to abandon the social saving approach (1983). Instead, he assessed the economic impact of Italian railway services in terms of market integration (1983).

All these criticisms suggest that to compare the alternative transport services offered by railways and by roads and canals in, say, 1865, achieves simply that and nothing else. To deduce from those figures how much national income benefited from railways in 1865 would be to ignore the extent of the railway's responsibility for the development of that economic structure in the first place. Such was the all-pervasive influence of the railways that we can never accurately answer the question, how rapidly would the economy have grown without a railway system? The control experiment, the essential resort of the pure scientist, can never be available to the historian.

Ultimately, therefore, all the social saving debate can have discussed with any accuracy was the relative efficiency of different modes of transport in particular years. Even this must suffer from its static quality, the insufficiency of extant data and the fact that the railway did not compete over all routes either because the relationship was one of complementarity or that the terrain was unsuitable or simply that the competition had been eliminated. Although the new economic historians have put firmly to rest some of the more ridiculous railway superlatives of the Jenks generation one is bound to bemoan the excessive concentration of academic effort into disputing this specific issue when much of the railways' importance remains underinvestigated. The ultimate futility of the social saving debate is summed up in the words of its initiator who surely could not have imagined what was to follow his original work:

> Certainly the new economic history has done little to change our perception of the sequence of events that constitute the history of modern transportation. Nor has it eroded the proposition that the collective impact of advances in transportation technology during the nineteenth century was of such a magnitude as to warrant the title of a 'transportation revolution'. (Fogel, 1979, 48).

Notes

1. P. Deane, 'New estimates of Gross National Product for the United Kingdom, 1830–1914', *Review of Income and Wealth* 14, 1968; C. H. Feinstein, 'Capital formation in Great Britain', in P. Mathias and M. M. Postan (eds) *The Cambridge Economic History of Europe* VII(1), Cambridge, 1978.
2. C. K. Hyde, *Technological Change and the British Iron Industry, 1700–1870*, Princeton, 1977.

6 The Motor Vehicle Industry

This chapter examines the origins, development and economic impact of the motor vehicle up to the early 1920s. Beyond these pioneering days the industry grew in importance and its structure was significantly altered. However, many modern features of the industry such as mass production, oligopoly, overseas investment and marketing policies found their origins in the pre-1918 period. In some respects the car industry throws wider light upon the comparative economic performances of European countries. France's volume leadership of the European vehicle industry casts doubt upon her alleged economic retardation at the end of the nineteenth century, while the steady progress of British motor engineering questions her supposed technological backwardness. Historians have dwelt upon the inability of the European vehicle industry to keep pace with the expansion of its American counterpart which they seek to explain either in terms of entrepreneurial conservatism or an inadequate market. Growth in Europe was, nonetheless, rapid and its economic impact requires some assessment.

ORIGINS

Technological developments rather than the pull of the market explain the emergence of the vehicle industry. A market did not exist but had to be created, initially among sportsmen, enthusiasts and the wealthy but already before the First World War it reached a wider middle-class audience. One historian has alleged a crisis in horse-drawn conveyance which turned many to look for alternative transport. Calculating that the average horse consumed the product of a four or five acre field each year, he concludes that this conflicted with the needs of a growing human population (Barker, 1987, 4–5). The decline of horse-drawn transport was, however, a gradual process compared with the rapid rise of the motor industry. Agricultural output and productivity were rising helped by horse manure fertiliser and European farmers complained of the flood of cheap Russian and American food imports. The United States, the leading car-maker, certainly faced no subsistency conflict. Instead, entrepreneurs responded to developments in technology or entered the industry when their existing product faced a slump in demand.

The motor vehicle evolved from two lines of technology; the power source and the vehicle design. The earliest mechanical road vehicles date from Joseph Cugnot's work in Paris in the 1760s and 1770s. The development of the railway locomotive in the early nineteenth century encouraged lateral developments in road transport such as Trevithick's steam road vehicles. In the 1820s and 1830s steam coaches were experimented with in England but none proved commercially viable because the weight of their steam boilers, engine and fuel meant low speeds, difficulties building a suitable vehicle for the engine and damage to road surfaces.

The boom in the electrical industry at the end of the nineteenth century encouraged the development of electrical road vehicles. From the late 1880s electric trams were adopted in many American cities after Frank Sprague successfully demonstrated a system of electric traction at Richmond, Virginia in 1888. Trams spread to German and French cities in the 1890s and to Britain and elsewhere in Europe at the end of the decade (McKay, 67–74). In the 1890s there was a boom in electric taxis in London, Paris and Berlin. At the 1899 Paris car show 63 types of electric car were displayed by 19 companies (Laux, 1976, 91). By 1901 interest in electric cars had collapsed in the wake of their shortcomings: frequent recharging of batteries was expensive and inconvenient and many were too heavy to be supported by pneumatic tyres. Their short range became an increasing disadvantage as motoring spread outside the urban environment. Electric vehicles found greater popularity in the United States where their ease of starting and operation suited the larger body of women drivers and the poor state of rural roads prevented their short range from being a major impediment.

Many of these problems did not face urban public transport services: routes were short and regular while the problems of recharging heavy batteries was overcome by transferring the electricity from a generator to the motor through overhead electric cables. Environmental objections were overcome by designing stylish supporting poles or attaching the cables to brackets mounted upon roadside buildings. Alternatively, power was received from an insulated conduit in the roadbed. As a result, it was not until after the First World War that the lower-cost and more flexible motor bus superseded the tram. In contrast to many other transport developments tramway services were built and operated by the private sector in continental Europe but by the public in Britain. Three firms dominated tramway construction in Germany and built systems in many other countries. Thomson-Houston, backed by American finance, was dominant in France. Consortiums of Belgian, French and German banks provided the finance for tramway installation in many cities including Warsaw, Naples, Turin, Cologne, Frankfurt, Munich, Florence, and Trieste. In Britain the failure of private tramway initiatives in the early 1890s contrasted to the success of municipal experiments in gas and water to encourage further local government intervention.

The internal combustion engine provided the solution to the draw-backs of the electric car. In the early 1860s Étienne Lenoir developed an engine which was similar in operation to a steam engine but ignited the fuel by a spark plug. He initially used gas as a fuel but soon realised that petrol vapour could be burnt by using a carburet-tor. In the following decades Lenoir's design was improved upon by other engineers particularly Nicholas Otto who produced a four-stroke engine in 1876. These engines remained comparatively slow and heavy but in 1883 Gottlieb Daimler patented his design, based on a hot-tube ignition system, for a high speed, light internal combustion engine. At 600 revolutions per minute it was five or six times as fast as many other designs and at 90 kg was only a few per cent of its competitors' weight (Barker, 1987, 11–12). Daimler, like most en-gine developers, was not responding to a need for motorised road transport and initially showed more interest in engines for boats, trams, airships and manufacturing industry.

Advances were also necessary in metalworking, chassis design, electrical apparatus, tyres, suspension and lubricants. The cycle industry set the technological precedent with many interchangeable standardised parts made on specialised machine tools. Light tubular frames, ball bearings, chain drive, pneumatic tyres, shaft drive, gears, wire wheels and brake cables were among the many features inherited from the bicycle. Michelin in France and Dunlop in Ireland took out patents for the pneumatic tyre in the late 1880s which reduced the weight of the vehicle and increased its speed.

The production of motorised cycles, tricycles and 'voiturettes' (small cars with single-cylinder engines) posed engineering problems relevant to the emerging car industry. In 1886 Karl Benz adapted one of Otto's engines for use in a tricycle which is often regarded as the first effectively functioning motor vehicle. He used a belt to transmit power to a differential shaft from which two chains drove the rear wheels. In 1895 De Dion-Bouton, one of the pioneers of the French motor industry, produced a petrol-driven tricycle with an electric ignition. Its cheapness helped it to compete with the four-wheeled vehicles which began to appear on the market in the 1890s.

While many of the earliest technical developments originated in Germany, France and Britain soon produced new inventions and outstanding engineers. Paris's leading school of engineering, the École Centrale des Arts et Manufactures, trained many vehicle engineers including René Panhard and Emile Levassor. Britain, helped by technical schools like the City and Guilds of London Institute, produced such outstanding engineers as Lanchester, Napier and Maudsley, which questions the assumption of Britain's technical backwardness. Technology flowed freely between countries as inventors sought to exploit or protect their patents by licensing them abroad. A representative of Daimler, Edouard Sarazin, who was also a friend of Levassor, approached Panhard et Levassor in 1887 to manufacture the Daimler engine in order to protect the patent in France. The movement of engineers between countries acted as a further source of technology transfer. Louis Coatalen brought his experience of three French vehicle firms to Humber and Hillman.

The commercial beginnings of the industry were to be found in France. When Panhard et Levassor took the licence for the manufacture of Daimler engines in France in 1887 they did not envisage large scale production of engines, let alone vehicles. It was not until 1890–1 that they began to produce vehicles with the help of Peugeot who provided the chassis. Panhard et Levassor ran one of the largest metalworking concerns in Paris where they manufactured a range of machines and tools. The Peugeot family owned two major metalworking concerns in Montbéliard. With the appearance of the safety bicycle in 1885, they diversified into cycle production. Within a few years they became interested in applying mechanical power to their cycles and in 1889 manufactured a modified version of Léon Serpollet's steam tricycle before joining forces with Panhard et Levassor.

Panhard et Levassor and Peugeot were in many ways typical of the pioneer French motor firms most of whose origins can be traced to engineering or cycle production. Darracq, Clément, Chenard et Walcker, Rochet-Schneider and Richard began as cycle firms while Decauville (railway equipment), Lorraine-Dietrich (railway car builders), Delaunay-Belleville (ship's boilers) and Mors (electrical equipment) came from the engineering industry. Some were newly created enterprises including Renault and De Dion-Bouton. Renault emerged in 1898 out of the mechanical talents of Louis who successfully converted the De Dion-Bouton tricycle into a small car and incorporated a direct drive mechanism into it.

Humber, Rover, Swift and Singer all came from the cycle industry while an engineering background characterised Crossley, Ruston, Hornsby (engine makers), Vauxhall (marine engineering), Royce and Brush (electrical engineering). New firms included Austin, Argyll, Hillman, Lanchester, Morris and Standard. Like Renault, many of the new British firms drew heavily upon the technical and business acumen of their founders. Herbert Austin was a thrusting, dynamic inventor-entrepreneur who learned his engineering with the Wolseley Sheep Shearing Machine Company in Britain and Australia which extended its manufacturing operations to machine tools and cars before Austin left to form his own organisation in 1905.

Besides Daimler and Benz, the German firms of Stoewer and Dürkopp came from engineering while Opel and Adler had been cycle makers. At least ten metalworking firms had begun vehicle production in Belgium by 1901 including Vivinus. Other entrants included Germain, who had manufactured railway equipment, cycle makers Minerva and the National Armament Company. Early motor manufacture in Italy drew upon machine shops, railway equipment builders and cycle makers although some successful firms had no previous history. Fiat was formed in 1899 through the efforts of a group of cycle mechanics, financiers, industrialists and professionals. Sporadic and small scale production took place in other cities with a background in machining, cycle and carriage making including Barcelona, Geneva, Zurich, Vienna, Prague, Budapest, Amsterdam and Copenhagen. In Austria-Hungary Tatra emerged from carriage production, Praga from machine engineering and Laurin and Klement from cycle manufacturing (Purs, 194).

Diversification from engineering and cycle firms often resulted from necessity rather than as part of a long term plan. When Pierre Michaux fitted a crank and pedals to the front wheel of a two-wheeled vehicle in the 1860s he laid the technological foundation of the cycle industry but it was the depression in the craft industries which led to its rapid expansion in France and England. Likewise, a recession in the cycle industry in the late 1890s encouraged many firms to diversify into vehicle production. The introduction of the safety bicycle in 1885, the patenting of the pneumatic tyre in 1888 and the growth of a specialist press, helped popularise cycling. A boom in the flotation of cycle companies ensued in the mid-1890s which led to an over expansion of the industry. Britain had been the leading exporter of cycles and parts but now faced stiff competition from cheaper models in France and Germany. Most damaging were the McKinley duties in 1890 of 35–45 per cent which caused British cycle exports to America to collapse from £255 000 in 1892 to £6000 in 1898 (A. Harrison, 1969, 291). The number of cycle firms based in Coventry, the centre of the industry in Britain, declined from 75 in 1898 to 49 in 1912 (Thoms and Donnelly, 27–8).

The experience of Rover suggests that diversification was the product of necessity in a declining market. Rover conducted experiments with motor cars in the late 1880s and early 1890s but were unconvinced of their prospects and continued production for the booming cycle industry. By 1903 a decline in profits, prices and sales caused the firm to diversify into motor cycles. This proved a failure and was halted in 1906 to be replaced by car production which was immediately successful. By the following year Rover accounted for ten per cent of British car production (Foreman-Peck, 1983, 187). Humber experimented with car production when it went into the red in 1899. Singer and Swift, though, planned their transition from cycle to motor vehicle more carefully by using the profits of the former to finance early development of the latter. This ability to convert from an older technological structure to a newer one questions the assumption that Britain's poor economic performance between 1870 and 1930 was due to overcommitment to an outdated industrial structure.[1] In France De Dietrich turned to car manufacture in 1897 when the prospects looked poor for the manufacture of railway equipment. Hotchkiss abandoned the armaments market in 1903 and Delaunay-Belleville abandoned the production of ship's engines for similar reasons.

The established firm brought internal economies to motor vehicle production, particularly its managerial experience, its capital, its market and marketing network and its company reputation. Diversification presented few technical problems as most firms were operating in a related field. Many purchased a licence to manufacture an existing design of vehicle. In 1897 De Dietrich manufactured a vehicle designed by Amédée Bollée. Sometimes the firm acted as no more than an assembler, buying the engine, the car body and most of the components. This minimised the amount of fixed capital required by the early firms, some of whom could adapt existing capital, though it increased their working capital needs. The system operated on an international scale with many British, German, Belgian and Italian firms importing French chassis and adding locally produced bodies. Rochet-Schneider sold the manufacturing rights to its vehicles in Switzerland, Belgium and Italy. In Britain this system provided work for former coach builders such as Vincent's of Reading and Egerton's of Ipswich. In Germany, Opel imported Darracq and Renault chassis while Adler initially used De Dion-Bouton engines.

Many vehicle firms bought plant and machinery cheaply from ailing cycle firms. Liquidity flow was aided by the practice of vehicle buyers paying a third on order and the remainder on completion. However, the seasonal and yearly fluctuations in the demand for cars could create liquidity problems and often left firms reliant upon the good will of banks. The Clarendon Motor Company collapsed in 1906 when Lloyds and Midland banks refused overdraft facilities (Thoms and Donnelly, 56–7). This helps to explain the high failure rate among early motor manufacturers: only 113 of 293 motor firms established in Britain before the First World War survived to 1914 (Saul, 23).

Finance came from the resources of the existing firms or from family, friends, local interests, banks and business contacts. The Renault brothers drew on family wealth in the textile business. Opel tapped the family's sewing machine and cycle interests. Fiat was initially supported by two wealthy aristocrats and Austin by a steel manufacturer. Many cycle firms went public in the flotation boom of the mid 1890s which enabled them to raise further finance for diversification on the back of the existing company. Sometimes money was raised by a public flotation though the risks of new technology and, in Britain, fraudulent company promoters, discouraged investors. In 1895 the notorious Harry Lawson formed the Daimler Motor Syndicate in order to acquire the Daimler patent in Britain. Shortly afterwards he established the British Motor Syndicate (BMS) to obtain patents over other cars and therefore achieve a monopoly over car production in Britain. In the following year he floated the Great Horseless Carriage Company (GHCC) which paid BMS the inflated amount of £500 000 for patent rights (Barker, 1987, 31–2). Lawson and his friends as the main shareholders in BMS were substantial beneficiaries. By October 1897 the value of GHCC shares had fallen from £10 to 22s. 6d. (Richardson, 19). Ernest Hooley made a financial 'killing' by inflating the capital in firms floated by him. The French use of patent rights to build cars and publicise them in races has been contrasted to their abuse in Britain (Barker, 1987, 35). When investor confidence did return finance was attracted from a wide social base including the nobility, businessmen, tradesmen and professionals. Glossy prospectuses listing aristocrats as directors, bribes of financial journalists and the exploitation of speculative fevers attracted public money although many of the smaller firms remained undersubscribed.

Overseas investment played a limited role in financing the industry. Extensive British investments were made in the French car industry, particularly between 1903 and 1906 when firms such as Darracq, Rochet-Schneider and Delahaye became English-owned companies. The reasons for this are unclear given that company regulations in England were less restrictive and required a smaller proportion of capital to be initially subscribed and paid up. British overseas investments were already very high and the French motor industry offered a way into a new industry with existing, experienced firms.

The geographical origins of the industry lay in towns renowned for their light engineering, metalwork and bicycle industries. In Britain this meant Coventry, Birmingham and Wolverhampton, though also Manchester, Derby and London. Coventry attracted firms such as Rover, Swift, Humber and Singer because it had been a centre of the cycle industry, coachbuilding and other light engineering and craft industries. In France it was chiefly Paris together with Lyons, Bordeaux, Le Mans and Marseilles. Exceptionally, Peugeot was based in Montbéliard where geographical and religious links made it possible to borrow industrial techniques and money from Switzerland and Germany. The insufficiency of local labour was overcome by importing it from other region's and providing company housing. In Italy, production was concentrated at Milan and Turin but in Germany there was a greater geographical spread of manufacture which took in such towns as Berlin, Cannstatt, Russelsheim, Stettin and Bielefeld. The pull of the market was important for Paris which attracted many wealthy sportsmen from at home and abroad. The earliest car sales were completed directly between producer and purchaser. The unreliability of early vehicles and the paucity of repair and servicing facilities emphasised the importance of market proximity. Early provincial firms like Peugeot and De Dietrich took care to establish service facilities in the capital. Paris was, as Laux concludes, a 'magnetic attraction on the automobile industry, as in so many other aspects of French life' (Bardou et al, 59). Clearly substantial economies of localisation existed in the early motor industry.

Although London, New York, Berlin and Rome did not rival Paris as a centre of the automobile industry in the early years the original market was predominantly urban. The poor state of the roads outside the cities and the absence of petrol stations and repair facilities restricted the geographical spread of motoring into rural areas. The comparatively poor state of German and the good condition of French roads at the end of the nineteenth century may go some way to explaining the differing levels of interest in the motor car. Moreover, civic services, such as fire, police, street maintenance and taxis showed a strong early demand for the motor car.

PRODUCTION

In 1896 Panhard et Levassor produced half of the French vehicle output of 320 but interest soon spread to other firms including the Mors brothers, who were producing a vehicle of their own design by 1898, and De Dion-Bouton whose steam tricycle proved highly popular. Press publicity and road races heightened interest and by 1898 the existing firms were struggling to keep pace with demand. Delivery dates lengthened and new firms entered the industry in search of high profits. Panhard et Levassor reorganised production in order to raise their output to 450 by 1899 and 1000 by 1902 (Laux, 1976, 36–8). Many of the earliest sales by Parisian motor firms were to foreigners and within a few years a market and new producers emerged in other European countries, particularly Britain, Germany and Italy.

By 1900, 800 vehicles were being produced in Germany and 175 in the United Kingdom, well behind the French output of nearly 5000.

Table 6.1   World Motor Vehicle Production, 1900–24

	1900	1907	1913	1924
United States	4 000	45 000	485 000	3 504 000
France	4 800	25 000	45 000	145 000
United Kingdom	175	12 000	34 000	147 000
Germany	800	4 000	23 000	49 000*
Canada	–	–	18 000	135 000
Italy	–	2 500	8 000	50 000*

* 1925

Sources: Mitchell, 1975, 467–8; Bardou et al, 15; Laux, 1976, 196; Foreman-Peck, 1982, 871; Blaich, 1981, 110.

French and German output grew by 25 per cent per annum to 1907 compared with 85 per cent in the United Kingdom. From 1907 to 1913, French production grew at a more modest 10 per cent per annum and that of the UK at 20 per cent while German growth accelerated to 35 per cent. Thus by 1913 France (45 000) remained Europe's leading vehicle producer but her lead had been shortened by the UK (34 000) and Germany (23 000). The sustained growth of west European car output before 1914 gives the lies to the suggestion that it was a response to the challenge of Ford which did not arrive in Britain until 1911 and France until 1913 (Richardson). Italy was also an important producer with an output of 8000. Elsewhere in Europe sporadic and small scale vehicle production began in Russia, Sweden, Belgium, Spain, Switzerland, Austria-Hungary and the Czechoslovakian lands.

The First World War forced further expansion upon the motor industry although now it was military vehicles rather than civilian cars. High wartime demand came to an end in 1918, but the organisational advances it had forced upon the motor industry were permanent and ensured a continued high level of output. The gap between French and British production continued to narrow and by 1924 British output was the greater. German output, faced with national economic and political problems, expanded more slowly and was surpassed by Italy by 1924. The leading world producer of motor vehicles at the time of the First World War was the United States. She had surpassed France's early lead by 1905, was producing half a million vehicles by the outbreak of war and 3.5 million by 1924. A 35 per cent growth rate and high productivity were achieved by the reorganisation of production into what became known as flow assembly methods and was commonly associated with Henry Ford. Ford followed the practices of other American industries by producing on a large scale a standardised commodity of interchangeable parts and manufactured entirely on a single site by a carefully supervised but unskilled workforce. Production was organised in the form of an assembly line with the vehicle gradually moving around the factory to pass through each successive process until it was completed. Division of labour was extensive with each process being subdivided into a series of simple tasks. His Ford 'T' model, introduced in 1908, proved a brilliant success because of its cheapness, ease of repair and rugged design.

The delayed transition of such technology, it is frequently alleged, limited the expansion of European output although there is no agreement as to whether blame lay with European engineers, manu-

facturers, salesmen or the labour force. However, the belated introduction of 'Fordism', as it became known, was economically rational
since neither the market nor the manufacturing environment suited
the widespread adoption of American manufacturing methods before
the First World War. Some elements of Fordism were adopted
though with limited success and against opposition particularly from
the workforce. European car makers were aware of the nature of
American mass production with the establishment of Ford factories
in Manchester and Bordeaux. Renault and Fiat sent personnel to
America to study their methods. France's pre-war leadership of the
European car industry, however, was not due to her earlier adoption
of mass production which was no more prevalent than in Britain or
Italy. When things changed after the war it was British producers,
Morris and Austin, who began to corner the market. France's initial
hegemony can be explained by her earlier development of vehicle
technology combined with the commercial acumen to exploit it.
British development was hampered by financial mistrust resulting
from Lawson's speculative exploits. In Germany, Benz was the
leading world producer to 1900 but the firm fell behind when its
namesake clashed with his partners over the technical modernisation
of his basic designs.

France also dominated early motorcycle production. In 1896 Michel and Eugene Werner began production of small front-wheel drive
motorcycles. In 1900 they introduced a larger 1.75 hp engine which
was too heavy for the front wheel and so was placed above the pedal
crank and drove the rear wheel. In 1903 the firm was bought out by
an English company and within a few years ownership and manufacture of motor cycles had moved to Britain and America (Laux, 1976,
96–7).

No European manufacturer, excluding Ford of Britain, produced
as many cars as the principal twelve American firms before the First
World War. The average output of the European market leaders was
only ten per cent of their American counterparts. Ford was the
leading American car maker and arrived in Europe in 1911 when it
began assembling cars in Manchester from components manufactured in America. The substitution of local parts occurred gradually
with the development of a British components industry and as a
result of the McKenna import duty on cars and parts in 1915. Ford
soon established itself as the largest European producer ahead of
Peugeot, Renault and Benz and produced double the output of any
other firm in Britain. The low output of European firms can be

Table 6.2 Market Leaders in the European and American Car Industries, 1913

Europe		USA	
Firm	*Units*	*Firm*	*Units*
Ford (GB)	6 100	Ford	202 700
Peugeot (F)	5 000	Willys-Overland	37 400
Renault (F)	4 700	Studebaker-Overland	32 000
Benz (G)	4 500	Buick	26 700
Darracq (F)	3 500	Cadillac	17 300
Opel (G)	3 200	Maxwell	17 000
Fiat (I)	3 100	Hupmobile	12 500
Wolseley (GB)	3 000	Reo	7 600
Berliet (F)	3 000	Oakland	7 000
De Dion Bouton (F)	2 800	Hudson	6 400
Humber (GB)	2 500	Chalmers	6 000
Brennabor (G)	2 400	Chevrolet-Little	6 000
Average Output	3 700	Average Output	31 600

Sources: Laux, 1976, 199; Bardou et al, 74.

explained by the small and varied nature of demand rather than by entrepreneurial conservatism. While some manufacturers such as Lanchester showed more interest in technical excellence than commercial viability, most successful firms before 1913 understood the nature of the market. Panhard et Levassor, Rochet-Schneider, Daimler, Rolls-Royce and Romeo succeeded by concentrating upon the luxury market where profits were good. The French were renowned for their designs although Daimler's Mercedes and Rolls Royce's 'Silver Ghost' soon achieved great popularity. To produce cheaper cars might endanger a firm's reputation in a market where competition was as much based upon product as price.

The lower end of the market developed gradually with Peugeot, Berliet and Fiat expanding to fill the demand. Fiat's output leapt from 300 vehicles in 1906 to 3000 by 1913 and its share of Italian production rose from five to 50 per cent (Bigazzi, 76). Renault expanded from 1200 cars in 1905 to 4700 by 1909 helped by a large demand for taxi cabs from 1905 (Laux, 1976, 139–43). The crisis in the industry in 1907–8 caused a 'shake-out' as weak firms formed during the boom a few years earlier collapsed and others were forced to adapt and recognise the growing demand for a small, cheap car. Rochet-Schneider's failure to diversify may explain its deteriorating results up to 1914. Singer, Standard and Hillman all adapted their production to reach the small-car market. Morris was the most successful British firm to produce a cheap car before 1914 with the 'Morris Oxford' which sold at £175. Neither this nor the 'Singer 10' at £195 could match the Ford 'T' price of £125–135, although there was more to the market than price competition (Church, 1982, 14; Bardou et al, 71). Austin and Darracq, though, found little success with small cars before 1914. For most European firms the policy was one of diversification into a range of different models which addressed the stratified nature of demand and left various options for expansion. Ford's concentration upon a single model seemed to work in the embryonic pre-war industry but was exposed as overcommitment in the more competitive environment of the 1920s.

Some aspects of the American system could be achieved at low levels of production. High quality, specialist machine tools were imported into Europe particularly in France and Italy where the machine tool industry was less developed than in Britain and Germany. In Britain, Humber and Rover used special-purpose machine tools widely. The single model policy, though at the other end of the market, was pursued with great success by Rolls Royce which manufactured only the 'Silver Ghost' up to 1925. A feature of 'Fordism' which found little support in Europe before 1914 was that of single-site vertical integration. At their Highland Park and River Rouge sites, Ford undertook every process of production from iron foundry to completed vehicle. Many of the earliest British firms assembled adaptations of imported French designs. Clément Talbot sold Talbots assembled from French Clément parts while De Dion and Aster engines were widely used. In Germany Opel began by selling Renault and Darracq chassis while Isotta Fraschini imported Renault cars into Italy. Most early French firms were small-scale assemblers, drawing upon the emerging components industry of Paris. The booms in the car industry around 1898 and 1904–5 encouraged the development of a European components industry. In Britain, Smith's produced carburettors, acetylene lamps, generators and lighting while Lucas experimented with integrated lighting and starting systems. In France and Germany component firms supplied the most up-to-date equipment and sometimes on credit. In Czechoslovakia, however, the absence of a components industry restrained expansion of the motor industry as firms had to rely upon imports of many parts including tyres and glass.

The uncertain and varied nature of demand together with the changing technology of the industry and the greater capital costs discouraged integrated production. Most saw greater operational flexibility and reduced financial pressure from continuing to draw upon specialist suppliers. The English engineer and manufacturer Lanchester, went against the tide by producing the components for his vehicles but this only served to overstretch his finances, push up their price and discourage customers aware of the dangers of techno- logical obsolescence and uncertainty of replacement. The firm's downfall in 1904 was not unrelated to this policy (Kingsford). Even the larger English firms such as Rover and Wolseley relied heavily upon component suppliers.

It was the organisation of factory work which was the most distinc- tive feature of the Ford system. Instead of small teams of workers building a car, the moving assembly line was introduced so that each car moved on from one stage of production to the next around the factory with different personnel taking responsibility for just one of a large number of simple tasks. The flow assembly system appeared in the United States as early as 1903 and by 1912 Ford had introduced a moving conveyor. These methods were used only sporadically in Europe before 1914. The Lorraine-Dietrich works at Argenteuil, though not large scale, introduced an assembly line in 1907 while Sunbeam and Wolseley concentrated on making cars in large batches and increasing worker specialisation.

One of the major aims behind the introduction of flow assembly methods in America was to overcome the shortage of skilled labour. Increased division of labour facilitated de-skilling while careful supervision and increased wages helped to promote labour produc- tivity. Scientific time and work studies calculated the most efficient means of performing different tasks ('Taylorism'). There was no shortage of workers, skilled or unskilled, in Europe which reduced the incentive for labour and factory reorganisation. 'Taylorism' created most interest in France where Renault and Panhard et Levassor both sent representatives to study American methods. Attempts to introduce it, however, led to labour unrest particularly among skilled workers who made much of the de-humanising nature of the assembly line. In Britain, changes in working conditions and practices led to industrial unrest including a lockout in 1897–8 by employers in the metalworking trades. European manufacturers had more success in introducing piece-rate wages which were seen by many American companies as boosting productivity. By 1914 around half of British car workers were on piece rates and probably a higher proportion in France and Germany (Bardou et al, 66). Rather than introduce piece rates, Ford took a 'stick and carrot' approach offering improved wages and conditions but firing anyone working slowly or involved in organising unions. This attitude was followed by Panhard et Levassor who offered welfare and pension funds to its workforce but sacked union organisers. In spite of improvements in labour efficiency, which spread further during the 1920s, labour productivity remained well below its level in the USA: in 1927 it took 300 man-days of labour to build the average French car but only 70 in the United States (Bardou et al, 102).

Judging the Ford system as a whole, Renault came closest to its imitation before 1914. From its origins in a small workshop in 1898 producing a few handmade cars, Renault emerged as a major volume car producer before 1914 by pioneering the 'industrial imperative' of large scale integrated production on one site which enabled lower prices and a wider market (Fridenson, 1972). Renault cars were still expensive in relation to Fords and the basis of their early success was repeated large orders for a standard vehicle, the taxi cab, although a range of other models were also produced. Renault favoured large-scale integration for the sake of independence from suppliers rather than as a means of scale economies. The company experienced obstacles to its plans particularly from its workforce when it attempted to introduce a form of 'Taylorism' after 1908. In 1912–13 the workforce went on strike when the company introduced time studies.

The First World War created the conditions for the 'Americanisation' of the European car industry. The war led to a large increase in the demand for a limited range of standard military vehicles and equipment with a heavy emphasis upon reliability and rugged design. The urgency with which these vehicles were required encouraged a search for increased productivity through improved methods and products and caused governments to offer firms generous terms to expand their productive capacity. At the same time, conscription removed many of the skilled workers upon whom the industry relied and created a general labour shortage. Thus the war created a large standardised demand, financial support and a labour shortage. On the other hand, production facilities were sometimes the victim of warfare: Panhard et Levassor's factory at Reims was destroyed and Peugeot's Lille factory plundered. The development and production of new models was frequently held back as attention was concentrated upon military vehicles, such was the fate of Morris's Cowley model which was ready for production by 1915, as a competitor to the

Ford 'T'. In the wake of neutrality for most of the war, the American car industry increased its output lead over Europe.

The stimulus of the war can be seen by the quadrupling of the number of buildings, machines and employees in the French motor industry and a diversification of output into military vehicles, aircraft and shells (Bardou et al, 80–1). The industry was organised into groups each producing a particular military item. Renault, Citroën and Peugeot dominated these groups which reinforced their pre-war leadership. Their large size enabled them to handle government orders and it appears that Citroën and Renault, at least, held influence within political circles. Assembly-line production was introduced by several larger firms including Berliet in 1917. Moreover, the Ministry of Armaments required the installation of conveyors in some factories where there was a predominance of women workers.

The British motor industry also expanded and diversified under the impact of the First World War with the pre-war leaders again dominant. The aircraft industry began to emerge during the war. By 1918 aircraft engines were produced in Manchester, Coventry, Birmingham, Derby, London, Sheffield and Clydeside. Austin produced shells, aircraft and their engines by expanding its Longbridge site, by building new factories with government support and integrating production. Morris introduced mass production flow techniques based on Taylorism to cope with the wartime demand. These benefits proved their worth after 1918 by helping Morris to outproduce Ford UK in the highly competitive conditions of the 1920s. During the war, however, Ford remained much the largest vehicle manufacturer in Britain, providing a range of cars, trucks and ambulances.

Fiat was the main beneficiary of the wartime expansion of the Italian motor industry. Its output of vehicles grew from 5000 in 1914 to 16 000 by 1918, which was greater than that of Ford UK, while also expanding production of aviation engines. By 1918 it was the third largest business in Italy (Bardou et al, 82). Growth was achieved by expanding capacity, particularly in the construction of a new plant at Turin in 1916, and increasing its pre-war drift towards Fordism. Romeo, Itala and Lancia also expanded and prospered but, as small luxury producers, were not equipped to take full advantage of the wartime opportunities. Similarly, the smallness of Russian car firms caused the government to place many wartime orders with foreign firms some of which sold licences to Russian companies or established new plants there. Renault built new factories at Petrograd in

1914 and Rybinsk in 1916 while Fiat and Citroën sold licences.

The leading German firms raised their output and profits during the war. The production of aircraft engines expanded although there was less diversification away from vehicles and little impact upon production methods. Adler, Benz, Mercedes and Opel received government car orders while Benz, Bussing, Mercedes, Opel and Krupps took most of the lorry requisitions. The failure to turn to new methods of production is not easily explained. Before the war there was little evidence of mass production among the market leaders. In wartime there was less resort to unskilled labour which had necessitated organisational changes in other countries. The failure to make this transition held back German progress in the changed conditions of the 1920s. In Austria-Hungary existing pre-war firms, such as Laurin-Klement, Nesselsdorf, Praga, Austro-Daimler, Graf und Stift and WAF, expanded output and diversified into aviation and lorry production.

Motor manufacturers in those European countries which remained outside the hostilities derived few benefits from neutrality. The decline of a small vehicle industry in Switzerland, Spain and Denmark was slowed down or temporarily halted, but no country appears to have gained significant long term benefits. It was overwhelmingly the needs of the war economy which gave birth to a modern car industry, particularly in those countries and companies which had laid the foundations, admittedly tenuous, before 1914.

Neutrality to 1917 brought benefits to the American car industry though it is doubtful that this amounted to the 'bonanza for American automobile makers' alleged by Fridenson (Bardou et al, 84). Although European governments placed orders for munitions with American firms, the real boom was in the domestic car market. Ford rigorously pursued price-cutting policies which caused vertical integration and assembly methods to spread further through the industry as firms struggled to compete with Ford. Ford's policies opened up a middle range car market at about $700–800 for a car with more power and style than the Ford 'T' which led firms such as Dodge and Chevrolet to enter the industry (Bardou et al, 84). These firms differed from Ford by competing on the basis of product differentiation rather than price and buying-in components from suppliers or producing them in a separate factory in place of Ford's single site integration.

The transition back to peacetime production created a series of problems including debts from expansion, inappropriate capacity, bottlenecks in the supply of components and raw materials and an uncertain market. In 1918 Leyland faced overdrafts, unpaid excess profits tax and a flooded second-hand market for military vehicles. The firm changed its name in order to raise further finance through a share issue without Treasury scrutiny. This backfired, though, when the firm consequentially missed out on the wartime tax refund for useful industries (Turner). The transition was most difficult for companies which had abandoned car production during the war; as a result their capacity was inappropriate and they were four years behind in the rapidly changing technology of the industry. This was the experience of much of the Coventry car industry although Rover managed to keep its link with car production by subcontracting some of its military work. Morris continued to manufacture a small number of Oxfords and Cowleys during the war so that in 1918 it had a reputable collection of up-to-date models. In Italy, Fiat benefited from its wartime car production while Romeo had manufactured munitions and Fraschini and Bianchi aircraft engines.

The immediate post-war consumer boom instilled a rapid growth of car production. In Britain, there was a 50 per cent rise in the number of firms between 1919 and 1922 together with 40 new makes of car (Richardson, 95). Within a few years overproduction and the collapse of the boom hit the car industry and a period of intense competition ensued which involved price and product wars and efficiency drives. The uncertainty of the post-war market dictated circumspection and an attitude of 'wait and see'. In France, Berliet and Citroën were confident of a sustained growth in motoring and adopted mass production, introducing moving conveyor belts and importing steel presses from the United States. The collapse of the boom, the prolonged interwar depression and the realisation that the European market, although becoming more standardised, was not to be as homogenous as America, brought the downfall of some over-committed companies. The 1920–1 crisis nearly bankrupted Berliet and reduced its subsequent importance within the industry. Citroën survived by financial support from family and business friends. Renault and Peugeot waited until at least 1922 before committing themselves to a path of growth.

Austin and Morris were the postwar leaders of the British motor industry. Aware of the growing demand for a cheap standardised car, they began to produce the Austin Seven and the Morris Cowley in large numbers, production of the latter reaching 63 000 by 1924 (Bardou et al, 105). Both were innovative in production and style and began to push the Ford 'T' out of the market. Their smaller engines minimised the cost of the horse-power tax. Ford continued to reduce prices but refused to update and adapt the 'T' according to the needs of the European market; it was not until 1923, for example, that a right-hand drive version was introduced for the British market. Sales of the 'T' declined and Ford found themselves overcommitted to a single model. The policy was a life-saver for Austin which had been pushed close to bankruptcy in 1921 by concentrating upon the more expensive 'Austin 20' (Church, 1979). Austin and Morris, like Renault and Peugeot, took care to avoid overcommitment to the American system; output was increased by extending the division of labour principle and introducing various innovations. Morris initially rejected vertical integration and continued to buy parts from the reputable components industry. This reduced capital requirements and gave operations more flexibility in a changing environment although in the immediate postwar years production was sometimes delayed by supply bottlenecks.

The technology of the German car industry changed comparatively little during the war and even in the 1920s only Opel went over to assembly-line methods. The depreciating Reichsmark provided a temporary export boom and a hundred new firms were established between 1919 and 1924 but this ended with the 1924 currency stabilisation (Blaich, 1981, 94). The technology lag attracted American firms like Ford and GM but the construction techniques of German firms remained backward and inhibited the long term expansion of the industry. In Italy, Fiat built upon its wartime growth and moved further towards mass production. At the same time, there remained a niche in the market for the small companies such as Romeo which concentrated upon a luxury car market and diversification into such areas as aircraft engines. Bigazzi, however, points out that differences in company attitudes were moderated by the cultural climate causing Fiat to temper Fordism with paternalism (Bigazzi, 78).

SALES AND MARKETING

Except for the earliest years of Paris motoring, Britain was the largest European market for vehicles both absolutely and on a per capita comparison. In 1913 a quarter of a million vehicles were registered in Britain which was twice the figure for France and nearly four times that of Germany. Per capita ownership in Britain was also greater than that of the United States until about 1907. With British output initially slow to develop, only one vehicle was produced to every five owned in Britain in 1907 compared with less than one in two in France, one in three in the United States and one in four in Germany. The more rapid subsequent growth of British output and an acceleration in the French market caused these figures to converge by the mid-1920s.

The early discrepancies of output and ownership ratios was made possible by the high proportion of exports. In 1907 half of French production was exported which represented more than half of the world's vehicle exports (Bardou et al, 20). With the rise of the American industry, France's share of world vehicle exports fell to a third in 1913 but she remained the largest European exporter. After the war Canada and the United States accounted for nearly 80 per cent of exports (Foreman-Peck, 1982, 868). Britain was the major market for French vehicles before 1914 though smaller volumes went to many other countries including Belgium, Algeria, Germany, the United States, Argentina, Brazil, Italy, Russia and Spain. Even these figures may understate the true size of French exports because many foreign customers, particularly the wealthy and sportsmen, purchased a car while in Paris and took it home with them. Laux believes more cars may have been imported into Britain from France in 1908–10 by this manner than through official imports (Bardou et al, 72). The main growth of British exports came after 1909 and was concentrated upon Australia, New Zealand and other Empire countries. German exports expanded just before the First World War to reach 36 per cent of production and were concentrated upon Russia, Austria-Hungary, Argentina and Brazil (Bardou et al, 71–2).

France's early penetration of the British market was helped by the absence of import duties before 1915. The intra-European car trade was aided by low duties in Germany (2–3 per cent), Italy (4–6 per cent), France (8–12 per cent), and Belgium (12 per cent). French sales to the United States occurred behind a high duty of 45 per cent (Bardou et al, 21). Most of these vehicles, however, were in the top end of the range where quality was more important than price. America's poor showing in the French car market was explained by the inability of the manufacturers to understand the qualitative and varied nature of the European market. Ford's dwindling fortunes in Britain after 1918 have already been explained.

The successful capture of the British market by French car makers has been attributed to the backwardness of British producers who

Table 6.3 Vehicle Ownership in Europe and America, 1907–21

	1907		1913		1920–1	
	Vehicles regist'd	*Inhabitants per vehicle*	*Vehicles regist'd*	*Inhabitants per vehicle*	*Vehicles regist'd*	*Inhabitants per vehicle*
UNITED STATES	143 200	608	1 258 000	77	9 240 000	11
GREAT BRITAIN	63 500	640	250 000	165	363 000	118
FRANCE	40 000	981	125 000	318	236 400	164
GERMANY	16 200	3 800	70 600	950	90 900	695[†]
BELGIUM	7 800	924	9 600	773[*]	20 700	358
ITALY	6 100	5 600	17 000	2 100	49 500	767
CANADA	2 100	3 100	50 600	151	408 800	21

Notes: [*] Based on 1910 population figure
      [†] Based on 1925 population figure

Sources: Bardou et al, 20, 72, 90; Laux, 1976, 196; Mitchell, 1975, 19–24, 639–42; M. C. Urquhart and K. A. H. Buckley, *Historical Statistics of Canada,* Toronto, 1965, 14, 550. B. R. Mitchell, *International Historical Statistics. The Americas and Australasia,* London, 1983, 50.

Table 6.4   Destination of French Vehicle Exports, 1907 and 1913 (%)

	United Kingdom	Belgium	Algeria	Germany	United States
1907	42	11	–	10	8
1913	24	18	10	9	–

	Argentina	Brazil	Italy	Spain	Russia	Others
1907	4	3	3	3	–	18
1913	8	4	3	3	3	19

Source: Laux, 1976, 99, 101.

concentrated upon technical perfection above commercial viability and failed to introduce a cheap low-horsepower car (Saul). Another historian has explained it in terms of the economies of scale of French firms (Foreman-Peck, 1979). However, French car makers were not significantly more advanced or efficient in their production techniques than the British. Cheap cars were as rare in France as in Britain and were not what the market demanded. Nor can the French firms be praised for their overseas marketing techniques. Only Renault, Darracq and Panhard et Levassor had reasonable overseas marketing organisations. Church suggests that French success had more to do with their early technological lead over Britain and the dynamism of British importing agents like Edge, Friswell and Rolls (1982).

The expansion of the market was accompanied by a change in its nature. The earliest car buyers tended to be enthusiasts, sportsmen and the wealthy, while motor cycles found a larger market further down the social scale. From this small base the car market gradually spread to cover the military, the professions, the business community, farmers, civic amenities and passenger and freight services. The élite nature of early car buyers reflected the high price in relation to incomes. In Germany in 1906 a small car cost around 6000 Reichsmark which compared with an average annual working-class income of around 900 marks and 2200 for a middle-class professional (Nübel, 64). Motor cycles were about a sixth of the price. The high price and luxury status caused demand to fluctuate considerably according to economic conditions which led companies and agents to introduce sales methods such as instalment selling to stabilise demand. With demand highly elastic, price-reducing productivity improvements brought many new buyers into the market. Car shows, clubs, races, press support, patronage by the influential, infrastructure improvements, the removal of legal obstacles, rising incomes, falling prices and the First World War all had a place in the growth of European vehicle ownership to 850 000 by 1920, thirty years after its original inception.

Exhibitions and motor shows began to draw public attention to vehicles. The 1889 Paris Exposition included examples of steam tricycles, petrol cars and motor engines and by the 1890s motor shows had become an annual event. What seemed to attract most publicity for the industry, however, was the road race. Originally designed as road tests for new vehicles, they developed into competitive annual events, particularly in France. The 1894 race over 78 miles from Paris to Rouen and back attracted much interest and press publicity in France and throughout Europe. The 732-mile race between Paris and Bordeaux in 1895 confirmed the supremacy of petrol over steam when eight out of the eleven petrol vehicles finished the course but only one of the six steamers (Barker, 1987, 19–20). Panhard et Levassor's vehicle finished the course in 48 hours stopping only for routine maintenance. Such durability confirmed that the motor car had passed through the experimental stage and could be purchased by the non-enthusiast. One historian has concluded that the 1895 race 'was for motor vehicles what the Rainhill trials had been for railways' (Barker, 1987, 20). The races became longer and more demanding; Paris to Marseilles in 1896, to Amsterdam in 1898, Vienna in 1902 and Madrid in 1903. Most early road tests took place in France because of greater interest, more cars, better roads and the sympathy of road authorities. In Britain, the London to Brighton race in 1896 followed by the London to Edinburgh race, stimulated interest in car ownership and led to a boom in sales in the last few years of the century. In Germany there was little interest in road races.

Publicity for motor shows and races took the form of handbills, posters and catalogues. The press was also an important means of disseminating information about the industry. Several French car firms owned daily newspapers while the press baron, Lord Northcliffe, was one of the earliest car owners and publicists in England. A specialist press for the industry developed rapidly; sometimes as cycle journals extended their interests. *Motor*, for example, was previously *Motor Cycling* and originally *Cycling*. *La Locomotion Automobile* in 1894 was the first specialist motor journal but was soon followed by others including *Autocar* from 1895 which was formed by William

Iliffe, proprietor of the *Cyclist*. *L'Auto*, established in 1900, was selling 20 000 copies within a few months and 125 000 by 1913 (Fridenson, 1987, 131). Most readers were not car owners but their interest and desire for ownership were whetted by such publications. The press may have increased the market for motor vehicles but did not always give motorists helpful or unbiased advice. Henry Sturmey, editor of *Autocar*, invested heavily in Harry Lawson's fraudulent company ventures and supported him in published articles. Engineering and technical journals such as *La Revue Industrielle* and *L'Industrie Electrique* published details of technical developments in the car industry. Several journals appeared in Germany including *Technik* from 1897 and *Motorwagen* the following year.

Automobile clubs served as an additional focus point for the growing interest in motor vehicles. The Automobile Club de France (ACF) was formed in 1895 by De Dion and had attracted 1000 members by 1897 (Laux, 1976, 28–31). Its concentration of membership among the rich and prominent in society, helped by high subscription fees, confirmed the élite social basis of early motoring. The Touring Club de France originally, formed by cycling enthusiasts in 1890, provided a less exclusive meeting point. Its membership numbered 20 000 by 1895 and included many who were not car owners but would form the nucleus of the growing number of motorists in the years leading up to 1914 (Bardou et al, 16). The Automobile Club of Britain and Ireland (ACBI, later the RAC) was founded in 1897. Its initial social basis was very similar to that of the ACF with a founders' list which included four hereditary peers and many gentlemen, solicitors and doctors, but in subsequent years the membership expanded and became less exclusive. In the same year the Mid-European Automobile Club was established in Berlin but by 1902 there were only 900 members of automobile clubs among the major German cities (Laux, 1976, 77–8).

The clubs performed many important tasks in encouraging the popularity and viability of motoring. The Touring Club de France improved road signs, published maps and encouraged regional hotels and hostels for cyclists and motorists. Frequently, they arranged motor shows and races or published journals and manuals. The Richmond motor show in 1899 was arranged by the ACBI and *L'Auto* magazine was founded by the ACF. Above all else the clubs acted as a rallying point and a national voice for the motorist. Motor traders organisations such as the Society of Motor Manufacturers and Traders (1902) and the British Motor Trade Association (1910) helped stimulate the car market by arranging publicity shows and setting price guidelines.

Infrastructura! improvements, while in many ways a response to early motoring, also served to spread the habit, particularly in rural areas. An expansion of the road network and an improvement in the quality of roads took place in many countries with the coming of the motor vehicle. Stronger surfaces were required and, therefore, the use of tarmacadam was extended in Britain and asphalt emulsion in France and Germany. New and cheaper construction techniques were introduced in the post-war rebuilding and modernisation programmes of the 1920s. Regular petrol supplies were provided earliest in France. Elsewhere the supply was intermittent including in Britain which had only 41 petrol stores in 1898 all located in the south of the country, and Germany where high import duties existed (Barker, 1987, 45; Blaich, 1981, 151). German vehicle ownership may also have been discouraged by the superior comfort, reliability and cheapness of its rail system.

Governments had no clear policy towards the motor industry although some measures influenced its development. High import duties to 65 per cent of the vehicle's price and a luxury tax hindered the development of motoring in Czechoslovakia (Purš, 195). In western Europe, tariffs and taxes remained low until wartime when they were increased in order to raise money and discourage expenditure on 'wasteful' luxuries. In Britain, the McKenna duties of 1915 imposed a 33 per cent duty on car imports. This was maintained after the war and extended to include parts and commercial vehicles in 1926. In 1921 the British government introduced a car tax, towards the cost of road maintenance and other infrastructure, whose incidence varied with the horsepower of the car and thereby encouraged a market shift towards smaller-engined cars. French and Italian tariffs were also increased sharply after 1918. In Italy duties reached 100–200 per cent. In Britain the Locomotive Act of 1865 was designed to safeguard road users against the earliest mechanically-powered vehicles. It limited the speed of steam traction engines to 4 mph in open country and 2 mph in built up areas and required a man with a red flag to precede the vehicle by 60 yards as a warning to other road users. This 'Red Flag' Act has been seen as an obstruction to the development of motoring but in fact was repealed as soon as pressure for its abolition emerged from among the small élite of early motorists. In 1896 the speed limit was increased to 12 mph and in 1903 to 20 mph (Barker, 1987, 29–30). Its fate reflected the growing influence of the car interest helped by its national organisations and patronage by key figures. Unlike the young working-class radicals in the bicycle clubs of the 1880s and 1890s, the motor car found its support among the influential and leaders of society including King Edward VII.

Many of the modern marketing methods of the car industry were developed during this period, including the growth of dealerships, instalment-buying and 'trade-ins'. The earliest car firms sold directly to the purchaser since they were dealing with a small and personalised market. The buyer might visit the factory during construction and subsequently return for servicing and repairs. As output and sales rose and the product became more standardised direct selling was replaced by a system of agents and dealers. Independent agents appeared in Britain as a link between the growing domestic market and the large French car industry. Charles Rolls imported various luxury French models into England before joining forces with Henry Royce in 1907 to concentrate upon sales of their 'Silver Ghost'. Mann Egerton were established in 1898 in Norwich and, like Rolls Royce, were a partnership of engineering knowledge and motoring enthusiasm. Rolls concentrated upon selling cars in London where there was a large and wealthy population. For Mann Egerton, Norwich was a regional capital close to the fashionable Broads. Dealership networks also emerged when agents signed franchise agreements with car manufacturers to sell their vehicles in a particular area. By 1913 Renault had 94 and Panhard et Levasor 58 agents selling their cars (Fridenson, 1987, 130). Expansion overseas gave Austin dealerships in France, Scandinavia, India and Japan by 1909 (Church, 1981, 80–1). The development of sales regions by the larger firms enabled them to distribute cars and offer after-sales services. By 1913 Renault and Panhard et Levassor each had four regional branches (Fridenson, 1987, 130–1).

Before 1914 most dealers were given plenty of leeway by the car companies to pursue their own policies including the sale of other makes. After 1918, under American influence and through necessity in a highly competitive market, car companies began to impose more stringent requirements upon dealers. In 1919 Ford sacked many of its dealers in England and hired new ones under the more rigorous conditions that they must sell Ford cars exclusively and offer good repair and service facilities. Ford's position in Europe declined in the 1920s largely as a result of pursuing sales and marketing policies more suited to North America than to Europe. Their highly successful pre-war agent in Britain, Percival Perry, was sacked and replaced by a series of American agents insufficiently attuned to the needs of the British market. European firms exercised closer control over their dealers but rarely to the same degree as did Ford. Exclusive dealing was often not enforced, particularly where the different makes were not directly in competition, but Peugeot, Renault, and Berliet dealers agreed to sell at catalogue prices from 1919. Closer dealer supervision, at any rate, gave companies a clearer idea of sales and, therefore, production targets and enabled them to offer technical, commercial and financial assistance to dealers.

When vehicles were first sold directly to purchasers the prospective buyer paid one third of the cost at the time of ordering and the balance upon delivery. In looking to reach a wider and less wealthy market the practice of payment by instalments was introduced. Charles Rolls was one of the first to introduce it in 1903 when he accepted twenty per cent deposit upon delivery followed by four quarterly payments at an annual interest rate of 5 per cent. Car firms sold vehicles to the dealers at a 10 or 20 per cent discount and allowed them some credit, which gave the dealers the liquidity necessary to sell cars by instalments (Fridenson, 1987, 130). In France, several financial institutions including the Automobile Bank specialised in car loans, although instalment selling was less common than in Britain. Some firms introduced hire purchase schemes during depressed years when fewer people could afford the cost of a new car; such was the policy of Rover during the 1908 downturn. Frequent updating of models together with a policy of 'trade-ins' encouraged owners to change their cars regularly.

Instalment selling and the second hand market, however, were only just emerging before the First World War. It was in the 1920s that these policies became more commonplace. Other sales problems remained unsolved before the war, especially the lack of opportunities to inspect and test cars before purchase, the delays between order and delivery and the difficulty obtaining replacement parts. The solutions to many of these problems in the 1920s grew organically out of the pre-war developments although they were helped along by the changes which the war brought to the industry. With larger, standardised, cheaper production geared to a market of narrowing income levels and which regarded the car as less of a luxury and more of a utility, mass marketing became inevitable.

The reason why Britain had a larger per capita, as well as absolute, car market, than the rest of Europe, is not easy to explain. The activities of British dealers in publicising the motor car and developing appropriate sales and marketing policies played a part, as did the fact that the average per capita income in the UK ($243) was higher than in France ($185) and Germany ($146) in 1914 (Bardou et al, 47). By 1913, France's per capita ownership of vehicles was coming closer to that of Britain, but Germany remained well behind. The slowness of German firms to adopt new marketing techniques and the social conservatism and rural isolation of the German upper classes may help to explain the small market. By the 1920s when the motor car was filtering down to a middle-class market in France and Britain, the prosperity of the German middle classes was disintegrating under the impact of hyper-inflation. A temporary rise in sales in the 1920s was due to 'currency dumping' as Germans bought into goods of any sort before the Reichsmark, and therefore their savings, disintegrated. In these difficult economic circumstances, motor cycles predominated over cars in Germany until the 1930s.

THE ECONOMIC EFFECTS OF THE MOTOR VEHICLE INDUSTRY

The historiography of the motor vehicle has given little consideration to its importance within the economy or its contribution to economic development. There has been no general evaluation or Fogel-like quantification of its importance in spite of the view of one historian that 'no other product yielded so rich a harvest of forward and backward linkages' (Landes, 443). Even one recent book, whose professed aim was to assess the economic effects of the car, retreated into a detailed discussion of the evolution of the industry (Barker, 1987). Similarly, there is little work on the efficiency of the motor vehicle compared with railways, coastal shipping and horse-drawn conveyance which approach was the starting point of Fogel and Fishlow's work.

As a major growth industry, historians looked to the railways to explain the contemporaneous early industrialisation of France, Germany and Britain in the middle decades of the nineteenth century. By the time the motor car arrived these economies, which dominated vehicle production, had passed through their early phase of economic development. Britain and France witnessed low growth at the end of the nineteenth century and therefore there could be no search for a dynamic leading sector. This is an oversimplified and false view of European development before 1914. There was plenty of growth and structural change in the French and British, as well as German, economies in the two decades before the First World War and the motor vehicle industry played an important part in the changes which were taking place. The car industry affected only certain sectors and regions particularly the so-called 'new industries' such as steel, aluminium, rubber and petroleum products. While railway construction took the form of social overhead capital largely expended in the initial phases of the industry, in the car industry construction capital increased with the expansion of the industry and therefore its greatest influence came after 1918. The impact of the car industry on transport patterns was also very different from that of the railways because of the greater flexibility of the road network.

Within the car industry capital was widely dispersed among manufacturers, engine-makers, coach-builders and component firms which makes its aggregate calculation very difficult. Total investment in the industry before 1914 was less than that of the railway and therefore its multiplier effect upon economic growth and its influence upon methods of financing was probably less. In Britain the industry only took up a few per cent of the value of new share issues before 1914. It was the dynamic growth of investment and its periodic nature which made for the industry's importance. Some idea of the pace of investment growth can be gleaned from the rapid expansion of output indicated earlier. Of the six largest industrial sectors in France, only metalworking significantly increased its share of total output in the two decades leading up to 1914. The car industry emerged as the largest industry in this sector. Investment in the motor industry occurred in spurts which may have influenced the trade cycle in the short term. The boom in the car industry in the mid to late 1890s contributed to the economic climacteric of those years. In 1896 thirteen per cent of new issues in Britain came from the car, cycle and related industries, imparting a pro-cyclical effect upon economic activity (A. Harrison, 1981, 169). Similarly, the substantial expansion of the industry in the First World War may have had a role in the 'overheating' of the economy by 1918. Investment cycles in the vehicle industry would appear to be pro-cyclical. The high income elasticity of demand for cars encouraged the concentration of sales into boom periods such as 1905–6.

The rapid growth of investment in the French car industry may question the traditional view that the relative slowdown in the French economy at the end of the nineteenth century was due to a capital shortage. The French motor industry demonstrated dynamic growth unrestrained by insufficient investment. On the other hand, since the capital requirements of the motor industry were relatively modest this industry may have expanded in place of others for this very reason.

Expansion of the motor industry sparked off increased investment and output in other industries, many of them in the early stages of development. The motor industry took up eight per cent of aluminium output in France in 1913 and up to twenty per cent of its domestic consumption. About half of French aluminium output was taken up by exports, often to car industries abroad. Thus vehicle demand was important in the growth of French aluminium production from 360 tons in 1895 to 13 483 by 1913. The motor industry only took up about two per cent of French steel output but it was a principal customer for steel alloys and high quality steels and encouraged research into the growing field of alloys (Laux, 1976, 206). Wood was often used for part of the bodywork. Paint, rubber, and electrical products and systems were naturally in high demand. Some car firms also manufactured aviation engines and aircraft. Fiat and Rolls Royce developed a strong reputation in this field but French firms dominated early aviation production. By 1909 Renault, Panhard et Levassor, De Dion-Bouton, Mors, Darracq and Clément were all building aviation engines. By 1913 France was the leading aircraft maker, and during the war produced 92 000 engines and 52 000 frames. There were some firms who had no connection with the car industry such as Voisin brothers, Seguin brothers and Armand Deperdussin but Laux correctly concludes that 'such achievements in aircraft production, especially of engines, rested primarily on the foundation of the large automobile industry' (1976, 206).

The industry was emerging as an important employer of labour by the time of the First World War. In France it employed 100 000 making cars and in related areas such as garages, road repairs and administration in 1913 (Laux, 1976, 178). Indeed, the factory workers were only a minority of those whose work involved the construction and operation of motor vehicles. The assembly methods of production greatly enhanced labour productivity and set important precedents for manufacturing techniques in the new consumer durable industries both in terms of labour organisation and the development of standardised components and products.

The effects of car production were concentrated geographically as well as sectorally. In Britain the car industry was mainly concentrated in Midlands towns together with Manchester and London. Coventry produced 28 per cent of the national total of vehicles in 1913. By 1911 cycle and car makers employed 20 per cent of the city's population with components and related industries employing many more (Thoms and Donnelly, 44–5). Labour was also attracted into the city from the surrounding areas of rural Warwickshire and the traditional engineering areas of Birmingham, Lancashire and Cheshire. The car industry was especially valuable for Coventry because it pulled her out of economic decline when her cycle industry declined in the 1890s. In France the Parisian domination of the industry was less important for such a large city. The car industry may have been more important to the development of provincial towns and cities such as Lyons, Montbéliard, Le Mans and Lunéville.

A large proportion of production was traded abroad. France was the major exporter and Britain the major importer. Thus in 1913 France had a positive trade balance in motor vehicles of 207 million francs and the United Kingdom a deficit of 55 million francs. However, the influence of the industry upon the Balance of Payments was greater than this. Raw materials and components were heavily traded: 75 per cent of French rubber exports were tyres, a trade which was growing by 20 per cent a year before 1914 and was equivalent to half the value of her car exports. Britain imported electrical components from Germany and the United States. The aviation products of car firms were exported particularly by the French who earned 12 million francs in this manner in 1913 (Laux, 1976, 206–7). Oil and petrol were also prominent in foreign trade, particularly as the sources of production were concentrated in Russia and America. Britain imported in excess of 100 million gallons of crude oil and 'petrol spirit' in 1913 (Richardson, 205). She appears, therefore, to have been a major trade deficit country for vehicles and related products. This is given greater weight in the knowledge that she had a surplus in previous transport products such as shipbuilding and coal. British exports of motorcycles, however, were seven times greater than imports in 1911 (Barker, 1987, 43).

The economic impact of the motor vehicle as a service industry has also received little attention from historians. Vehicle ownership stimulated a wide range of related activities which included garages, road construction and repairs, car parks, driving schools, insurance, public transport, retailing services, government administration, hire firms and tourism. Car registration and driving licences were introduced in Britain in 1903 and the British School of Motoring was created in 1910 although there was no formal test until 1934. In

Table 6.5 Foreign Trade in Motor Vehicles, 1907 and 1913
(million francs)

	1907			1913		
	Exports	Imports	Balance	Exports	Imports	Balance
France	144.4 (57)	8.7 (5)	+135.7	227.4 (33)	19.9 (9)	+207.5
United Kingdom	33.2 (13)	104.0 (60)	− 70.8	109.1 (16)	164.0 (70)	− 54.9
United States	28.5 (11)	25.0 (15)	+ 3.5	170.0 (25)	10.5 (5)	+159.5
Italy	20.2 (8)	8.3 (5)	+ 11.9	38.7* (6)	11.5* (5)	+ 27.2
Germany	17.8 (7)	22.2 (13)	− 4.4	107.1 (16)	17.8 (8)	+ 89.3
Belgium	10.0 (4)	4.4 (3)	+ 5.6	31.7* (5)	10.1* (4)	+ 21.6
Total	254.1	172.6		684.0	233.8	

Notes: Percentage of total in parentheses.
    * 1912

Sources: Laux, 1976, 209; Foreman-Peck, 1982, 868.

France, driving licences were introduced as early as 1891 although registration plates had to wait until 1909. In 1891 Carless, Capel and Leonard began marketing 'motor spirit' in Britain. By 1906 they had 1300 retail agents among garages, motor and cycle firms, iron-mongers and village stores (Richardson, 202). In France, where Deutsch was busy establishing depots throughout the country, petrol could be obtained in most medium-sized towns by the mid-1890s. Petrol was sold by the can rather than directly through pumps until after 1918.

The spread of motor vehicles led to the gradual decline of horse-drawn carriages and the more rapid demise of horse-drawn omni-buses. Nineteen-thirteen witnessed the last horse-drawn omnibus in Paris but there remained 222 000 horse-drawn carriages in France in 1909 (Fridenson, 1981, 139). Motorised transport took over first in the cities; the long distance competition with the railways for passen-gers and freight did not happen until after 1918. It was over short distances that the flexibility of motorised road transport first enabled it to compete with the railways. The competition over short distances was mainly between vehicle and horse. Helped by the invention of the taximeter there were 7000 motor taxis in London, 5000 in Paris and 2000 in Berlin by 1911 (Bardou et al, 21–2). Sixty-three per cent of French car registrations were in urban areas in 1901 although this had fallen to 45 per cent by 1918 as improved roads and services extended ownership into small towns and villages (Fridenson, 1987, 133). In the process it extended the suburban developments associ-ated with earlier road improvements and the coming of the railway. The huge growth in the use of passenger transport services associated with the electric tram systems had a similar effect. The average number of 'streetcar' rides per capita in major German cities grew from 39 to 137 in 1890–1910 (McKay, 94). Often outer suburbs expanded rapidly after the arrival of tramway services. McKay has identified such 'streetcar suburbs' in Brussels and Manchester (209–20). The greater flexibility of urban road transport by 1914 may have mitigated the problems of ribbon development associated with early road improvements and the railways. However, a map of Manchester in 1913 still indicates star-shaped expansion around the major transport links (McKay, 218).

One of the consequences of the coming of the railway had been to force many road hauliers out of long distance commerce into short hauls often connecting with railway termini: such was the experience of Pickfords. Pickfords were not alone in converting to the use of motor vehicles although in some cases the horse remained an effective competitor. The fact that the move to short hauls was already under way in the nineteenth century made the transition to motorised transport more straightforward. It also suggests that many of the developments in retailing and wholesaling long associated with the motor vehicle were already under way in the later nineteenth century. The motor vehicle extended this process and encouraged manufacturing firms to establish their own transport fleet rather than rely upon specialist haulage firms who maintained a stable of horses. Thus, the motorisation of road transport may have encouraged the vertical integration of manufacturing, wholesaling and retailing processes. More research is required to establish whether this was the case.

Note

1. H. W. Richardson, 'Overcommitment in Britain before 1930', *Oxf. Econ. Papers*, 17, 1965.

Bibliography

TRANSPORT AND ECONOMIC DEVELOPMENT

Transport Economics

BONAVIA, M. R. *The Economics of Transport.* London, 1936.
BUTTON, K. J. *Transport Economics.* London, 1982.
COLE, S. *Applied Transport Economics.* London, 1987.
GLAISTER, S. *Fundamentals of Transport Economics.* Oxford, 1981.
GWILLIAM, K. M. and MACKIE, P. J. *Economics and Transport Policy.* London, 1975.
KIRKALDY, A. W. and EVANS, A. D. *The History and Economics of Transport.* London, 1915.
MILNE, A. M. *The Economics of Inland Transport.* London, 1955.
O'LOUGHLIN, C. *The Economics of Sea Transport.* Oxford, 1967.
STUBBS, P. C., TYSON, W. J. and DALVI, M. Q. *Transport Economics.* London, 1980.
THOMSON, J. M. *Modern Transport Economics.* Harmondsworth, 1974.

Economic Development

BAXTER, R. D. Railway extension and its results. *Jnl Stat. Society*, 29, 1866.
BEROV, L. Transport costs and their role in trade in the Balkan lands in the sixteenth to nineteenth centuries. *Bulg. Hist. Rev.*, 3, 1975.
COOTNER, P. H. The role of railroads in United States economic growth. *Jnl Econ. Hist.*, 23, 1963.
FREEMAN, M. Introduction. Aldcroft and Freeman (eds) *Transport.* 1983.
FROMM, G. (ed.) *Transport Investment and Economic Development.* Washington, 1965.
GAULTHIER, H. L. Geography, transport and regional development. *Econ. Geog.*, 46, 1970.
GEARY, F. Balanced and unbalanced growth in nineteenth-century Europe. *Jnl Europ. Econ. Hist.*, 17, 1988.
GERSCHENKRON, A. *Economic Backwardness in Historical Perspective.* Cambridge, Mass., 1968.
HABERLER, G. and STERN, R. M. *Equilibrium and Growth in the World Economy: Economic Essays by Ragnar Nurske.* Cambridge, Mass., 1962.
HEYMANN, H. The objectives of transportation. Fromm (ed.) *Transport Investment.* 1965.

HIRSCH, L. V. and KLEIN, M. S. (eds) *The Impact of Highway Investment on Development*. Washington, 1966.

HIRSCHMAN, A. O. *The Strategy of Economic Development*. New Haven, 1958.

HUNTER, H. Transport in Soviet and Chinese development. *Econ. Devt and Cult. Change*, 14, 1965.

JENSEN, J. H. and ROSEGGER, G. Transferring technology to a peripheral economy. The case of the lower Danube transport development, 1856–1928. *Techn. and Cult.*, 19, 1978.

LAYARD, R. *Cost-Benefit Analysis: Selected Readings*. Reading, 1972.

LEWIS, W. A. Economic development with unlimited supplies of labour. *Manchester School Econ. & Soc. Studies*, 22, 1954.

MALTHUR, A. Balanced and unbalanced growth: a reconciliatory view. *Oxf. Econ. Papers*, 18, 1966.

MISHAN, E. J. *Cost-Benefit Analysis*. London, 1975.

NATH, S. V. The theory of balanced growth. *Oxf. Econ. Papers*, 14, 1962.

NURSKE, R. *Problems of Capital Formation in Underdeveloped Countries*. Oxford, 1953.

O'BRIEN, P. K. Transport and economic growth in western Europe, 1830–1914. *Jnl Europ. Econ. Hist.*, 11, 1982.

OWEN, W. *Strategy for Mobility*. Washington, 1964.

PREST, A. R. *Transport Economics in Developing Countries*. London, 1969.

ROSENSTEIN-RODAN, P. N. Problems of industrialisation of eastern and south-eastern Europe. *Econ. Jnl*, 53, 1943.

ROSTOW, W. W. *The Process of Economic Growth*. New York, 1962.

ROSTOW, W. W. *The Stages of Economic Growth*. London, 1960.

SALVEMINI, B. Transport and economic development. *Jnl Europ. Econ. Hist.*, 2, 1973.

SCHUMPETER, J. E. *The Theory of Economic Development*. Cambridge, Mass., 1934.

SCITOVSKY, T. Two concepts of external economies. *Jnl Pol. Economy*, 62, 1954.

SHARP, C. H. Transport and regional development with special reference to Britain. *Transport Policy and Decision-Making*, 1, 1980.

SMITH, A. *An Inquiry into the Nature and Causes of the Wealth of Nations*. (2 vols). London, 1776.

TEHERANIAN, M., HAKIMZADEH, F. and VIDALE, M. L. *Communications Policy for National Development*. London, 1977.

WILSON, C. Transport as a factor in the history of economic development. *Jnl Europ. Econ. Hist.*, 2, 1973.

WILSON, G. W. Towards a theory of transport and development. Hirsch and Klein (eds) *Impact of Highway Investment*. 1966.

YOUNGSON, A. J. *Overhead Capital: A Study in Development Economics*. Edinburgh, 1967.

General Surveys

ALDCROFT, D. H. and FREEMAN, M. J. (eds)   *Transport in the Industrial Revolution*. Manchester, 1983.

ALDCROFT, D. H.   *Studies in British Transport History, 1870–1970*. Newton Abbot, 1974.

ALDERMAN, G.   The Victorian Transport Revolution. *Hist. Jnl*, 14, 1971.

BAGWELL, P. S.   *The Transport Revolution from 1770*. London, 1974.

BARKER, T. C. and SAVAGE, C. I.   *An Economic History of Transport in Britain*. London, 1959.

BLUM, J.   Transportation and industry in Austria, 1815–48. *Jnl Mod. Hist.*, 15, 1943.

CARON, F.   *An Economic History of Modern France*. London, 1979.

CROUZET, F.   *The Victorian Economy*. London, 1982.

DYOS, H. J. and ALDCROFT, D. H.   *British Transport: an Economic Survey from the Seventeenth Century to the Twentieth*. London, 1969.

FLANAGAN, P. J.   *Transport in Ireland, 1880–1910*. Dublin, 1969.

FLINN, M. W.   *The Origins of the Industrial Revolution*. London, 1966.

FREEMAN, M. J. and ALDCROFT, D. H. (eds)   *Transport in Victorian Britain*. Manchester, 1988.

GATRELL, P.   *The Tsarist Economy, 1850–1917*. London, 1986.

GIRARD, L.   Transport. M. M. Postan and P. Mathias (eds) *The Cambridge Economic History of Europe* vol. 6 (1). Cambridge, 1965.

HARRISON, R. J.   *An Economic History of Modern Spain*. Manchester, 1978.

HUGHES, J. R. T.   *Industrialisation in Economic History*. New York, 1970.

KEMP, T.   *Historical Patterns of Industrialisation*. Harlow, 1978.

JACKMAN, W. T.   *The Development of Transportation in Modern England*. Cambridge, 1916.

KENNEDY, L. and OLLERENSHAW, P. (eds)   *An Economic History of Ulster, 1820–1939*. Manchester, 1985.

LANDES, D. S.   *The Unbound Prometheus, Technological Change and Industrial Development in Western Europe from 1750 to the Present*. Cambridge, 1969.

MADRAZO, S.   *El Sistema de Transportes en España, 1750–1850*. (2 vols). Madrid, 1984.

MILWARD, A. S. and SAUL, S. B.   *The Development of the Economies of Continental Europe, 1850–1914*. Cambridge, Mass., 1977.

MILWARD, A. S. and SAUL, S. B.   *The Economic Development of Continental Europe, 1780–1870*. London, 1973.

MITCHELL, B. R.   *European Historical Statistics, 1750–1970*. London, 1975.

NADAL, J.   *El Fracaso de la Revolucíon Industrial en España, 1814–1913*. Barcelona, 1975.

POLLARD, S.   *Peaceful Conquest. The Industrialisation of Europe, 1760–1970*. Oxford, 1981.

POUNDS, N. J. G.   *An Historical Geography of Europe, 1800–1914*. Cambridge, 1985.
PRICE, R.   *An Economic History of Modern France, 1730–1914*. London, 1981.
PRICE, R.   *The Modernisation of Rural France: Communication Networks and Agricultural Markets*. London, 1983.
SYMONS, L. and WHITE, C. (eds)   *Russian Transport*. London, 1975.
TAMES, R.   *The Transport Revolution in the Nineteenth Century*. Oxford, 1971.
TOUTAIN, J. C.   Les transports en France de 1830 à 1965. *Hist. Quantitative de l'Économie Française* 9, 1967. (1).
TOUTAIN, J. C.   *Les Transports en France de 1830 à 1965*. Paris, 1967. (2).
TORTELLA, G.   *Banking, Railroads and Industry in Spain, 1829–74*. New York, 1977.
TREBILCOCK, C.   *The Industrialisation of the Continental Powers, 1780–1914*. Harlow, 1981.
VOIGT, F.   *Die Entwicklung des Verkehrssystems*. Berlin, 1965.

ROAD AND RIVER TRANSPORT

General

GINARLIS, J. E.   Capital formation in road and canal transport. J. P. P. Higgins and S. Pollard (eds) *Aspects of Capital Formation in Great Britain, 1750–1850*. London, 1971.
LEPETIT, B.   *Chemins de terre et voies d'eau: réseaux de transports et organisation de l'espace en France, 1740–1840*. Paris, 1984.

Road Transport

ALBERT, W.   The Justices' rates for land carriage, 1748–1827, reconsidered. *Tspt Hist.*, 1, 1968.
ALBERT, W.   *The Turnpike Road System in England, 1663–1840*. Cambridge, 1972.
ALBERT, W.   The turnpike trusts. Aldcroft and Freeman (eds) *Transport*. 1983.
ARBELLOT, G.   La grande mutation des routes en France au XVIIIème siècle. *Ann. E. S. C.*, 28, 1973.
AUSTEN, B.   The impact of the mail coach on public coach services in England and Wales, 1784–1840. *Jnl Tspt Hist.*, 3rd ser, 2, 1981.
CAVAILLES, H.   *La Route française. Son histoire, sa fonction*. Paris, 1946.
CHARTRES, J. A.   On the road with Professor Wilson. *Econ. Hist. Rev.*, 2nd ser., 33, 1980.
CHARTRES, J. A.   Road carrying in England in the seventeenth century: myth and reality. *Econ. Hist. Rev.*, 2nd ser., 30, 1977.

CHARTRES, J. A. and TURNBULL, G. L. Road Transport. Aldcroft and Freeman (eds) *Transport*. 1983.

COCKER, J. de Een groot wegenwerk in de achttiende eeuw. *Jaarboek van het Heemkundig Genootschap van het land van Rode*. 1969.

COPELAND, J. *Roads and Their Traffic, 1750–1850*. Newton Abbot, 1968.

DICKINSON, G. C. The development of suburban road passenger transport in Leeds, 1840–95. *Jnl Tspt Hist.*, 4, 1960.

EVERITT, A. Country carriers in the nineteenth century. *Jnl Tspt Hist.*, new ser., 3, 1975–6.

FRIZ, G. *Le Strade dello Stàto Pontifício nel XIX sècolo, 1844–70*. Rome, 1967.

GENICOT, L. Études sur la construction des routes en Belgique. *Bull. Inst. Rech. Écon. Soc.*, 10, 12, 13, 1938, 1946, 1947.

HALDANE, A. R. B. *The Drove Roads of Scotland*. Nelson, 1952.

HEY, D. *Packmen, Carriers and Packhorse Roads. Trade and Communications in North Derbyshire and South Yorkshire*. Leicester, 1980.

HUGHES, M. Telford, Parnell and the Great Irish Road. *Jnl Tspt Hist.*, 6, 1963–4.

IMBERDIS, F. *Le Réseau routier de l'Auvergne au XVIIIème siècle*. Paris, 1967.

LEON, P. La conquête de l'espace national. F. Braudel and E. Labrousse (eds) *Histoire économique et sociale de la France*, vol 3. Paris, 1976.

MINONZIO, J-F. Les transports publics de voyageurs en Côte d'Or à la veille de l'ouverture du chemin de fer, 1845–9. *Ann. Bourg.*, 42, 1970.

PAWSON, E. *Transport and the Economy: the Turnpike Roads of Eighteenth-Century Britain*. London, 1977.

PLACQ, G. Le développement du réseau routier belge de 1830 à 1940. *Bull. Inst. Rech. Écon. Soc.*, 17, 1951.

POUSSOU, J. P. Sur le rôle des transports terrestres dans l'économie du sud-ouest au XVIIIème siècle. *Ann. Midi.* 90, 1978.

REVERDY, G. *Histoire des grandes liaisons françaises*. Paris, 1982.

RINGROSE, D. R. Transportation and economic stagnation in eighteenth-century Castile. *Jnl Econ. Hist.*, 28, 1968.

RINGROSE, D. R. *Transport and Economic Stagnation in Spain, 1750–1850*. Durham, NC, 1970.

SUMMERSON, J. N. *Georgian London*. London, 1945.

THIMME, P. Strassenbau und Strassenpolitik in Deutschland zur Zeit der Grundung des Zollvereins, 1825–35. *Vierteljahrschrift für Soz-Wirtgesch.*, 21, 1931.

THOMPSON, F. M. L. (ed.) *Horses in European Economic History: a Preliminary Canter*. Reading, 1983.

TURNBULL, G. Provincial road carrying in England in the eighteenth century. *Jnl Tspt Hist.*, new ser., 4, 1977.

TURNBULL, G. State regulation in the eighteenth-century English economy: another look at carriers' rates. *Jnl Tspt Hist.*, 3rd ser, 6, 1985.

TURNBULL, G. *Traffic and Transport: An Economic History of Pickfords*. London, 1979.

WILLAN, T. S.   The Justices of the Peace and the rates of land carriage. *Jnl Tspt Hist.*, 5, 1961–2.

WILSON, C.   Land carriage in the seventeenth century. *Econ. Hist. Rev.*, 2nd ser., 33, 1980.

Inland Waterways

BARKER, T. C.   Lancashire coal, Cheshire salt and the rise of Liverpool. *Trans. Hist. Society Lancs. & Cheshire*, 103, 1951.

BAULT, T. L.   Les voies navigables et l'industrialisation du Nord de la France. *Rev. Nord*, 61, 1979.

BERGASSE, J. D. (ed.)   *Le Canal du Midi: trois siècles de batallerie et de voyages*. Millau, 1983.

BIERMER, M.   Der Rhein-Elbe Kanal. *Jb. für Gesetsgebung, Verwaltung und Volkswirt im Deutschen Reich*, 24, 1900.

BOURQUIN, M-H.   L'approvisionnement de Paris en bois de la Régence à la Révolution. *Études d'histoire du droit parisien*. Paris, 1970.

BOUVIER, J.   Une dynastie d'affaires lyonnaise au XIXème siècle: les Bonnardel. *Rev. Hist. Mod. Contemp.*, 2, 1955.

BUCHER, G. R.   Le commerce du port de Chalon au XVIIIème siècle. *Ann. Bourg.*, 61, 1979.

CERMAKIAN, J.   *The Moselle. River and Canal from the Roman Empire to the European Economic Community*. Toronto, 1975.

CHARLES, A.   L'isolement de Bordeaux et l'insuffisance des voies de communication en Gironde au début du Second Empire. *Ann. Midi*, 72, 1960.

COCULA-VAILLIÈRES, A. M.   *Les gens de la rivière de Dordogne, 1750–1850*. Paris, 1979.

DUCKHAM, B. F.   Canals and river navigations. Aldcroft and Freeman (eds) *Transport*. 1983.

DUCKHAM, B. F.   The founding of Goole: an early nineteenth-century canal port. *Industrial Archaeology*, 4, 1967.

DUCKHAM, B. F.   The navigation of the Yorkshire Ouse during the nineteenth century. *Jnl Tspt Hist.*, 6, 1963–4.

DUCKHAM, B. F.   Selby and the Aire and Calder Navigation, 1774–1826. *Jnl Tspt Hist.*, 7, 1965–6.

ECKERT, C.   Rheinschiffahrt im XIX Jahrhundert. *Statts- und sozialwissenschaftliche Forschungen*, 18, 1900.

FARNIE, D. A.   *The Manchester Ship Canal and the Rise of the Port of Manchester*. Manchester, 1980.

FILLITZ, F.   Die Donauschiffahrt vom Einst zum Jetzt. *Der Donauraum*, 2, 1957.

FORTIN, A.   Les chemins de fer et les voies navigables du Pas-de-Calais durant le Second Empire. *Rev. Nord*, 53, 1971.

FUCHS, K.   Die Lahn als Schiffahrtsweg im 19 Jahrhundert. *Nassauische Ann.*, 75, 1964.

GASNIER, G.   La navigation sur la Loire et ses affluents vers 1785. *Ann. de Bretagne*, 36, 1924–5.

GEIGER, R.   Planning the French canals: the Becquey Plan of 1820–2. *Jnl Econ. Hist.*, 44, 1984.

GLASSL, H.   Der Ausbau der ungarischen Wasserstrassen in den letzten Regierungsjahren Maria Teresias. *Ungarn Jahrbuch*, 1970.

GROSSKREUTZ, H.   *Privatkapital und Kanalbau in Frankreich, 1814–48: eine Fallstudie zur Rolle der Banken in der französischen Industrialisierung*. Berlin, 1977.

HADFIELD, C.   *The Canal Age*. Newton Abbot, 1968.

HAJNAL, H.   *The Danube. Its Historical, Political and Economic Importance*. The Hague, 1920.

HAMMOND, W. E.   The development of the Marne-Rhine Canal and the Zollverein. *French Hist. Studs*, 3, 1964.

HANSEN, F. V.   *Canals and Waterways of Sweden*. Stockholm, 1915.

HANSON, P.   Soviet inland waterways. *Jnl Tspt Hist.*, 6, 1963–4.

HAYWOOD, R. M.   The development of steamboats on the Volga river and its tributaries, 1817–56. *Res. Econ. Hist.*, 6, 1981.

IONESCU, T.   L'échange maritime de marchandises entre les principautés danubiennes et la France durant la période 1829–48. *Rev. Roumaine Hist.*, 13, 1974.

JONES, E.   A transport private saving calculation for the brewers Truman, Hanbury and Buxton, 1815–63. *Jnl Tspt Hist.*, 3rd ser., 7, 1986.

LEON, P.   La navigation intérieure en France. *Rev. Écon. Int.*, 3, 1904.

LESKOSCHEK, F.   Schiffahrt und Flosserei auf der Drau. *Zt Hist. Ver. Steiermk*, 63, 1972.

LINDSAY, J.   The Aberdeenshire Canal, 1805–54. *Jnl Tspt Hist.*, 6, 1963–4.

LINDSAY, J.   *The Canals of Scotland*. Newton Abbot, 1968.

MACAIGNE, R.   *Le canal de Saint-Quentin*. Paris, 1934.

MALET, H.   *Bridgewater: the Canal Duke, 1736–1803*. Manchester, 1977.

MEAD, W. R.   The genesis of waterway improvement in Finland. *Terra* 81, 1969.

MELLOR, R. E. H.   *The Rhine: a Study in the Geography of Water Transport*. Aberdeen, 1983.

MERGER, M.   Le programme Baudin: un effort pour faire renaître la navigation intérieure. *Transports et voies de communication*. Actes du 18ème colloque de l'Association interuniversitaire de l'Est. Dijon, 1977.

MILKEREIT, G.   *Das Projekt der Moselkanalisierung, ein Problem der westdeutschen Eisen- und Stahlindustrie*. Cologne, 1967.

NEWEKLOVSKY, E.   Die Eisenschiffahrt auf der Enns. *Oberösterreich Heimatsblätter*, 3, 1949.

PASKALEVA, V.   Le rôle de la navigation à vapeur sur le bas Danube dans l'établissement de liens entre l'Europe Centrale et Constantinople jusqu'à la guerre de Crimée. *Bulg. Hist. Rev.*, 4, 1976.

PILKINGTON, R.   Canals: inland waterways outside Britain. C. Singer, E. J. Holmyard, A. R. Hall and T. I. Williams (eds) *A History of Technology* vol. 4. Oxford, 1958.

PINON, P. and KRIEGEL, A.   L'achèvement des canaux sous le Restauration et la Monarchie de Juillet. *Ann. des Ponts-et-Chaussées*, new ser., 19, 1981.

POLLINS, H.   The Swansea Canal. *Jnl Tspt Hist.*, 1, 1953–4.

RATCLIFFE, B. M.   The business elite and the development of Paris: intervention in ports and entrepots, 1814–34. *Jnl Europ. Econ. Hist.*, 14, 1985.

RIVET, F.   American technique and steam navigation on the Saône and the Rhône, 1827–50. *Jnl Econ. Hist.*. 16, 1956.

RIVET, F.   *La Navigation à vapeur sur la Saône et le Rhône, 1783–1863.* Paris, 1962.

ROOT, H-J.   Die Entwicklung der Verkehrsstroöme und der Verkehrsstruktur auf der Elbe während des 19 Jahrhunderts, unter besonderer Berücksichtigung der wirtschaftlichen Entwicklung im Verkehrsgebiet. *Jahrbuch Wirtgeschichte*, 1975.

SCHAWACHT, J. H.   *Schiffahrt und Guterverker zwischen den Hafen des deutschen Niederrheins (inbesondere Koln) und Rotterdam vom Ende des 18 bis zur mitte des 19 Jahrhunderts.* Cologne, 1975.

SCHULTE, F.   Die Rheinschiffahrt und die Eisenbahnen. *Schriften des Vereins für Sozialpolitik*, 102, 1905.

SKEMPTON, A. W.   Canals and river navigations before 1750. C. Singer, E. J. Holmyard, A. R. Hall and T. I. Williams (eds) *A History of Technology* vol. 3. Cambridge, 1957.

VALDENAIRE, A.   Das Leben und wirken des Johann Gottfried Tulla. *Zt Gesch. des Oberrheins*, 42, 1929–30.

VRIES, J. de   *Barges and Capitalism. Passenger Transportation in the Dutch Economy, 1632–1839.* Utrecht, 1981.

WARD, J. R.   *The Finance of Canal Building in Eighteenth-Century England.* Oxford, 1974.

WATERWAYS ASSOCIATION,   *Digest of the Report and Recommendations of the Royal Commission on Canals.* Birmingham, 1913.

WILLAN, T. S.   *The Navigation of the River Wear in the Eighteenth Century.* Manchester, 1951.

WILLAN, T. S.   *River Navigation in England.* Manchester, 1936.

ZORN, W.   Neue Teile der historischen Wirtschaftkarte der Rheinland. *Rheinische Vierteljahrsblätter*, 31, 1966–7.

SHIPPING INDUSTRY

General

ALANEN, A. J.   *Der Aussenhandel und die Schiffahrt Finnlands im 18 Jahrhundert.* Helsinki, 1957.

ALEXANDER, D. and OMMER, R. (eds)   *Volumes not Values.* Newfoundland, 1979.

CHARLIAT, P.   *Trois siècles d'économie maritime français.* Paris, 1931.

COTTRELL, P. and ALDCROFT, D. H. (eds)   *Shipping, Trade and Commerce.* Leicester, 1981.

DAVIS, R.   *The Rise of the English Shipping Industry in the Seventeenth and Eighteenth Centuries.* Newton Abbot, 1962.

DOUGHTY, M. *Merchant Shipping and War*. London, 1982.
FAYLE, C. E. *A Short History of the World's Shipping Industry*. London, 1933.
FAYLE, C. E. *The War and the Shipping Industry*. London, 1927.
FISCHER, L. R. and PANTING, G. (eds) *Change and Adaptation in Maritime History. The North Atlantic Fleets in the Nineteenth Century*. Newfoundland, 1985.
FRITZ, M. Shipping in Sweden, 1850–1913. *Scand. Econ. Hist. Rev.* 28, 1980.
HAUTALA, K. From the Black Sea to the Atlantic. Finnish merchant shipping in the late nineteenth century. *Scand. Econ. Hist. Rev.* 19, 1971.
HOGBERG, S. *Utrikeshandel och sjöfart pa 1700 – talet*. Lund, 1969.
JACKSON, G. Scottish shipping. Cottrell and Aldcroft (eds) *Shipping, Trade and Commerce*. 1981.
JACKSON, G. The shipping industry. Freeman and Aldcroft (eds) *Transport*. 1988.
KENT, H. S. K. *War and Trade in the Northern Seas. Anglo-Scandinavian Economic Relations in the Mid Eighteenth Century*. Cambridge, 1973.
KIRKALDY, W. A. *British Shipping*. London, 1914.
KRESSE, W. The shipping industry in Germany, 1850–1914. Fischer and Panting (eds) *Change and Adaptation*. 1985.
MATTHEWS, K. and PANTING, G. (eds) *Ships and Shipbuilding in the North Atlantic Region*. Newfoundland, 1978.
MOLLAT, M. (ed.) *Les Grandes voies maritimes dans le monde*. Paris, 1965.
MOLTMANN, B. H. *Geschichte der deutschen Handelsschiffahrt*. Hamburg, 1981.
NORDVIK, H. W. The shipping industries of the Scandinavian countries, 1850–1914. Fischer and Panting (eds) *Change and Adaptation*. 1985.
PALMER, S. The British shipping industry, 1850–1914. Fischer and Panting (eds) *Change and Adaptation*. 1985.
PALMER, S. and WILLIAMS, G. (eds) *Charted and Uncharted Waters*. London, 1982.
PARKINSON, C. N. (ed.) *Trade Winds*. London, 1948.
SYRETT, D. *Shipping and the American War, 1775–83*. London, 1970.

Companies, Shipowning, Investment and Insurance

BARBANCE, M. *Histoire de la Compagnie Générale Transatlantique: un siècle d'exploitation maritime*. Paris, 1955.
BESSELL, G. O. *Norddeutscher Lloyd, 1857–1957. Geschichte einer bremischen Reederei*. Bremen, 1957.
BINDER, J. *Rot-Weiss-Rot auf Blauen Wellen*. Vienna, 1979.
BOITEUX, L. A. *La fortune de la mer: le besoin de sécurité et les débuts de l'assurance maritime*. Paris, 1967.
BRAMSEN, B. *A Hundred Years under Dannebrog: the History of the Dannebrog Shipping Company, 1883–1983*. Copenhagen, 1983.
COONS, R. E. *Steamships, Statesmen and Bureaucrats. Austrian Policy*

towards the Steam Navigation Company of the Austrian Lloyd, 1836–48.
Wiesbaden, 1975.

CORLEY, T. A. B. *A History of the Burmah Oil Company, 1886–1924.*
London, 1983.

COTTRELL, P. The steamship on the Mersey, 1815–80: investment and
ownership. Cottrell and Aldcroft (eds) *Shipping, Trade and Commerce.*
1981.

CRAIG, R. Aspects of tramp shipping and ownership. Matthews and
Panting (eds) *Ships and Shipbuilding.* 1978.

DAVIES, P. N. *Sir Alfred Jones.* London, 1978. (1).

DAVIES, P. N. and BOURN, A. M. Lord Kylsant and the Royal Mail.
Bus. Hist., 14, 1972.

DAVIES, P. N. *The Trade Makers. Elder Dempster in West Africa,
1852–1972.* London, 1973.

DENOIX, L. La Compagnie des Indes au XVIIIème siècle. Ses activités
diverse. *Rev. Hist. Écon. Soc.*, 34, 1956.

FERRIER, R. W. *The History of the British Petroleum Company. I: The
Developing Years, 1901–32.* Cambridge, 1982.

FISCHER, L. R. and NORDVIK, H. W. Floating capital: investment in
the Canadian and Norwegian merchant marines in comparative perspective, 1850–1914. *Scandinavian-Canadian Studies*, 3, 1988.

GERAINT JENKINS, J. *Evan Thomas Radcliffe.* Cardiff, 1982.

GREEN, E. and MOSS, M. *A Business of National Importance: The Royal
Mail Shipping Group, 1902–37.* London, 1982.

GRUVBERGER, N. *Sveriges utrikessjöfart, 1865–85. Företagsformer och
ägandestruktur.* Stockholm, 1965.

HARMS, O. *Deutsche-Australische Dampschiffs-Gesellschaft, Hamburg.*
Hamburg, 1933.

HYDE, F. E. *Blue Funnel: A History of Alfred Holt and Company of
Liverpool, 1865–1914.* Liverpool, 1956.

HYDE, F. E. *Cunard and the North Atlantic, 1840–1973.* London, 1975.

HYDE, F. E. *Shipping Enterprise and Management, 1830–1939: Harrisons
of Liverpool.* Liverpool, 1967.

JOHN, A. H. The London Assurance Company and the marine insurance
market of the eighteenth century. *Economica*, 25, 1958.

JONES, S. *Two Centuries of Overseas Trading: the Origins and Growth of
the Inchcape Group.* London, 1986.

KAUKIAINEN, Y. Finland's peasant seafarers and Stockholm. *Scand.
Econ. Hist. Rev.*, 19, 1971.

KONINCKX, C. *The First and Second Charters of the Swedish East India
Company, 1731–66.* Courtrai, 1980.

KRESSE, W. *Materialien zur Entwicklungsgeschichte der Hamburger
Handelsflotte, 1765–1823.* Hamburg, 1966.

LAMAR, C. *Albert Ballin.* Princeton, 1967.

MARRINER, S. and HYDE, F. E. *The Senior: John Samuel Swire,
1825–98. Management in the Far Eastern Shipping Trades.* Liverpool,
1967.

MATHIES, O. *Hamburgs Reederei, 1814–1914.* Hamburg, 1924.

MILNE, T. E. British shipping in the nineteenth century: a study of the

Ben Line papers. P. L. Payne (ed.) *Studies in Scottish Business History*. London, 1967.

MOLLAT, M. (ed.) *Sociétés et compagnies de commerce en Orient et dans l'Océan Indien*. Paris, 1970.

MOREL GIBBS, J. *Morels of Cardiff*. Cardiff, 1982.

NAKAGAWA, K. and YUI, T. (eds) *Shipping Business in the Late Nineteenth and Twentieth Centuries*. Tokyo, 1985.

ORBELL, J. *From Cape to Cape. The History of Lyle Shipping Company*. Edinburgh, 1978.

PALMER, S. 'The most indefatigable activity': the General Steam Navigation Company, 1824–50. *Jnl Tspt Hist.*, 3rd ser., 3, 1982. (1).

PORTER, A. *Victorian Shipping Business and Imperial Policy: Donald Currie and the Castle Line and Southern Africa*. Woodbridge, 1986.

SCHMACK, K. *J. C. Godeffroy und Sohn. Kaufleute zu Hamburg*. Hamburg, 1938.

SMYTH, H. P. *The B & I Line: A History of the British and Irish Steam Packet Company*. Dublin, 1984.

SPOEHR, F. M. *White Falcon*. Palo Alto, 1963.

SPOONER, F. C. *Risks at Sea. Amsterdam Insurance and Maritime Europe, 1766–80*. Cambridge, 1983.

SUTTON, J. *Lords of the East. The East India Company and its Ships*. London, 1981.

TAYLOR, J. *Ellermans: A Wealth of Shipping*. London, 1976.

VILLE, S. *English Shipowning during the Industrial Revolution*. Manchester, 1987.

VILLE, S. Patterns of shipping investment in the port of Newcastle upon Tyne, 1750–1850. *Northern Hist.*, 25, 1989.

WRIGHT, C. and FAYLE, C. *A History of Lloyds*. London, 1928.

Shipbuilding and Technological Change

ALBION, R. G. *Forests and Sea Power. The Timber Problem of the Royal Navy, 1652–1862*. Cambridge, Mass., 1926.

BAMFORD, P. W. *Forests and French Sea Power, 1660–1789*. London, 1956.

CAMPBELL, R. H. Scottish shipbuilding: its rise and progress. *Scottish Geog. Magazine* 80, 1964.

CRAIG, R. *Steam Tramps and Cargo Liners, 1850–1950*. London, 1980.

FLETCHER, M. E. From coal to oil in British shipping. *Jnl Tspt Hist.*, new ser., 3, 1975.

GJOLBERG, O. The substitution of steam for sail in Norwegian ocean shipping, 1866–1914. A study in the economics of diffusion. *Scand. Econ. Hist. Rev.*, 28, 1980.

GOMEZ-MENDOZA, A. Government and the development of modern shipbuilding in Spain, 1850–1935. *Jnl Tspt Hist.*, 3rd ser., 9, 1988.

GRAHAM, G. S. The ascendancy of the sailing ship, 1850–85. *Econ. Hist. Rev.*, new ser., 9, 1956–7.

GREENHILL, B. *The Life and Death of the Merchant Sailing Ship, 1815–1965.* London, 1980.

HARLEY, C. K. The shift from sailing ships to steamships, 1850–90: a study in technological change and its diffusion. D. N. McCloskey (ed.) *Essays on a Mature Economy: Britain after 1840.* London, 1971.

HARRIS, J. R. Copper and Shipping in the Eighteenth Century. *Econ. Hist. Rev.*, 2nd ser., 19, 1966.

HENNING, G. and TRACE, K. Britain and the motorship: a case of the delayed adoption of new technology. *Jnl Econ. Hist.*, 35, 1975.

HORNBY, O. and NILSSON, C. A. The transition from sail to steam in the Danish merchant fleet, 1865–1910. *Scand. Econ. Hist. Rev.*, 28, 1980.

KAUKIAINEN, Y. The transition from sail to steam in Finnish shipping, 1850–1914. *Scand. Econ. Hist. Rev.*, 28, 1980.

KUUSE, J. The relations between the Swedish shipbuilding industry and other industries, 1900–80. Slaven and Kuuse (eds) *Scottish and Scandinavian Shipbuilding.* 1981.

LAEISZ, C. F. Shipbuilding in Germany. *Trans. Inst. Nav. Arch.*, 39, 1897.

LECKEBUSCH, G. *Die Beziehungen der deutschen Seeschiffswerftsen zur Eisenindustrie an der Ruhr in der Zeit von 1850 bis 1930.* Cologne, 1963.

LEHMANN-FELKOWSKI, G. (ed.) *The Shipbuilding Industry of Germany.* London, 1904.

LORENZ, E. H. Two patterns of development: the labour process in the British and the French shipbuilding industries, 1880–1930. *Jnl Europ. Econ. Hist.*, 13, 1984.

McGOWAN, A. *The Century before Steam. The Development of the Sailing Ship, 1700–1820.* London, 1980.

MAYWALD, K. The construction costs and the value of the British merchant fleet, 1850–1938. *Scot. Jnl. Pol. Econ.*, 3, 1956.

MOLLAT, M. (ed.) *Les Origines de la navigation à vapeur.* Paris, 1970.

OLSSON, K. Tankers and the technical development of the Swedish shipbuilding industry. Slaven and Kuuse (eds) *Scottish and Scandinavian Shipbuilding.* 1981.

OOSTEN, F. C. van *Schepen onder Stoom. De Geborte van het Stoomschip.* Bussum, 1972.

PALMER, S. R. Experience, experiment and economics: factors in the construction of early merchant steamships. Matthews and Panting (eds) *Ships and Shipbuilding.* 1978.

POLLARD, S. British and World Shipbuilding, 1890–1914: a study in comparative costs. *Jnl Econ. Hist.*, 17, 1957.

POLLARD, S. and ROBERTSON, P. *The British Shipbuilding Industry, 1870–1914.* London, 1979.

RATCLIFFE, M. *Liquid Gold Ships: A History of the Tanker, 1859–1984.* London, 1985.

REES, G. Copper sheathing: an example of technological diffusion in the English merchant fleet. *Jnl Tspt Hist.*, new ser., 1, 1971–2.

ROBERTSON, P. L. Technical education in the British shipbuilding and marine engineering industries, 1863–1914. *Econ. Hist. Rev.*, 2nd ser., 27, 1974.

RUSSO, G.   Fifty years progress of shipbuilding in Italy. *Trans. Inst. Nav. Arch.*, 53, 1911.

SCHWARTZ, T. and von HALLE, E. L.   *Schiffbauindustrie in Deutschland und im Auslande.* Berlin, 1902.

SLAVEN, A.   British shipbuilders: market trends and order book patterns between the wars. *Jnl Tspt Hist.*, 3rd ser., 3, 1982.

SLAVEN A. and KUSSE, J. (eds)   *Scottish and Scandinavian Shipbuilding: Development Problems in Historical Perspective.* Gothenburg, 1981.

SLAVEN, A.   The shipbuilding industry. R. Church (ed.) *The Dynamics of Victorian Business.* London, 1980.

UNGER, R. W.   *Dutch Shipbuilding before 1800.* Amsterdam, 1978.

WALKER, F. and SLAVEN, A. (eds)   *European Shipbuilding: One Hundred Years of Change.* London, 1984.

Deployment and Trades

ACHILLES, F. W.   *Seeschiffe im Binnenland.* Hamburg, 1985.

ALBION, R. G.   British shipping and Latin America, 1806–1914. *Jnl Econ. Hist.*, 4, 1951.

ALDCROFT, D. H.   The eclipse of British coastal shipping, 1913–21. *Jnl Tspt Hist.*, 6, 1963–4.

ANDERSON, B. L. and RICHARDSON, D.   Market structure and the profits of the British African trade in the late eighteenth century: a comment. *Jnl Econ. Hist.*, 43, 1983.

ANSTEY, R.   *The Atlantic Slave Trade and British Abolition, 1760–1810.* London, 1975. (1).

ANSTEY, R.   The volume and profitability of the British slave trade, 1761–1807. S. L. Engerman and E. D. Genovese (eds) *Race and Slavery in the Western Hemisphere.* Princeton, 1975. (2).

ANSTEY, R. and HAIR, P. E. H. (eds)   *Liverpool, the African Slave Trade and Abolition.* Widnes, 1976.

ARMSTRONG, J. and BAGWELL, P. S.   Coastal shipping. Aldcroft and Freeman (eds) *Transport.* 1983.

ASTROM, S-E.   North European timber exports to Great Britain, 1760–1810. Cottrell and Aldcroft (eds) *Shipping, Trade and Commerce.* 1981.

BAGWELL, P. S. and ARMSTRONG, J.   Coastal shipping. Freeman and Aldcroft, (eds) *Transport.* 1988.

BAMFORD, P. W.   French shipping in northern European trade, 1660–1789. *Jnl Mod. Hist.*, 26, 1954.

BOS, R. W.   *Brits-Nederlandse Handel en Scheepvaart, 1870–1914: een Analyse van Machtsafbrokkeling op een Markt.* Wageningen, 1978.

BROEZE, F. J. A.   British intercontinental shipping and Australia, 1813–50. *Jnl Tspt Hist.*, new ser., 4, 1977–8.

CHANNON, G.   The Aberdeen beef trade with London, a study in steamship and railway competition. *Tspt Hist.*, 2, 1969.

CIESLAK, E.   Aspects of the Baltic seaborne trade in the eighteenth century: the trade relations between Sweden, Poland, Russia and Prussia. *Jnl Europ. Econ. Hist.*, 12, 1983.

COLIN, A.   *La Navigation commerciale au XIXème siècle.* Paris, 1901.

CROWHURST, P. W.   *The Defence of British Trade, 1689–1815.* Folkestone, 1977.

CROWHURST, P. W.   Profitability in French privateering, 1793–1815. *Bus. Hist.*, 24, 1982.

DARITY, W.   The numbers game and the profitability of the British trade in slaves. *Jnl Econ. Hist.*, 45, 1985.

DAVIES, P. N.   The development of the liner trades. Matthews and Panting (eds) *Ships and Shipbuilding.* 1978. (2).

DAVIES, P. N.   The impact of the expatriate shipping lines on the economic development of British West Africa. *Bus. Hist.*, 19, 1977.

EMMER, D. C.   A history of the Dutch slave trade: a bibliographical survey. *Jnl Econ. Hist.*, 32, 1972.

ENGERMAN, S. L.   The slave trade and British capital formation in the eighteenth century: a comment on the Williams thesis. *Bus. Hist. Rev.*, 46, 1972.

FAIRLIE, S.   Shipping in the Anglo-Russian grain trade to 1870. *M. Hist.*, 1, 1971.

FARNIE, D. A.   *East and West of Suez: The Suez Canal in History, 1854–1956.* Oxford, 1969.

FELDBAEK, O.   Danish East India trade, 1772–1807: statistics and structure. *Scand. Econ. Hist. Rev.*, 26, 1978.

FISCHER, L. R. and NORDVIK, H. W.   The Nordic challenge to British domination in the Baltic timber trade to Britain, 1863–1913. L. R. Fischer and H. W. Nordvik (eds) *Shipping and Trade in the Northern Seas, 1600–1939.* 1988.

FISHER, H. E. S.   *The Portugal Trade.* London, 1971.

FLETCHER, M. E.   The Suez Canal and world shipping, 1869–1914. *Jnl Econ. Hist.*, 18, 1958.

FREDRICKSON, J. W.   American shipping in the trade with northern Europe, 1783–1860. *Scand. Econ. Hist. Rev.*, 4, 1956.

GRAY, M.   *The Fishing Industries of Scotland, 1770–1914.* Oxford, 1978.

GREENBERG, M.   *British Trade and the Opening of China, 1800–42.* Cambridge, 1951.

GREENHILL, R. G.   Latin America's export trades and British shipping, 1850–1914. Alexander and Ommer (eds) *Volumes not Values.* 1979.

GREEN-PEDERSEN, S. E.   The scope and structure of the Danish negro slave trade. *Scand. Econ. Hist. Rev.*, 19, 1971.

HYDE, F. E.   The expansion of Liverpool's carrying trade with the Far East and Australia, 1860–1914. *Trans. Royal Hist. Soc.*, 5th ser., 6, 1956.

HYDE, F. E.   *Far Eastern Trade, 1860–1914.* London, 1973.

INIKORI, J. E.   Market structure and the profits of the British Africa trade in the late eighteenth century. *Jnl Econ. Hist.*, 41, 1981.

JACKSON, G.   *The British Whaling Trade.* London, 1978.

KLEIN, H. S.   *The Middle Passage: Comparative Studies in the Atlantic Slave Trade.* Princeton, 1978.

KLEIN, H. S.   The Portuguese slave trade from Angola in the eighteenth century. *Jnl Econ. Hist.*, 32, 1972.

KLUDAS, A.   *Die grossen deutschen Passagierschiffe*. Oldenburg, 1971.

KRANTZ, O.   The competition between railways and domestic shipping in Sweden, 1870–1914. *Econ. & Hist.*, 15, 1972.

KRAWEHL, O. E.   *Hamburgs Schiffs- und Warenverkehr mit England und den englischen Kolonien, 1814–60*. Cologne, 1977.

KRESSE, W.   *Die Fahrtgebiete der Hamburger Handelsflotte, 1824–88*. Hamburg, 1972.

KNOPPERS, J. T.   *Dutch Trade with Russia from the Time of Peter I to Alexander I: A Quantitative Study in Eighteenth Century Shipping*. Amsterdam, 1976.

LEUBUSCHER, C.   *The West African Shipping Trade, 1909–59*. Leyden, 1963.

LINDBLAD, T.   Swedish shipping with the Netherlands in the second half of the eighteenth century. *Scand. Econ. Hist. Rev.*, 27, 1979.

MOLLAT, M. (ed.)   *Histoire des pêches maritimes en France*. Toulouse, 1987.

MERRITT, J. E.   The triangular trade. *Bus. Hist.*, 3, 1960–1.

OSEAU, W.   *Hamburgs Grönlandfahrt auf Walfischfang und Robbenschlag von 17–19 Jahrhundert*. Gluckstadt, 1955.

PALMER, S. R.   The British coal export trade, 1850–1913. Alexander and Ommer (eds) *Volumes not Values*. 1979.

PAVELKA, H.   *Englisch-österreichische Wirtschaftsbeziehungen in der ersten Hälfte des 19 Jahrhunderts*. Cologne, 1968.

PIETERS, L. J.   A hundred years of sea communication between England and the Netherlands. *Jnl Tspt Hist.*, 6, 1964.

PLATT, D. C. M.   *Latin America and British Trade, 1806–1914*. London, 1972.

RAGATZ, L. J.   *The Fall of the Planter Class in the British Caribbean, 1763–1833*. New York, 1963.

ROBERT, H.   *Les Trafics coloniaux de La Rochelle au XVIIIème siècle*. Poitiers, 1960.

SOLHAUG, T.   *De norske fiskeriers historie, 1815–80*. Bergen, 1976.

SPIEKMAN, H.   *De Ontwikkeling van de Amsterdamse petroleumhaven*. Haarlem, 1958.

STEIN, R. L.   *The French Slave Trade in the Eighteenth Century. An Old Regime Business*. Madison, Wis., 1979.

TARRADE, J.   *Le Commerce colonial de la France à la fin de l'Ancien Régime: l'evolution du régime de l'exclusif de 1763 à 1789*. Paris, 1973.

THOMAS, R. P. and BEAN, R. N.   The fishers of men: the profits of the slave trade. *Jnl Econ. Hist.*, 34, 1974.

THORBURN, T.   *Sveriges Inrikes Sjöfart, 1818–1949*. Uddevalla, 1958.

THORNER, D.   *Investment in Empire. British Railway and Steam Shipping Enterprise in India, 1825–49*. London, 1950.

UNGER, W. S.   *Het Archief der Middelburgsche Commercie Compagnie*. The Hague, 1951.

UTAAKER, K.   Norwegian shipping activities between foreign ports, 1815–35. *Sjöfartshistorisk Arbok* 1973.

UTTERSTROM, G.   Migratory labour and the herring fisheries of Western Sweden in the eighteenth century. *Scand. Econ. Hist. Rev.*, 7, 1959.

VELSCHOW, T.   Voyages of the Danish Asiatic Company to India and China, 1772–92. *Scand. Econ. Hist. Rev.*, 20, 1972.

WIGRAM, C. and SAMUDA, J. D. S.   The influence of the Suez Canal on ocean navigation. *Trans. Inst. Nav. Arch.*, 11, 1870.

WILLIAMS, D. M.   Abolition and the re-deployment of the slave fleet, 1807–11. *Bus. Hist.*, new ser., 2, 1973–4.

WILLIAMS, E.   *Capitalism and Slavery*. Chapel Hill, NC, 1945.

International Competition

ALDCROFT, D. H.   British shipping and foreign competition: the Anglo–German rivalry, 1870–1914. D. H. Aldcroft, *Studies in British Transport History, 1870–1970*. London, 1974.

BUCCHEIM, C.   Aspects of nineteenth-century Anglo-German trade rivalry reconsidered. *Jnl Econ. Hist.*, 41, 1981.

DEAKIN, B. M.   *Shipping Conferences*. Cambridge, 1973.

HOFFMAN, R. J. S.   *Great Britain and the German Trade Rivalry, 1875–1914*. Philadelphia, 1933.

MEEKER, R.   *A History of Shipping Subsidies*. New York, 1905.

MOORE, K. A.   *The Early History of Freight Conferences*. London, 1981.

STURMEY, S. G.   *British Shipping and World Competition*. London, 1962.

VALE, V.   *The American Peril: Challenge to Britain on the North Atlantic, 1901–4*. Manchester, 1984.

Ports and Port Activity

ACKER, J. van   *Anvers: d'escale romaine à port mondial*. Antwerp, 1975.

ALDCROFT, D. H.   Port congestion and the shipping boom of 1919–20. *Bus. Hist.*, 3, 1960–1.

BOULLE, P. H.   Slave trade, commercial organisation and industrial growth in eighteenth century Nantes. *Rev. Française Hist. d'Outre Mer*, 59, 1972.

BROEZE, F. J. A.   *De Stad Schiedam: de Schiedamsche Scheepsreederij en de Nederlandse vaart op Oost-Indië omstreeks 1840*. Hague, 1978.

CABANTOUS, A. (ed.)   *Histoire de Dunkerque*. Toulouse, 1983.

CLARK, J. G.   *La Rochelle and the Atlantic Economy during the Eighteenth Century*. Baltimore, 1981.

DARDEL, P.   *Navires et marchandises dans les ports de Rouen et du Havre au XVIIIème siècle*. Paris, 1963.

DERMIGNY, L.   *Naissance et croissance d'un port: Sète de 1666 à 1880*. Montpelier, 1955.

DIJK, H. van   *Rotterdam 1810–80, aspecten van een stedelijke samenleving*. Schiedam, 1976.

ENGELSING, R.   *Bremen als Auswandererhafen, 1683–1880*. Bremen, 1961.

FISHER, H. E. S. Lisbon, its English merchant community and the Mediterranean in the eighteenth century. Cottrell and Aldcroft (eds) *Shipping, Trade and Commerce*. 1981.

HARRIS, J. R. (ed.) *Liverpool and Merseyside. Essays in the Economic and Social History of the Port and its Hinterland*. London, 1969.

HAZEWINKEL, J. F. Le développement d'Amsterdam. *Ann. Geog.*, 25, 1932.

HYDE, F. E. *Liverpool and the Mersey. The Development of a Port, 1700–1970*. Newton Abbot, 1971.

JACKSON, G. *Hull in the Eighteenth Century*. London, 1972.

JACKSON, G. Port competition on the Humber: docks, railways and steamships in the nineteenth century. E. M. Sigsworth (ed.) *Ports and Resorts in the Regions*. Hull, 1980.

JACKSON, G. The ports. Aldcroft and Freeman (eds) *Transport*. 1983.

JACKSON, G. The ports. Freeman and Aldcroft (eds) *Transport*. 1988.

JAUPART, F. *L'Activité commerciale de Bayonne au XVIIIème siècle*. Bayonne, 1966.

JONES, S. A maritime history of the port of Whitby, 1700–1914. PhD Univ. London, 1982.

KENWOOD, A. G. Capital investment in docks, harbours and river improvements in north-eastern England, 1825–50. *Jnl Tspt Hist.*, new ser., 1, 1971–2.

MINCHINTON, W. *The Port of Bristol in the Eighteenth Century*. Bristol, 1962.

MOLLER, A. M. *Kobenhavns handelsflaade, 1814–32*. Copenhagen, 1974.

OSTENSJO, R. *Haugesund, 1835–95*. Haugesund, 1959.

PALMER, S. R. The character and organisation of the shipping industry of the port of London, 1815–49. PhD Univ. London, 1982. (2).

SCHLIEBS, H. Der Schiffbau und die Reederei Papenburgs von 1783 bis 1913. *Mitteilungen des Vereins für Gesch. und Landeskunde von Osnabruck* 52, 1930.

SNELLER, Z. W. *Geschiedenis van den Steenkolenhandel van Rotterdam*. Groningen, 1946.

TESSMER, F. H. *Bremische Handelsbeziehungen mit Australien von den Anfangen bis zum Beginn des 1 Weltkrieges*. Bremen, 1979.

VILLE, S. Shipping in the port of Newcastle, 1780–1800. *Jnl Tspt Hist.*, 3rd ser., 9, 1988.

WILLIAMS, J. E. Whitehaven in the Eighteenth Century. *Econ. Hist. Rev.*, new ser., 8, 1955–6.

Productivity, Profitability and Economic Development

ALANEN, A. Maritime trade and economic development in south Ostrobothnia. *Scand. Econ. Hist. Rev.*, 1, 1953.

ALDCROFT, D. H. The depression in British shipping, 1901–11. *Jnl Tspt Hist.*, 7, 1965–6.

BOGUCKA, M. The role of Baltic trade in European development from the sixteenth to the eighteenth centuries. *Jnl Europ. Econ. Hist.*, 9, 1980.

DARITY, W. The numbers game and the profitability of the British trade in slaves. *Jnl Econ. Hist.*, 45, 1985.

HYDE, F. E., PARKINSON, B. B. and MARRINER, S. The nature and profitability of the Liverpool slave trade. *Econ. Hist. Rev.*, new ser., 5, 1952–3.

KNAUERHASE, R. The compound steam engine and productivity changes in the German merchant marine fleet, 1871–87. *Jnl Econ. Hist.*, 28, 1968.

NORTH, D. C. Ocean freight rates and economic development, 1750–1913. *Jnl Econ. Hist.*, 18, 1958.

PORTER, A. Britain, the Cape Colony and Natal: capital, shipping and the imperial connection. *Econ. Hist. Rev.*, 2nd ser., 34, 1981.

REMOND, A. Études sur la circulation marchande en France aux XVIIIème et XIXème siècles. I: Les prix des transports marchands de la Révolution au Premier Empire. Paris, 1956.

STEIN, R. The profitability of the Nantes slave trade, 1783–92. *Jnl Econ. Hist.*, 35, 1975.

VILLE, S. Total factor productivity in the English shipping industry: the north-east coal trade, 1700–1850. *Econ. Hist. Rev.*, 2nd ser., 39, 1986.

WALTON, G. M. A measure of productivity change in American colonial shipping. *Econ. Hist. Rev.*, 2nd ser., 21, 1968.

WALTON, G. M. Productivity change in ocean shipping after 1870: a comment. *Jnl Econ. Hist.*, 30, 1970.

WALTON, G. M. Sources of productivity change in American colonial shipping, 1675–1775. *Econ. Hist. Rev.*, 2nd ser., 20, 1967.

RAILWAYS

General Accounts

AMES, E. A century of Russian railroad construction, 1837–1936. *Amer. Slav. & E. Europ. Rev.*, 6, 1947.

ARNAUTOVIC, D. *Histoire des chemins de fer yougoslaves, 1825–1937.* Paris, 1937.

ARTOLA, M. (ed.) *Los Ferrocarriles en España, 1844–1943* (2 vols). Madrid, 1978.

BEAVER, S. H. Railways in the Balkan peninsula. *Geog. Jnl*, 97, 1941.

BOUVIER, J. La 'grande crise' des compagnies ferroviaires suisses. *Ann. E. S. C.*, 11, 1956.

CARON, F. France. O'Brien (ed.) *Railways and Economic Development.* 1983.

CASARES ALONSO, A. *Estudio Histórico Económico de las Construcciones Ferroviarias Españolas en el siglo XIX* Madrid, 1973.

CRISPO, A. *Le ferrovie italiane.* Milan, 1940.

DUNHAM, A. L. How the first French railways were planned. *Jnl Econ. Hist.*, 1, 1941.

DUNHAM, A. L.   The Pioneer Period of European Railroads. Cambridge, Mass., 1946.
FENOALTEA, S.   (Italy). O'Brien (ed.) Railways and Economic Development. 1983.
FREMDLING, R.   (Germany). O'Brien (ed.) Railways and Economic Development. 1983.
GARBUTT, P. E.   The Russian Railways. London, 1949.
GOMEZ-MENDOZA, A.   Spain. O'Brien (ed.)   Railways and Economic Development. 1983.
GOURVISH, T. R.   Railways and the British Economy, 1830–1914. London, 1980.
HARTGERINK-KOOMANS, M.   Handelsbetrekkingen en spoorwegverbindingen in de eerste helft der 19de eeuw. Plannen tot spoorwegbouw in de noord-oostelijke provincies, 1845–54. Econ.–Hist. Jb., 26, 1956.
HAYWOOD, R. M.   The Beginnings of Railway Development in Russia in the Reign of Nicholas I, 1835–42. Durham, NC, 1969.
KARKAR, Y. N.   Railway Development in the Ottoman Empire, 1856–1914. New York, 1972.
KLEIN, A. A.   Von den Anfängen des Eisenbahnbaues in Österreich. Zt Hist. Ver. Steiermk, 55, 1964.
LAFFUT, M. Belgium. O'Brien (ed.)   Railways and Economic Development. 1983.
LAFFUT, M.   Les Chemins de fer belges, 1835–1913. L'établissement du réseau, étude descriptive et instruments de travail. Liège, 1974.
LAMALLE, U.   Histoire des chemins de fer belges. Brussels, 1943.
LeFRANC, G.   The French railroads, 1823–42. Jnl Econ. & Bus. Hist., 2, 1929–30.
MAY, A. J.   Trans-Balkan railway schemes. Jnl Mod. Hist., 24, 1952.
O'BRIEN, P. K. (ed.)   Railways and the Economic Development of Western Europe. London, 1983.
PICARD, A.   Les Chemins de fer français. (6 vols). Paris, 1884.
POLLINS, H.   British Railways: An Industrial History. Newton Abbot, 1971.
RENKIN, J.   Les chemins de fer de l'état belge. Rev. Écon. Int., 3, 1904.
RUDOLPH, M.   Geographie der Landstrassen und Eisenbahn von Norwegen. Petermanns Mitteilungen Erganzungsheft, 206, 1929.
SCHIVELBUSCH, W.   The Railway Journey: Trains and Travel in the Nineteenth Century. Oxford, 1980.
STUMPF, B.   Geschichte der deutschen Eisenbahnen. Mainz, 1960.
TAJANI, F.   Storia delle ferrovie italiane. Milan, 1939.
THORNER, D.   Great Britain and the development of India's railways. Jnl Econ. Hist., 11, 1951.
WESTWOOD, J.   A History of Russian Railways. London, 1964.
WINGATE, A.   Railway Building in Italy before Unification. Reading, 1970.

Case Studies

BAGWELL, P. S.   *The Railway Clearing House in the British Economy, 1842–1922*. London, 1968.

CARON, F.   *Histoire de l'exploitation d'un grand réseau. La Compagnie du chemin de fer du Nord, 1846–1937*. Paris, 1973.

CROUZET, F.   When the railways were built. A French engineering firm during the 'Great Depression' and after. S. Marriner (ed.) *Business and Businessmen*. Liverpool, 1978.

GARBUTT, P. E.   The Trans-Siberian Railway. *Jnl Tspt Hist.*, 1, 1953–4.

HARTGERINK-KOOMANS, M.   Amstersam, Rotterdam en de Rijnspoor, 1830–56. *Bijdragen voor de Geschiedenis der Nederlanden*, 13, 1958.

IRVING, R. J.   *The North Eastern Railway Company, 1870–1914*. Leicester, 1976.

JENSEN, J. H. and ROSSEGER, G.   British railway building along the lower Danube, 1856–69. *Slav. & E. Europ. Rev.*, 46, 1968.

JOHN, H.   Die Entwicklung des Eisenbahnetzes im Raum Marburg und Giessen. *Hessisches Jb. für Landesgesch.*, 9, 1959.

LANDI, P. L.   Intorno ad un progetto di etrada ferrata da Livorno a Genova, 1856–7. *Nuova Rivista Storica*, 56, 1972.

LAURENT, R.   *L'Octroi de Dijon au XIXème siècle*. Paris, 1960.

MAY, A. J.   The Novibazar railway project. *Jnl Mod. Hist.*, 10, 1938.

POPOV, R.   Autour du projet Austro-Hongrois pour la construction du chemin de fer de Novibazar. *Études Balkaniques*, 1970.

RATCLIFFE, B. M.   The building of the Paris–St Germain railway. *Jnl Tspt Hist.*, 2nd ser., 2, 1973.

RATCLIFFE, B. M.   The origins of the Paris–St Germain railway. *Jnl Tspt Hist.*, 2nd ser., 1, 1971–2.

ROBBINS, M.   The Balaklava Railway. *Jnl Tspt Hist.*, 1, 1953–4.

SOLOVYOVA, A. M.   The railway system in the mining area of southern Russia in the late nineteenth and early twentieth centuries. *Jnl Tspt Hist.*, 3rd ser., 5, 1984.

STEITZ, W.   *Die Entstehung der Köln–Mindener Eisenbahngesellschaft Ein Beitrag zur Frühgeschichte der deutschen Eisenbahn und des preussischen Aktienwesens*. Cologne, 1974.

WANK, S.   Aehrenthal and the Sanjak of Novibazar railway project. A reappraisal. *Slav. & E. Europ. Rev.*, 42, 1964.

Political Background

ALDERMAN, G.   *The Railway Interest*. Cambridge, 1973.

BLANCHARD, M.   The railway policy of the Second Empire. F. Crouzet, W. H. Chaloner and W. M. Stern (eds) *Essays in European Economic History, 1789–1914*. London, 1969.

COLLINS, D. N.   The Franco-Russian alliance and the Russian railways, 1891–1914. *Hist. Jnl*, 16, 1973.

EARLE, E. M.   *Turkey, the Great Powers, and the Bagdad Railway. A Study in Imperialism*. New York, 1924.

FREMDLING, R.   Freight rates and state budget, the role of the National Prussian Railways. *Jnl Europ. Econ. Hist.*, 9, 1980.

GISEVIUS, H. F.   *Zur Vorgeschichte des Preussisch-Sächsischen Eisenbahnkrieges: Verkehrspolitische Differenzen zwischen Preussen und Sachsen im Deutschen Bund.* Berlin, 1971.

LAFFUT, M.   La maturation des projets de chemin de fer en Belgique au XIXème siècle. *Aspect de l'administration belge au XIXème siècle.* Brussels, 1978. (Conference papers).

LAVERYCHEV, V. Y.   The trend towards state monopoly in pre-revolutionary Russia's railways. *Jnl Tspt Hist.*, 3rd ser., 6, 1985.

PRATT, E. A.   *Railways and Nationalisation.* London, 1911.

RATCLIFFE, B. M.   Railway imperialism. The example of the Pereires' Paris–St Germain company, 1835–46. *Bus. Hist.*, 18, 1976.

ROSENBERG, W. G.   The democratisation of Russia's railroads in 1917. *Amer. Hist. Rev.*, 86, 1981.

SPRING, D. W.   The trans-Persian railway project and Anglo–Russian relations, 1904–14. *Slav. & E. Europ. Rev.*, 54, 1976.

TAJANI, F.   Railway nationalisation in Italy. *Econ. Jnl*, 15, 1908.

TURNOCK, D.   The Romanian railway debate. A theme in political geography. *Jnl Tspt Hist.*, 2nd ser., 5, 1979.

Finance and Ownership

BONGAERTS, J. C.   Financing railways in the German states, 1840–60: a preliminary view. *Jnl Europ. Econ. Hist.*, 14, 1985.

BOUSQUET, G.   List et les chemins de fer. *Rev. Hist. Écon. Soc.*, 21, 1933.

BROADBRIDGE, S.   The early capital market: the Lancashire and Yorkshire Railway. *Econ. Hist. Rev.*, 2nd ser., 8, 1955–6.

BROADBRIDGE, S.   *Studies in Railway Expansion and the Capital Market in England, 1825–73.* London, 1970.

CAIN, P. J.   Railway Combination and Government, 1900–14. *Econ. Hist. Rev.*, 2nd ser., 25, 1972.

CAMERON, R. E.   Problems of French investment in Italian railways. A document of 1868. *Bus. Hist. Rev.*, 35, 1961.

CARON, F.   Railway Investment, 1850–1914. R. E. Cameron (ed.) *Essays in French Economic History.*

DONAGHY, T. J.   The Liverpool and Manchester Railway as an investment. *Jnl Tspt Hist.*, 7, 1965–6.

GILLE, B.   *Histoire de la Maison Rothschild, 1848–70.* Geneva, 1965.

GOURVISH, T. and REED, M. C.   The financing of Scottish railways before 1860: a comment. *Scot. Jnl Pol. Econ.*, 18, 1971.

GRUNWALD, K.   *Turkenhirsch: A Study of Baron Maurice de Hirsch. Entrepreneur and Philanthropist.* London, 1966.

GUILLAUME, P.   Les fortunes bordelaises. A. Dumard (ed.) *Les fortunes françaises au XIXème siècle.* Paris, 1973.

HARTSOUGH, M. L.   Business leaders in Cologne in the nineteenth century. *Jnl Econ. & Bus. Hist*, 3, 1929–30.

HAWKE, G. R. and REED, M. C.   Railway capital in the United Kingdom in the nineteenth century. *Econ. Hist. Rev.*, 2nd ser., 22, 1969.

HEDIN, L. E. Some notes on the financing of the Swedish railroads, 1860–1914. *Econ. & Hist.*, 10, 1967.

HENDERSON, W. O. Friedrich List, railway pioneer. W. H. Chaloner and B. M. Ratcliffe (eds) *Trade and Transport*. Manchester, 1977.

HIDY, M. E. (ed.) *British Investment in American Railways*. Charlottesville, 1970.

IRVING, R. J. The capitalisation of Britain's railways, 1830–1914. *Jnl Tspt Hist.*, 3rd ser., 5, 1984.

JENKS, L. H. Britain and American railway development. *Jnl Econ. Hist.*, 11, 1951.

JUTIKKALA, E. The problem of railway ownership in nineteenth-century Finland. *Scand. Econ. Hist. Rev.*, 18, 1970.

KURGAN-VAN HENTENRIJK, G. Aspects financiers de la réorganisation des chemins de fer belges: la reprise du réseau des bassins houillers du Hainaut par l'état, 1870–7. *Rev. de la Banque*, 8, 1975.

LEE, J. The construction costs of Irish railways, 1830–53. *Bus. Hist.*, 9, 1968.

LEE, J. The provision of capital for early Irish railways, 1830–53. *Irish Hist. Studs*, 16, 1968.

McLEAN, D. British finance and foreign policy in Turkey. The Smyrna–Aidin railway settlement, 1913–14. *Hist. Jnl*, 19, 1976.

MACPHERSON, W. J. Investment in Indian railways, 1845–75. *Econ. Hist. Rev.*, 2nd ser., 8, 1955–6.

MARNATA, F. *La Bourse et le financement des investissements*. Paris, 1973.

MICHIE, R. C. *Money, Mania and Markets: Investment, Company Formation and the Stock Exchange in the Nineteenth Century*. Edinburgh, 1981.

PICK, P. W. German railway construction in the Middle East. *Jb. des Instituts für Deutsche Gesch.*, 1975.

PLATT,D. C. M. *Foreign Finance in Continental Europe and the USA*. London, 1984.

POLLINS, H. Railway contractors and the financing of railway development in Britain. *Jnl Tspt Hist.*, 3, 1957–8.

RAM, K. V. British government, finance capitalists and the French Jibuti–Addis Ababa railway, 1898–1913. *Jnl Imper. & Commonw. Hist.*, 9, 1981.

REDLICH, F. Two nineteenth-century financiers and autobiographers. *Econ. & Hist.*, 10, 1967.

REED, M. C. *Investment in Railways in Britain, 1820–44*. London, 1975.

RICHARDS, A. S. The finance of the Liverpool and Manchester Railway again. *Econ. Hist. Rev.*, 2nd ser., 25, 1972.

RIEBER, A. J. The formation of La Grand Société des Chemins de Fer Russes. *Jahrbuch für Geschichte Osteuropas*, 21, 1973.

SODERLUND, E. F. The placing of the first Swedish railway loan. *Scand. Econ. Hist. Rev.*, 2nd ser., 11, 1963.

TARSAIDZE, A. American pioneers in Russian railroad building. *Russian Rev.*, 9, 1950.

VAGTS, D. F. Railroads, private enterprise and public policy. Germany and the United States, 1870–1920. N. Horn and J. Kocka (eds) *Recht und Entwicklung der Grossunternehmen im 19 und frühen 20 Jahrhundert.* Gottingen, 1979.

VAMPLEW, W.   Sources of Scottish railway share capital before 1860. *Scot. Jnl Pol. Econ.*, 17, 1970.

VAMPLEW, W.   Sources of Scottish railway share capital before 1860: a reply. *Scot. Jnl Pol. Econ.*, 18, 1971. (1).

Economic and Industrial Effects

ALDCROFT, D. H.   Railways and economic growth. *Jnl Tspt Hist.*, new ser., 1, 1971–2.

BLOEMERS, K.   Der Eisenbahntarif-Kampf. K. E. Born (ed.) *Moderne deutsche Wirtschaftgeschichte.* Cologne, 1966.

CAIN, P.   Traders versus railways: the genesis of the Railway and Canal Traffic Act of 1894. *Jnl Tspt Hist.*, new ser., 2, 1973–4.

DAVID, P. A.   Transport innovation and economic growth: Professor Fogel on and off the rails. *Econ. Hist. Rev.*, 2nd ser., 22, 1969.

DYOS, H. J.   Railways and housing in Victorian London. *Jnl Tspt Hist.*, 2, 1955.

FENOALTEA, S.   Railroads and Italian industrial growth, 1861–1913. *Explor. Econ. Hist.*, 9, 1972.

FISHLOW, A.   *American Railroads and the Transformation of the Ante-Bellum Economy.* Cambridge, Mass., 1965.

FOGEL, R. W.   Notes on the social saving controversy. *Jnl Econ. Hist.*, 39, 1979.

FOGEL, R. W.   A quantitative approach to the study of railroads in American economic growth: a report of some preliminary findings. *Jnl Econ. Hist.*, 22, 1962.

FOGEL, R. W.   *Railroads and American Economic Growth.* Baltimore, 1964.

FREMDLING, R.   *Eisenbahnen und deutsches Wirtschaftwachstum, 1840–79.* Dortmund, 1975.

FREMDLING, R.   Railways and German economic growth: a leading sector analysis with a comparison to the United States and Great Britain. *Jnl Econ. Hist.*, 37, 1977.

FREMDLING, R. and HOHORST, G.   Marktintegration der preussischen Wirtschaft im 19 Jahrhundert-Skizze eines Forschungsansatzes zur Fluktuation der Roggenpreise zwischen 1821 und 1865. R. Fremdling and R. Tilly (eds) *Industrialisierung und Raum.* Stuttgart, 1979.

GOMEZ-MENDOZA, A.   *Ferrocarriles y Cambio Económico en España, 1855–1913.* Madrid, 1982.

GOMEZ-MENDOZA, A.   Railways and Spanish economic growth in the late nineteenth century. PhD Univ. Oxford, 1981.

GOMEZ-MENDOZA, A.   Railways and Western economic development. *Tspt Hist.*, 11, 1980.

GUNDERSON, G.   The nature of social saving. *Econ. Hist. Rev.*, 2nd ser., 23, 1970.

HAWKE, G. R. *Railways and Economic Growth in England and Wales, 1840–70*. Oxford, 1970.

HAYDEN BOYD, J. and WALTON, G. M. The social savings from nineteenth-century rail passenger services. *Explor. Econ. Hist.*, 9, 1972.

HOLGERSSON, B. and NICANDER, E. The railroads and economic development in Sweden during the 1870s. *Econ. & Hist.*, 11, 1968.

HOLTFRERICH, C. *Quantitative Wirtschaftgeschichte des Ruhrkohlenbergbaus im 19 Jahrhundert*. Dortmund, 1973.

IRVING, R. J. The profitability and performance of British railways, 1870–1914. *Econ. Hist. Rev.*, 2nd ser., 31, 1978.

JENKS, L. H. Railroads as an economic force in American development. *Jnl Econ. Hist.*, 4, 1944.

KELLETT, J. R. *The Impact of Railways on Victorian Cities*. London, 1969.

KELLY, W. Railroad development and market integration in Russia: evidence on oil products and grain. *Jnl Econ. Hist.*, 36, 1976.

LOCKE, R. R. *Les Fonderies et forges d'Alais a l'époque des premiers chemins de fer, 1829–74: la création d'une entreprise moderne*. Paris, 1978.

McCLELLAND, P. D. Railroads, American growth and the New Economic History. *Jnl Econ Hist*, 28, 1968.

McCLELLAND, P. D. Social rates of return on American railroads in the nineteenth century. *Econ. Hist. Rev.*, 2nd ser., 25, 1972.

METZER, J. Railroad development and market integration: the case of Tsarist Russia. *Jnl Econ. Hist.*, 34, 1974.

METZER, J. Railroads in Tsarist Russia: direct gains and implications. *Explor. Econ. Hist.*, 13, 1976.

METZER, J. *Some Economic Aspects of Railroad Development in Tsarist Russia*. New York, 1977.

MITCHELL, B. R. The coming of the railway and United Kingdom economic growth. *Jnl Econ. Hist.*, 24, 1964.

MODIG, H. The backward linkage effect of railroads on Swedish industry, 1840–1914. *Swedish Jnl Econs*, 74, 1972.

O'BRIEN, P. K. *The New Economic History of the Railways*. London, 1977.

QUATAERT, D. Limited Revolution. The impact of the Anatolian railway on Turkish transportation and the provisioning of Istanbul, 1890–1908. *Bus. Hist. Rev.*, 51, 1977.

SCHREIBER, H. N. On the New Economic History and its limitations. *Agricultural Hist.*, 41, 1967.

VAMPLEW, W. Railways and the Scottish transport system in the nineteenth century. *Jnl Tspt Hist.*, 2nd ser., 1, 1971–2.

VAMPLEW, W. Railways and the transformation of the Scottish Economy. *Econ. Hist. Rev.*, 2nd ser., 24, 1971. (2).

WAGENBLASS, H. *Der Eisenbahnbau und das Wachstum der deutschen. Eisen- und Maschinenbauindustrie, 1835–60*. Stuttgart, 1973.

WHITE, C. The concept of social saving in theory and practice. *Econ. Hist. Rev.*, 29, 1976.

WHITE, C. A Russian attempt to calculate social savings. *Soviet Studies*, 28, 1976.

MOTOR VEHICLE INDUSTRY

ANDREWS, P. W. S. and BRUNNER, E. *The Life of Lord Nuffield.* Oxford, 1955.

ASTEN, H. A. M. van De Spyker van de Weg Gereden. *Econ.-en Soc. Hist. Jb.*, 33, 1970.

BARDOU, J-P., CHANARON, J-J., FRIDENSON, P. and LAUX, J. M. *The Automobile Revolution.* Chapel Hill, 1982.

BARJOT, D. Advances in road construction technology in France. Barker (ed.) *Spread of Motor Vehicles.* 1987.

BARKER, T. C. The delayed decline of the horse in the twentieth century. Thompson (ed.) *Horses in European Economic History.*

BARKER, T. C. (ed.) *The Economic and Social Effects of the Spread of Motor Vehicles.* London, 1987.

BARKER, T. C. The spread of motor vehicles before 1914. C. P. Kindleberger and G. di Tella (eds) *Economics in the Long View.* London, 1982.

BIGAZZI, D. Management strategies in the Italian car industry, 1906–45: Fiat and Alfa Romeo. Tolliday and Zeitlin (eds.) *Automobile Industry.*

BIRD, A. *De Dion-Bouton.* New York, 1971.

BIRD, A. *The Motor Car, 1765–1914.* London, 1960.

BISHOP, C. W. *La France et l'Automobile. Contribution française au développement économique et technique de l'automobilisme des origines à la deuxième guerre mondiale.* Paris, 1971.

BLAICH, F. The development of the distribution sector in the German car industry. Okochi and Shimokawa (eds) *Development of Mass Marketing.* 1981.

BLAICH, F. Why did the pioneer fall behind? Motorisation in Germany between the wars. Barker (ed.) *Spread of Motor Vehicles.* 1987.

CASTEELE-SCHWEITZER, S. van de André Citroën: l'aventurier de l'industrie. *Hist*, 56, 1983.

CASTRO VICENTE, M. de *Historia del Automóvil.* Barcelona, 1967.

CASTRONOVO, V. *Giovanni Agnelli.* Turin, 1971.

CHANARON, J-J. *L'Innovation dans la construction automobile.* Grenoble, 1973.

CHURCH, R. Family firms and managerial capitalism: the case of the international motor industry. *Bus. Hist.*, 28, 1986.

CHURCH, R. *Herbert Austin: The British Motor Car Industry to 1941.* London, 1979.

CHURCH, R. Innovation, monopoly and the supply of vehicle components in Britain, 1880–1930: the growth of Lucas. *Bus. Hist.*, 52, 1978.

CHURCH, R. The marketing of automobiles in Britain and the United States before 1939. Okochi and Shimokawa (eds) *Development of Mass Marketing.* 1981.

CHURCH, R. Markets and marketing in the British motor industry before 1914, with some French comparisons. *Jnl Tspt Hist.*, 3rd ser., 3, 1982.

CHURCH, R. Myths, men and motor cars. *Jnl Tspt Hist*, new ser., 4, 1977–8.

CIURO, J. *Historia del automóvil en España.* Barcelona, 1970.

DIXON, D. F.   Petrol distribution in the United Kingdom, 1900–50. *Bus. Hist.*, 6, 1963–4.

ENSOR, J.   *The Motor Industry*. London, 1971.

FLAGEOLET-LARDENOIS, M.   Une Firme pionniere: Panhard et Levassor jusqu'en 1918. *Mouvement Soc.*, 81, 1972.

FLOUD, R.   *The British Machine Tool Industry, 1850–1914*. Cambridge, 1976.

FOREMAN-PECK, J.   The American challenge of the twenties. Multinationals and the European motor industry. *Jnl Econ. Hist.*, 42, 1982.

FOREMAN-PECK, J.   Diversification and the growth of the firm: the Rover Company to 1914. *Bus. Hist.*, 25, 1983.

FOREMAN-PECK, J.   Tariff protection and economies of scale: the British motor industry before 1939. *Oxf. Econ. Papers*, new ser., 31, 1979.

FRIDENSON, P.   France États-Unis: genèse de l'usine nouvelle. *Recherches*, 32–3, 1978.

FRIDENSON, P.   French Automobile Marketing, 1890–1970. Okochi and Shimokawa (eds) *Development of Mass Marketing*. 1981.

FRIDENSON, P.   *Histoires des usines Renault. I: naissance de la grande entreprise, 1898–1939*. Paris, 1972.

FRIDENSON, P.   Some economic and social effects of motor vehicles in France since 1890. Barker (ed.) *Spread of Motor Vehicles*. 1987.

FRIDENSON, P.   Une Industrie nouvelle: l'automobile en France jusqu'en 1914. *Rev. Hist. Mod. Contemp.*, 19, 1972.

FRIDENSON, P.   Les Premiers inventeurs de l'automobile. *Hist.*, 73, 1984.

HARRISON, A. E.   The competitiveness of the British cycle industry, 1890–1914. *Econ. Hist. Rev.*, 2nd ser., 22, 1969.

HARRISON, A. E.   The origins and growth of the UK cycle industry to 1900. *Jnl Tspt Hist.*, 3rd ser., 6, 1985.

HARRISON, A. E.   Joint stock company flotation in the cycle, motor vehicle and related industries, 1882–1914. *Bus. Hist.*, 23, 1981.

HEATH, J.   Private bus services before 1930. *Local Historian*, 15, 1982.

HENRI, D.   La société anonyme des automobiles Peugeot de 1918 à 1930, histoire d'une stratégie d'expansion. Paris I, mémoire de maîtrise, 1983.

HEUSS, T.   *Robert Bosch: Leben und Leistung*. Tubingen, 1946.

HIBBS, J.   *The History of British Bus Services*. Newton Abbot, 1968.

ICKX, J.   *Ainsi naquit l'automobile*. (2 vols). Lausanne, 1961.

ICKX, J.   L'industrie automobile belge a débuté en 1895; elle est aujourd'hui une puissance a l'échelle mondiale. *Bull. de la Fédération des industries belges*, 25, 1970.

JACKSON, A. A.   *Semi-Detached London. Suburban Development, Life and Transport, 1900–39*. London, 1973.

JONES, G.   The growth and performance of British multinationals before 1939: the case of Dunlop. *Econ. Hist. Rev.*, 2nd ser, 37, 1984.

KINGSFORD, P. W.   The Lanchester Engineering Company Limited. *Bus. Hist.*, 3, 1960–1.

LARSEN, H. K. and NILSSON, C. A.   Consumption and production of bicycles in Denmark, 1890–1980. *Scand. Econ. Hist. Rev.*, 32, 1984.

LAUX, J. M.   Les Capitaux étrangers et l'industrie automobile. M.

Lévy-Leboyer (ed.) *La Position internationale de la France*. Paris, 1977.

LAUX, J. M. *In First Gear: The French Automobile Industry to 1914*. Liverpool, 1976.

LAUX, J. M. Rochet-Schneider and the French motor industry to 1914. *Bus. Hist.*, 8, 1966.

LAUX, J. M. Some notes on entrepreneurship in the early French automobile industry. *French Hist. Studies*, 3, 1963.

LEWCHUK, W. *American Technology and the British Vehicle Industry*. Cambridge, 1987.

LEWCHUK, W. The British motor vehicle industry, 1896–1982: the roots of decline. B. Elbaum and W. Lazonick (eds) *The Decline of the British Economy*. Oxford, 1986.

LEWCHUK, W. Fordism and British motor car employers, 1896–1932. H. Gospel and C. Littler (eds) *Managerial Strategies and Industrial Relations*. London, 1983.

LEWCHUK, W. The return to capital in the British motor vehicle industry, 1896–1939. *Bus. Hist.*, 27, 1985.

LLOYD, I. *Rolls Royce: The Growth of a Firm*. London, 1978.

McKAY, J. P. *Tramways and Trolleys: The Rise of Urban Mass Transport in Europe*. Princeton, 1976.

MAXCY, G. and SILBERSTON, A. *The Motor Industry*. London, 1959.

MAXCY, G. *The Multinational Motor Industry*. London, 1981.

NEVINS, A. *Ford: The Times, the Man, the Company*. New York, 1954.

NIXON, St JOHN C. *The Story of the Society of Motor Manufacturers and Traders, 1902–52*. London, 1952.

NOCKOLDS, H. *Lucas: The First Hundred Years*. London, 1976.

NORROY, M. *André Citroën, le précurseur*. Paris, 1973.

NÜBEL, O. The beginnings of the automobile in Germany. Barker (ed.) *Spread of Motor Vehicles*. 1987.

OKOCHI, A. and SHIMOKAWA, K. (eds) *Development of Mass Marketing: The Automobile and Retailing Industries*. Tokyo, 1981.

OVERY, R. J. *William Morris, Viscount Nuffield*. London, 1976.

PICARD, F. *L'Industrie automobile*. New York, 1973.

PINOL, A. Travail, travailleurs et production aux usines Berliet, 1912–47. Lyon II, mémoire de maîtrise, 1980.

PLOWDEN, W. *The Motor Car and Politics, 1896–1970*. London, 1971.

PURS, J. The internal combustion engine and the revolution in transport: the case of Czechoslovakia and some European comparisons. Barker (ed.) *Spread of Motor Vehicles*. 1987.

RICHARDSON, K. *The British Motor Industry, 1896–1939*. London, 1976.

SAUL, S. B. The motor industry in Britain to 1914. *Bus. Hist.*, 5, 1962–3.

SCHMITTO, F. *Automobilets Histoire og des Maend*. (2 vols). Copenhagen, 1938.

SCHWEITZER, S. *Des engrenages à la chaine, les usines Citroën, 1915–35*. Lyon, 1982.

SCOTT-MONCRIEFF, D., NIXON, St John and PAGET, C. *Three-Pointed Star*. London, 1955.

SEPER, H.   *Damals als die Pferde scheuten: Die Geschichte der Oesterreichischen Kraftfahrt.* Vienna, 1968.
SIEBERTZ, P.   *Gottlieb Daimler.* Munich, 1940.
SIEBERTZ, P.   *Karl Benz.* Stuttgart, 1950.
SLEEMAN, J.   The rise and decline of municipal transport. *Scot. Jnl Pol. Econ.*, 9, 1962.
THOMS, D. and DONNELLY, T.   *The Motor Car Industry in Coventry since the 1890s.* London 1985.
TOLLIDAY, S. and ZEITLIN, J. (eds)   *The Automobile Industry and its Workers.* Cambridge, 1986.
TURNER, G.   *The Leyland Papers.* London, 1971.
VLASIMSKY, J.   *Seventy-Five Years of Czechoslovak Automobile Manufacture, 1897–1972.* Bratislava, 1972.
WALDIS, A.   Les Débuts de l'industrie automobile en Suisse. *L'Anthologie automobile*, 1969.
WALDIS, A.   Early days of the Swiss motor car industry. *Sandoz Bull.*, 1965.
WHITING, R. C.   *A View from Cowley: the Impact of Industrialisation upon Oxford, 1918–39.* Oxford, 1983.
YAGO, G.   *The Decline of Transit: Urban Transporation in German and US Cities, 1900–70.* Cambridge, 1984.

JOURNAL ABBREVIATIONS

Amer. Hist. Rev.	*American Historical Review*
Amer. Slav. & E. Europ. Rev.	*American Slavic and East European Review*
Ann. Bourg.	*Annales de Bourgogne*
Ann. E. S. C.	*Annales: Économies-Sociétés-Civilisations*
Ann. Midi	*Annales du Midi*
Bulg. Hist. Rev.	*Bulgarian Historical Review*
Bull. Inst. Rech. Écon. Soc.	*Bulletin de l'Institut de Recherches économiques et Sociales*
Bus. Hist.	*Business History*
Bus. Hist. Rev.	*Business History Review*
Econ. Devt and Cult. Change	*Economic Development and Cultural Change*
Econ. Hist. Rev.	*Economic History Review*
Econ. Jnl	*Economic Journal*
Econ. & Hist.	*Economy & History*
Explor. Econ. Hist.	*Explorations in Economic History*
French Hist. Studs	*French Historical Studies*
Hist.	*l'Histoire*
Hist. Jnl	*Historical Journal*
Jnl Econ. & Bus. Hist.	*Journal of Economic and Business History*

Jnl Econ. Hist.	*Journal of Economic History*
Jnl Europ. Econ. Hist.	*Journal of European Economic History*
Jnl Imp. & Commonw. Hist.	*Journal of Imperial and Commonwealth History*
Jnl Mod. Hist.	*Journal of Modern History*
Jnl Pol. Economy	*Journal of Political Economy*
Jnl Stat. Society	*Journal of the Statistical Society*
Jnl Tspt Hist.	*Journal of Transport History*
M. Hist.	*Maritime History*
Oxf. Econ. Papers	*Oxford Economic Papers*
Rev. Écon. Int.	*Revue Économique Internationale*
Rev. Hist. Écon. Soc.	*Revue d'Histoire Économique et Sociale*
Rev. Hist. Mod. Contemp.	*Revue d'Histoire Moderne et Contemporaine*
Rev. Nord	*Revue du Nord*
Rev. Roumaine Hist.	*Revue Roumaine d'Histoire*
Scand. Econ. Hist. Rev.	*Scandinavian Economic History Review*
Scot. Jnl. Pol. Econ.	*Scottish Journal of Political Economy*
Slav. & E. Europ. Rev.	*Slavonic and East European Review*
Trans. Inst. Nav. Arch.	*Transactions of the Institute of Naval Architects*
Tspt Hist.	*Transport History*
Zt Hist. Ver. Steiermk	*Zeitschrift des Historischen Vereins für Steiermark*

Index